Balanced Literacy

Through Cooperative Learning & Active Engagement

Sharon Skidmore
& Jill Graber
In consultation with Jackie Minor

Kagan

Kagan Publishing
981 Calle Amanecer
San Clemente, CA 92673
1 (800) 933-2667
www.KaganOnline.com

ISBN: 978-1-933445-04-5

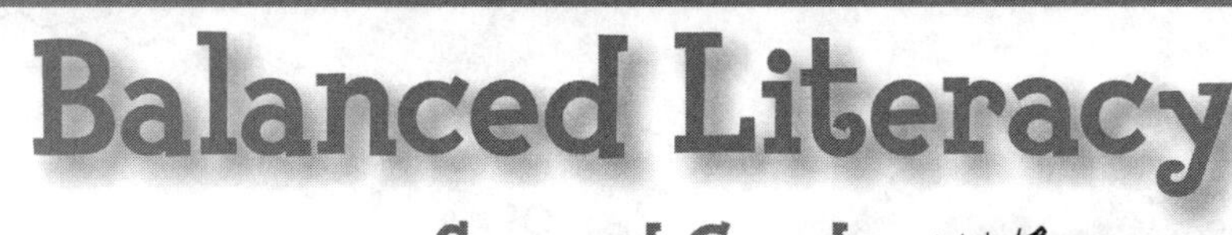

Second Grade

Introduction

Do you remember when you learned to ride a bike? You watched the neighborhood kids zooming down the street on their bikes. You knew you wanted to join them. You watched and listened carefully as your parents demonstrated and explained how to start and stop. Getting on the bike was a little scary at first. However, training wheels, the reassurance of supporting hands, and encouraging words gave you the confidence needed to successfully practice your new skill. With each practice, your ability grew and parental support was gradually withdrawn. Your new skills soon allowed you to ride your bike independently and successfully as you zoomed down the street with your neighborhood friends.

Just as learning to ride a bike requires a series of supported steps, literacy requires guiding the learner through scaffolded instruction. The balanced literacy components provide the framework for developing deep thinkers and strategic readers. Balanced literacy increases teachers' effectiveness as they explicitly instruct through varying degrees of demonstration and practice, teacher feedback, and ongoing assessment.

> *[Effective teachers provide] just the right amount of support that allows the learner to assume increasing control of the task. It's a gentle dance that requires careful leading, following, and occasionally sidestepping. Gradually, as students become competent, we reduce the amount of support we offer. Intrinsic to this belief is allowing enough time, support, and feedback.*
>
> Regie Routman

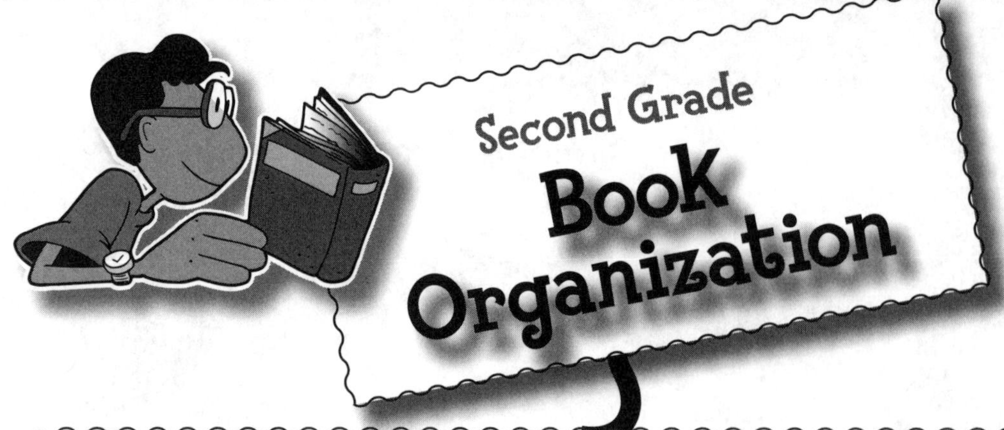

Second Grade Book Organization

In this book we have provided lessons and activities to support the balanced literacy components of aloud, shared, guided, and independent practice to strengthen national standards in comprehension, word study, vocabulary, fluency, and writing. Research emphasizes that learners need to acquire skills in these areas to be proficient readers and writers. Activities appropriate for second grade students have been developed for each of the four sections in this book, incorporating Kagan Cooperative Learning Structures.

As educators ourselves, we understand the limited time teachers have to develop student materials to support the literacy outcomes for their particular grade level. One of our goals for this book was to develop teacher-friendly materials. Therefore, you will find blackline masters (cards, spinners, cubes, and mats) designed to support the activities in each section. These are located directly behind the direction page for each cooperative learning structure. You may want to consider copying these pages onto cardstock, for durability. Blank templates have been included for some of the activities, giving you the flexibility to tailor activities to closely match specific literature or skills for your individual class.

The five national literacy standards of comprehension, word study, vocabulary, fluency, and writing are addressed in separate sections of this book, with the exception of vocabulary, which is included in both the Comprehension and Word Study sections.

Section 1: Comprehension

Section 2: Word Study

Section 3: Fluency

Section 4: Writing

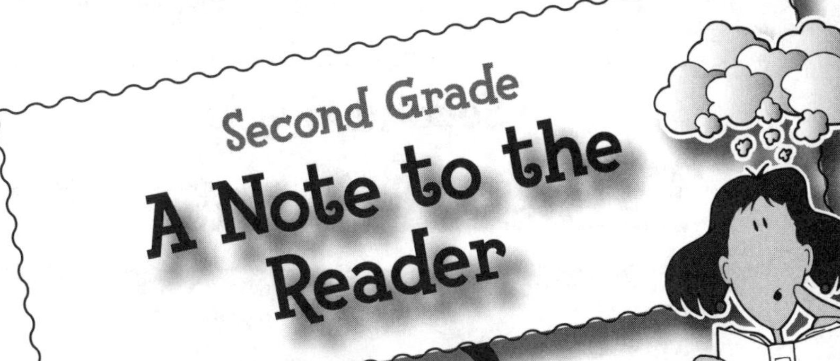

The ideas for this book are drawn from our combined experiences in the elementary classroom and as literacy coaches. As educators we are always striving to maximize learning and make every moment count as we endeavor to educate our students. It is our intention that this book will be a resource for you as you systematically think about literacy: What are the needs of my students? How can I best deliver instruction? What is the most effective use of instructional time?

When we combine balanced literacy and Kagan Cooperative Learning, our classroom practices become more purposeful and connected, resulting in increased student performance. We hope that this book will be a guide as you strive to improve instruction and enhance student learning.

A special thanks to Dr. Jacqueline Minor, our former Assistant Superintendent of Curriculum and Instruction and the present Director of Curriculum and Instruction for Kagan Professional Development, whose vision and knowledge continues to challenge us professionally. It has been with her involved guidance and encouragement that the ideas for the lessons and activities were organized for this book. Because of Jackie, this book has now become a reality.

Appreciations:

- **Illustrations:** Erin Kant
- **Graphic Designers and Layout Artists:**
  Alex Core
  Heather Malk
  Becky Herrington
- **Copyeditor:** Kim Fields
- **Publications Director:**
  Miguel Kagan

Second Grade

Table of Contents

Section 1

Comprehension

Comprehension Resources

Comprehension Activities and Lessons

Second Grade

Table of Contents Continued

Section 2
Word Study

Word Study Resources

Word Study Activities and Lessons

Second Grade

Table of Contents

Continued

Section 3

Fluency

Decoding and Strategy Resources

Fluency Resources

Fluency Activities

Second Grade

Table of Contents

Continued

Section 4

Writing

Writing Resources

Writing Activities

Comprehension

Word Study

Fluency

Writing

Comprehension

Comprehension

Comprehension research, as reviewed by the National Reading Panel (NICHD, 2000), suggests that students learn best when teachers are explicit in their instruction. This is most effectively accomplished when teachers tell students what they are expected to do and model their own thinking processes for the students (aloud). As students are encouraged to ask questions, discuss possible answers, and apply other comprehension strategies, active engagement increases (shared, guided, and independent).

Comprehension provides the purpose for all reading. Proficient readers are aware of their own thinking processes, making conscious decisions to apply different comprehension strategies as they read (e.g., awareness of text organizational patterns [text types and structures], figurative language meanings, vocabulary clarification, metacognition deepen comprehension).

Table of Comprehension Resources

		Balanced Literacy				
Page(s)	Resources	Aloud	Shared	Guided	Independent	Literature Circles
Metacognitive Awareness						
10	Metacognitive Awareness Descriptions					
12	Metacognitive Awareness Thinking Strategies Posters	●	●	●	●	●
14	Metacognitive Awareness Poster Cards	●	●	●	●	●
19	Metacognitive Awareness Poster Strips	●	●	●	●	●
24	Metacognitive Awareness Lesson Planning Form Shared Read Aloud	●	●			

Table of Comprehension Resources (continued)

		Balanced Literacy				
Page(s)	Resources	Aloud	Shared	Guided	Independent	Literature Circles
25	Book List for Metacognitive Awareness Shared Read Alouds	●	●			
Text Types and Text Structures						
27	Text Type, Text Structure, and Fact/ Opinion Resource Descriptions					
29	Four Text Types and Five Text Structures Resource Page	●	●	●	●	●
30	Four Text Types Resource Page	●	●	●	●	●
32	Text Structures Resource Page	●	●	●	●	●
33	Fact or Opinion? Resource Page	●	●	●	●	●

Table of Comprehension Activities and Lessons

Page(s)	Activities/Lessons	Blacklines	Balanced Literacy: Aloud	Shared	Guided	Independent	Literature Circles
36	Metacognitive Awareness Shared Read Aloud Comprehension Lesson	• Comprehension Lesson	●	●			
38	**Showdown Activities**						
39	Text Types (Narrative, Expository, Technical)	• Team Set • Student Set		●	●		
45	Text Features (Heading, Table of Contents, Glossary, Index, Caption)	• Team Set • Student Set		●	●		
49	Text Features (Map, Chart, Diagram, Timeline, Graph)	• Team Set • Student Set		●	●		
53	Fact or Opinion?	• Team Set • Student Set		●	●		
58	**Quiz-Quiz-Trade Activities**						
59	Cause–Effect	• 5 pages of question/ answer cards			●		
64	Emotions	• 7 pages of question/ answer cards			●		
71	Action Words—Verbs	• 8 pages of question/ answer cards			●		
79	Homophone Sentences	• 8 pages of question/ answer cards			●		
87	Homophones (it's, its)	• 7 pages of question/ answer cards			●		
94	Homophones (they're, there. their)	• 7 pages of question/ answer cards			●		
101	Homophones (are, our, hour)	• 7 pages of question/ answer cards			●		

Table of Comprehension Activities and Lessons (continued)

Page(s)	Activities/Lessons	Blacklines	Balanced Literacy: Aloud	Shared	Guided	Independent	Literature Circles
108	**Fan-N-Pick Activities**						
110	Text Features	• Fan-N-Pick Mat 2 pages of cards		●	●		
112	Story Elements (Fiction)	• Fan-N-Pick Mat 2 pages of cards		●	●		
114	Previewing Before Reading (Nonfiction)	• Fan-N-Pick Mat 2 pages of cards		●	●		
116	**Talking Chips Activity**						
117	Comprehension Story Element Cube	• Question Cube		●	●		
118	Comprehension Question Cube (Story Elements)	• Question Cube		●	●		
119	Comprehension Question Cube (Before Reading)	• Question Cube		●	●		
120	Comprehension Question Cube (After Reading)	• Question Cube		●	●		
121	Comprehension Question Cube (Reflection)	• Question Cube		●	●		
122	Questioning Cube	• Question Cube		●	●		
123	**RoundTable Consensus Activities**						
124	Vocabulary Spinner	• Spinner (Vocabulary) • 1 page of sentence cards		●	●		
128	Retelling (Fiction)	• Puzzle Pieces • Puzzle Mat		●	●		
130	Retelling (Nonfiction)	• Puzzle Pieces • Puzzle Mat		●	●		
132	Text Feature (Nonfiction)	• Puzzle Pieces • Puzzle Mat		●	●		

Table of Comprehension Activities and Lessons (continued)

Page(s)	Activities/Lessons	Blacklines	Balanced Literacy: Aloud	Shared	Guided	Independent	Literature Circles
134	**Solo and RallyCoach Activity**						
135	"Platypus" Anticipation Guide	• Anticipation Guide Sample • Answer Form • Anticipation Guide Blank Student Form	●	●	●	●	●
138	**Listen-Sketch-Draft Activity**						
139	Listen-Sketch-Draft	• Sample Page • Listen-Sketch-Draft Form	●	●	●	●	●
141	**Timed Pair Share Activity**						
142	Prediction Mat	• Prediction Mat • Blank Story Element Cards • Story Element Example Cards	●	●	●	●	●
145	**Jot Thoughts and Sorting Activity**						
146	Recall and Sorting Mat (Before and After Reading Knowledge)	• Recall Mat • Sorting Mat			●	●	●
148	**RallyCoach Activity**						
149	Text Structure	• Text Structure Sorting Mat • Cards			●	●	
151	Fact or Opinion?	• Fact or Opinion Sorting Mat • Fact or Opinion Cards			●	●	
155	Idioms	• Idiom Mat • Idiom Cards			●	●	
158	**Team Line-Ups Activity**						
159	Jumbled Sentences	• Word Cards			●		
161	Sequencing Events	• Event Cards			●		

Comprehension Resources

Resources/Materials Descriptions

How do we, as teachers, help our struggling readers improve their comprehension? We can show them how to build up their sight words, build their book list, and build time to practice reading. All of these activities are valuable but won't improve comprehension until we help students build a bridge . . . a bridge between their brains and the text.

Years of research have provided teachers with a list of comprehension strategies that good readers use while reading. Good readers are actively thinking while they read. They are aware when meaning has broken down, and they stop to fix the confusion. These strategies (Clarifying, Connecting, Deciding What Is Important, Evaluating, Inferring, Monitoring, Predicting, Prior Knowledge, Purpose Setting, Questioning, Responding Emotionally, Retelling/Summarizing, and Visualizing) become the thinking tools needed for bridge building.

Metacognitive awareness means that the reader is aware of his or her thinking during the reading of various types of texts. Through metacognitive awareness lessons, students learn to apply self-monitoring comprehension strategies. The components of balanced literacy become the avenue for the teaching and strengthening of these metacognitive comprehension strategies. Students are supported as they hear the teacher explain and use the strategies (aloud); observe the teacher use the strategies with text and participate at specific points (shared); practice the strategies with direct support and feedback (guided); and own the strategies through additional practice opportunities (independent).

Resources/Materials Descriptions (continued)

Metacognitive Awareness (Thinking Strategies) Poster (p. 12)

- This two-page poster identifies ten comprehension strategies for the teacher to use as a visual with modeling.
- It may be enlarged to use as a classroom poster or individually copied for students to keep in reading notebooks or journals for reference while reading.
- Now that students are aware that good readers think while reading, the teacher should model these strategies by stopping at various points during read aloud and explaining what she/he is thinking.
- Modeling of the use of these thinking strategies should be applied during the reading of various text types (narrative, expository, persuasive, and technical).

Metacognitive Awareness Poster Cards (p. 14) and Metacognitive Awareness Poster Strips (p. 19)

- As the teacher reads aloud, one strategy poster card or poster strip can be held up or referred to at a time, helping to focus the students' attention on the one strategy being modeled and explained.
- These cards or strips may be made into overhead transparencies to be used during shared read alouds.
- The cards may also be attached to a big book page with paper clips at the point in the text where the teacher stops to verbalize his/her thinking or when the students are sharing during **Timed Pair Share**.

Metacognitive Awareness Lesson Planning Form (Shared Read Aloud) (p. 24)

As the teacher continues to model the metacognitive awareness strategies, the Metacognitive Awareness Lesson Planning Form can be used to preplan specific, targeted comprehension strategies.

Book List for Metacognitive Awareness Shared Read Alouds (p. 25)

The book list is a resource for teacher read aloud, shared read aloud, or student literature circles that focus on metacognitive awareness (thinking) strategies.

Metacognitive Awareness Thinking Strategies Posters

Instructions: Enlarge for use as a classroom poster or make individual copies for students to keep as a reference in reading notebooks or journals.

What do I know about it?

(Prior Knowledge)

What might happen next?

(Predicting)

What do I wonder about?

(Questioning)

What is the picture in my mind?

(Visualizing)

Why do things happen?

(Inferring)

Metacognitive Awareness Thinking Strategies Posters

Instructions: Enlarge for use as a classroom poster or make individual copies for students to keep as a reference in reading notebooks or journals.

How does the character feel?

(Responding Emotionally)

What words or ideas don't I understand?

(Clarifying)

What is important in the text?

(Identifying Important Ideas)

How is it like something else?

(Making Connections)

- text to self
- text to text
- text to world

What was the text about?

(Retelling/Summarizing)

Metacognitive Awareness Poster Cards

Instructions: These cards may be copied on paper or made into overhead transparencies and cut apart to be used during teacher modeling or Timed Pair Share during shared read alouds.

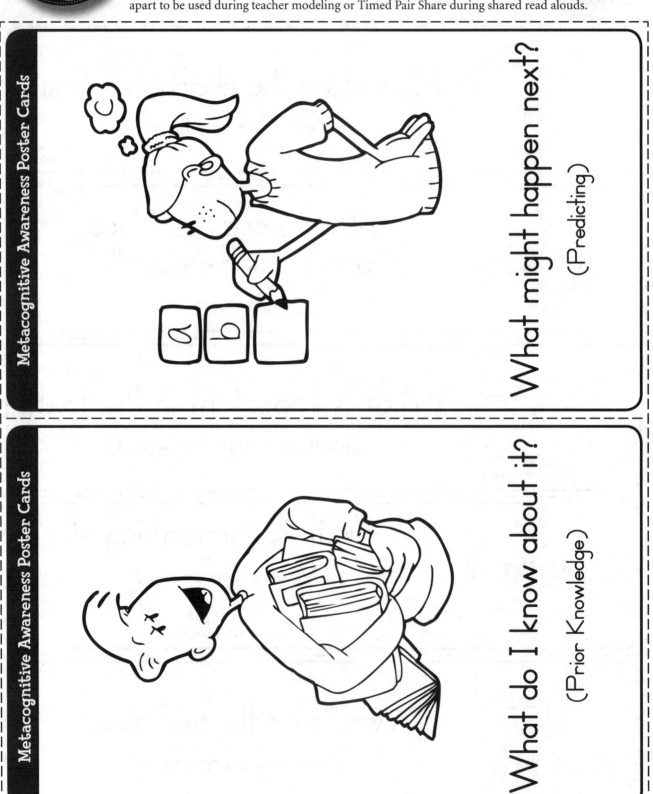

Metacognitive Awareness Poster Cards

What might happen next?

(Predicting)

Metacognitive Awareness Poster Cards

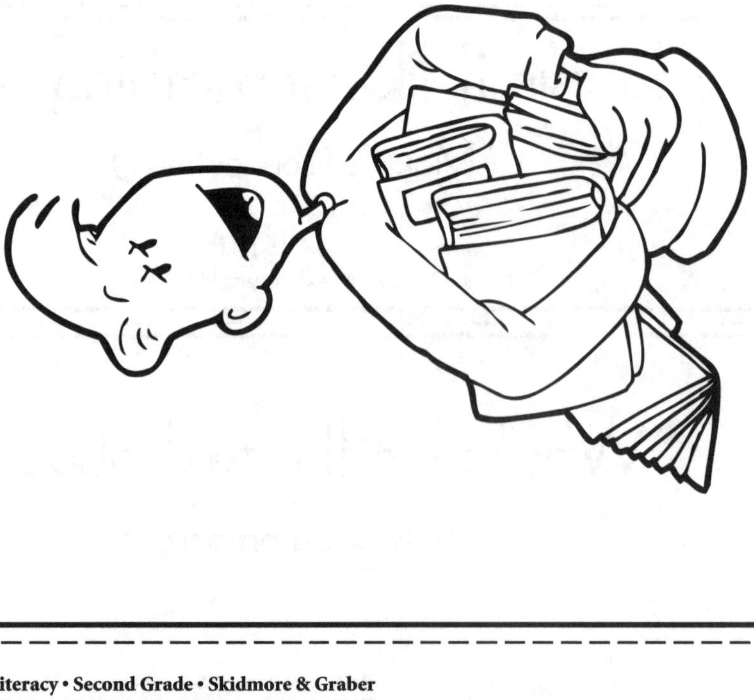

What do I know about it?

(Prior Knowledge)

Metacognitive Awareness Poster Cards

Instructions: These cards may be copied on paper or made into overhead transparencies and cut apart to be used during teacher modeling or Timed Pair Share during shared read alouds.

Metacognitive Awareness Poster Cards

What do I wonder about?

(Questioning)

Metacognitive Awareness Poster Cards

Instructions: These cards may be copied on paper or made into overhead transparencies and cut apart to be used during teacher modeling or Timed Pair Share during shared read alouds.

Metacognitive Awareness Poster Cards
How does the character feel?
(Responding Emotionally)

Metacognitive Awareness Poster Cards
WHY?
Why do things happen?
(Inferring)

Metacognitive Awareness Poster Cards

Instructions: These cards may be copied on paper or made into overhead transparencies and cut apart to be used during teacher modeling or Timed Pair Share during shared read alouds.

Metacognitive Awareness Poster Cards

explanation

What words or ideas don't I understand?

(Clarifying)

Metacognitive Awareness Poster Cards

Instructions: These cards may be copied on paper or made into overhead transparencies and cut apart to be used during teacher modeling or Timed Pair Share during shared read alouds.

Metacognitive Awareness Poster Cards
What was the text about?
(Retelling/Summarizing)

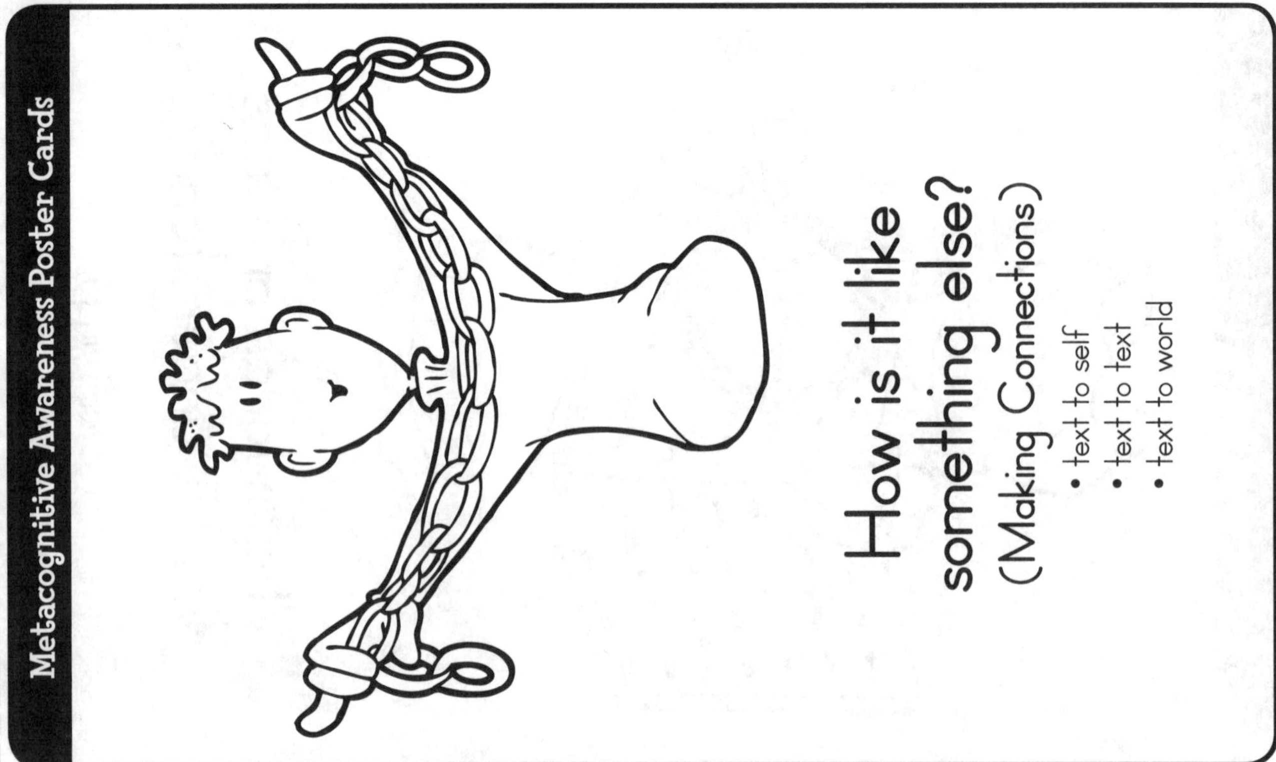

Metacognitive Awareness Poster Cards
How is it like something else?
(Making Connections)
• text to self
• text to text
• text to world

Metacognitive Awareness Poster Strips

Instructions: These strips may be copied on paper or made into overhead transparencies and cut apart to be used during teacher modeling or Timed Pair Share during shared read alouds.

Metacognitive Awareness Poster Strips

What do I know about it?

(Prior Knowledge)

Metacognitive Awareness Poster Strips

What might happen next?

(Predicting)

Metacognitive Awareness Poster Strips

Instructions: These strips may be copied on paper or made into overhead transparencies and cut apart to be used during teacher modeling or Timed Pair Share during shared read alouds.

Metacognitive Awareness Poster Strips

What do I wonder about?

(Questioning)

Metacognitive Awareness Poster Strips

What is the picture in my mind?

(Visualizing)

Metacognitive Awareness Poster Strips

Instructions: These strips may be copied on paper or made into overhead transparencies and cut apart to be used during teacher modeling or Timed Pair Share during shared read alouds.

Metacognitive Awareness Poster Strips

Why do things happen?

(Inferring)

WHY?

Metacognitive Awareness Poster Strips

How does the character feel?

(Responding Emotionally)

Metacognitive Awareness Poster Strips

Instructions: These strips may be copied on paper or made into overhead transparencies and cut apart to be used during teacher modeling or Timed Pair Share during shared read alouds.

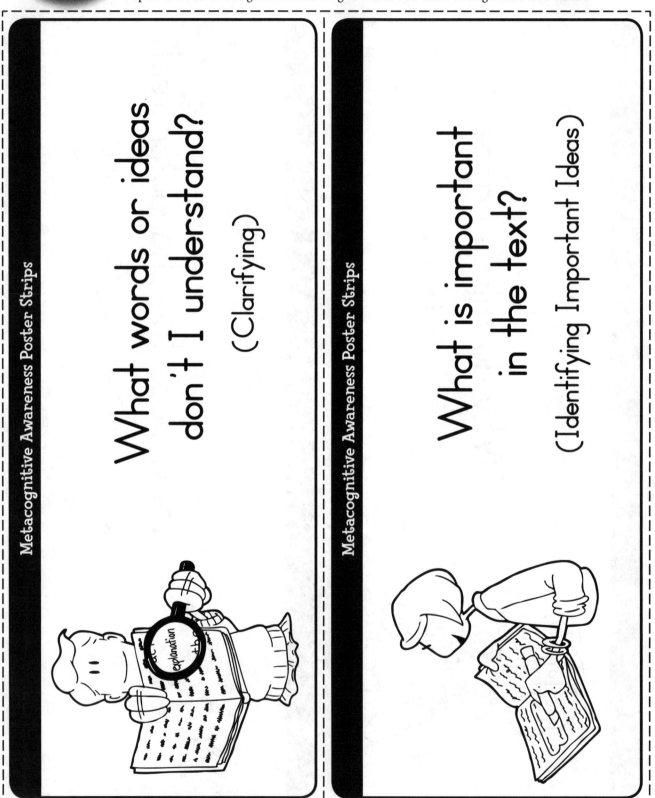

Metacognitive Awareness Poster Strips

What words or ideas don't I understand?

(Clarifying)

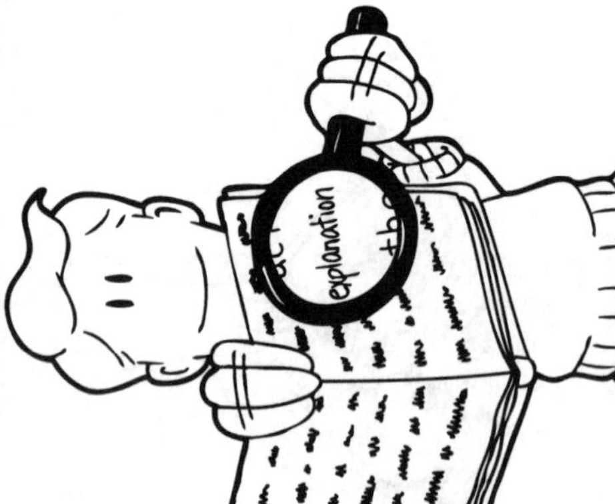

Metacognitive Awareness Poster Strips

What is important in the text?

(Identifying Important Ideas)

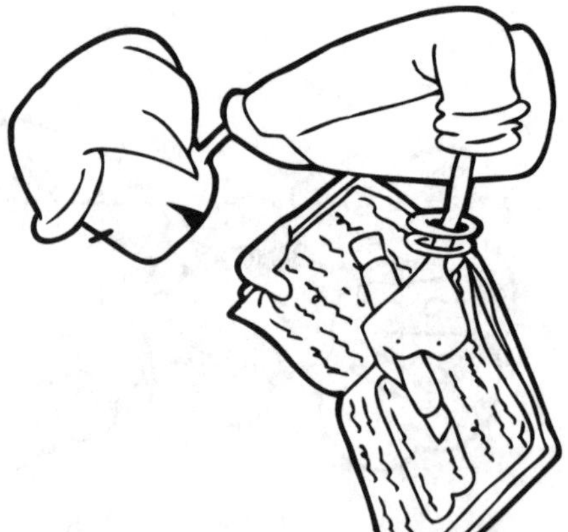

Metacognitive Awareness Poster Strips

Instructions: These strips may be copied on paper or made into overhead transparencies and cut apart to be used during teacher modeling or Timed Pair Share during shared read alouds.

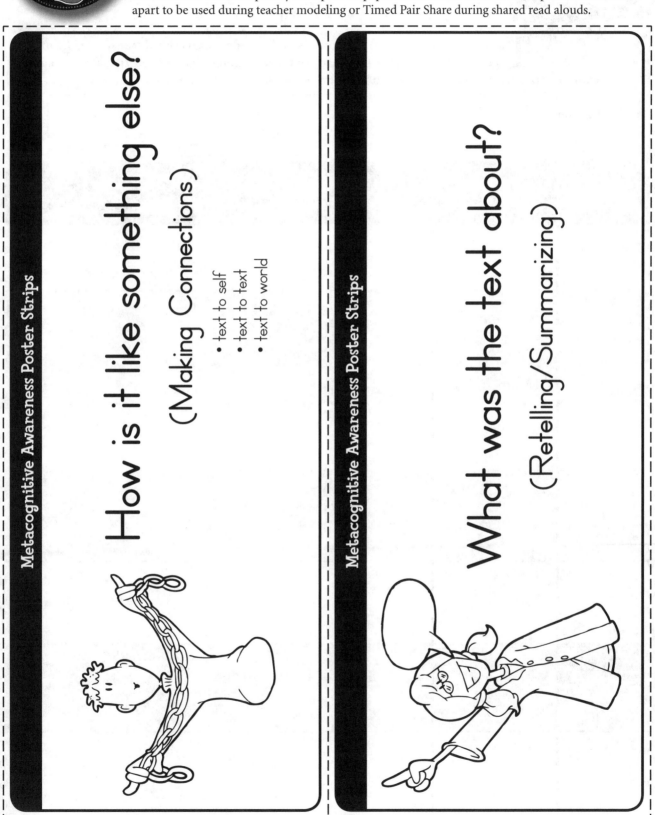

Metacognitive Awareness Poster Strips

How is it like something else?

(Making Connections)

- text to self
- text to text
- text to world

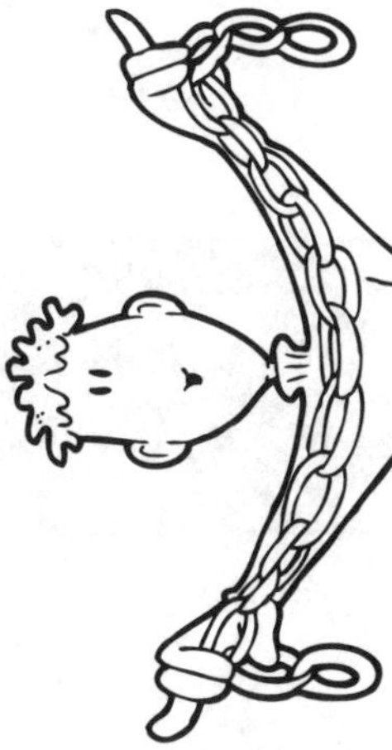

Metacognitive Awareness Poster Strips

What was the text about?

(Retelling/Summarizing)

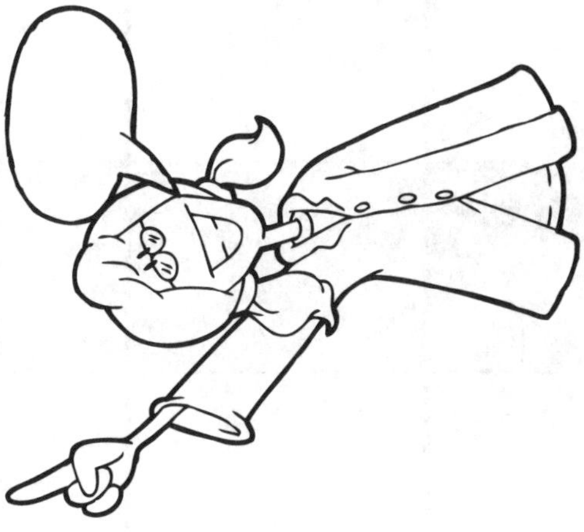

Metacognitive Awareness Lesson Planning Form

Shared Read Aloud

The teacher thinks aloud as she reads to the students. Overhead transparencies of specific pages from the book are used several times. Students participate by reading from the transparencies and then discussing the use of metacognitive strategies in teams.

Directions: Use this page to plan your lesson.

____

by: ______________________

Page	Reading Materials	Metacognitive Strategies (Teacher Think Aloud)

COMPREHENSION **Book List**

Metacognitive Awareness Shared Read Alouds

In addition to the following list of trade books, Big Books (both informational and literacy text) are ideal for Shared Read Alouds. Some of the books on the list may also be available in a Big Book format.

Book Title	Author
Song and Dance Man	Ackerman, Karen
America's Champion Swimmer	Adler, David A.
The Babe and I	Adler, David A.
Lou Gehrig, The Luckiest Man	Adler, David A.
Mama Played Baseball	Adler, David A.
Wagon Wheels	Brenner, Barbara
The Quiltmaker's Gift	Brumbeau, Jeff
Dandelions	Bunting, Eve
Fly Away Home	Bunting, Eve
Going Home	Bunting, Eve
Train to Somewhere	Bunting, Eve
Home Run	Burleigh, Robert
Verdi	Cannon, Janell
The Great Kapok Tree	Cherry, Lynne
The Josefina Story Quilt	Coerr, Eleanor
Miss Rumphius	Cooney, Barbara
Players in Pigtails	Corey, Shana
The Bat Boy and His Violin	Curtis, Gavin
Now One Foot, Now the Other	De Paola, Tomie
Sam Johnson and the Blue Ribbon Quilt	Ernst, Lisa Campbell
My Brother Martin: A Sister Remembers Growing Up with the Rev. Dr. Martin Luther King Jr.	Farris, Christine King
The Patchwork Quilt	Flournoy, Valerie
Teammates	Golenbock, Peter
Luka's Quilt	Guback, Georgia
Chrysanthemum	Henkes, Kevin
Lilly's Purple Plastic Purse	Henkes, Kevin
Sweet Clara and the Freedom Quilt	Hopkinson, Deborah
The Log Cabin Quilt	Howard, Ellen

COMPREHENSION **Book List**

Metacognitive Awareness Shared Read Alouds (continued)

Book Title	Author
The Boy and the Cloth of Dreams	Koralek, Jenny
Wilma Unlimited	Krull, Kathleen
It's Mine!	Lionni, Leo
The Rag Coat	Mills, Lauren
Uncle Jed's Barbershop	Mitchell, Margaree King.
The Drinking Gourd: A Story of the Underground Railroad	Monjo, F. N.
Lighthouse: A Story of Remembrance	Munsch, Robert
Almost to Freedom	Nelson, Vaunda Micheaux
The Keeping Quilt	Polacco, Patricia
Mrs. Katz and Tush	Polacco, Patricia
My Rotten Red-Headed Older Brother	Polacco, Patricia
Tar Beach	Ringgold, Faith
The Relatives Came	Rylant, Cynthia
When I Was Young in the Mountains	Rylant, Cynthia
Sylvester and the Magic Pebble	Steig, William
The Popcorn Dragon	Thayer, Jane
Alexander and the Terrible, Horrible, No Good, Very Bad Day	Viorst, Judith
Ira Sleeps Over	Waber, Bernard
Follow the Drinking Gourd	Winter, Jeanette
Owl Moon	Yolen, Jane

Text Type, Text Structure, and Fact/Opinion Resource Descriptions

Awareness of Text Types, Text Structures, and Fact/Opinion Benefits Readers' Comprehension

There are four general reasons why authors write. These are identified as text types. Identifying the text type of a passage lets the reader know what the author's goal was for writing the text. This knowledge allows the reader to set a purpose for reading.

Text structures are the organizational patterns found within the text types, which alert the reader to the arrangement of the text. Being aware of these structures and being able to identify them makes the text easier to understand. An author often chooses one main text structure for a piece, but may incorporate several of the structures throughout the writing.

Distinguishing between fact and opinion is a critical component of comprehension as the reader evaluates meaning. As students are exposed to a growing quantity of media, it is especially important that they recognize the differences between what is fact and what is someone's belief or view.

The following text type, text structure, and fact/opinion resources are for teacher and student use as instruction is scaffolded. The cooperative learning structures, Showdown and RallyCoach, located in this section of the book provide practice in identifying text types, identifying text structures using signal words in passages, and identifying the differences between fact and opinion.

Awareness of Text Types, Text Structures, and Fact/Opinion Benefits Readers' Comprehension (continued)

Four Text Types and Five Text Structures (p. 29)

This chart was designed as a resource allowing students to visualize both basic text type and text structure information. As students learn to identify the text structure(s) used in a text, a graphic organizer matching the organizational structure becomes a tool for increasing comprehension. The graphic organizers included here are basic examples, and students should be encouraged to experiment with the use of additional graphic organizers.

Four Text Types (p. 30)

There are four general reasons why authors write. These are identified as **text types**. Identifying the text type of a passage lets the reader know what the author's goal was for writing the text. This knowledge allows the reader to set a purpose for reading. These two pages, listing general characteristics of the four text types and examples of each, are resources for the teacher and students.

Text Types	
Narrative	**Technical**
Expository	**Persuasive**

**The Persuasive Text Type is introduced in second grade.*

Text Structures (p. 32)

Text structures are the organizational patterns found within the text types, which alert the reader to the arrangement of the text. Being aware of these structures and being able to identify them makes the text easier to understand. An author often chooses one main text structure for a piece, but may incorporate several of the structures throughout the writing. Signal words are frequently used by authors, which give hints about the text structure used in the writing. The chart on page 32 lists some of those words, as well as giving a brief description of the text structures.

Text Structures	
Sequence	**Description**
Problem and Solution	**Cause and Effect**
Compare and Contrast	

Fact or Opinion? Resource Page (p. 33)

This page lists key points for facts and opinions. It also lists signal words to help identify opinions and examples of fact and opinion statements.

Four Text Types

Text Type & Text Structures Resource Page

The four text types list four general reasons why authors write. Identifying the text type of a passage helps the reader set the purpose for reading and alerts the reader to the organization of the piece.

Narrative	Expository	Technical	Persuasive
• Entertains • Tells a story • Character(s), setting, problem, resolution	• Facts/ information • Text features (headings, bold words, charts, graphs, captions)	• Information to perform a task • Steps	• Author tries to convince reader to take a certain opinion or perform a certain action

Five Text Structures

Text structures are organizational patterns found within the text types. An author often chooses one main text structure for a piece but may incorporate several of the text structures throughout the piece.

Sequence	Problem and Solution	Compare and Contrast	Description	Cause and Effect
• Steps • Specific order 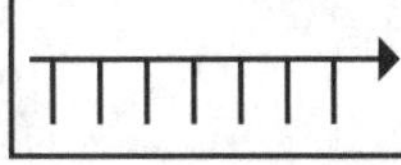 1. 2. 3. 4. 5.	• Problem, which is solved Problem Event Event Event Solution	• Comparing how things are the same/ different 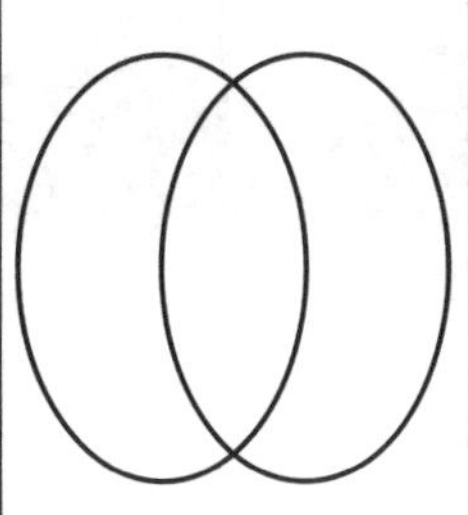	• Details 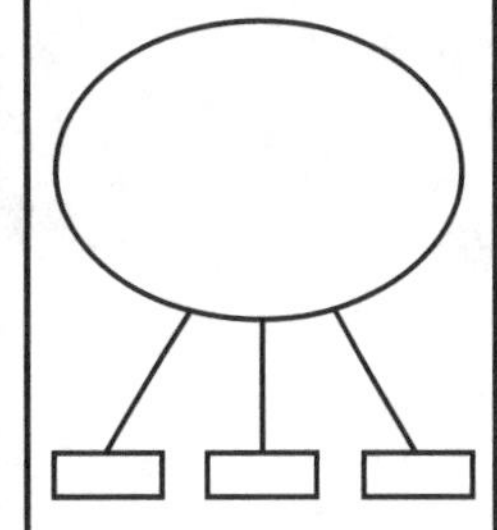	• Something causes something else to happen 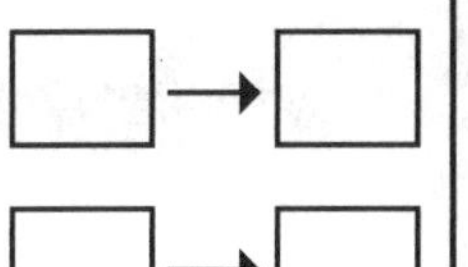

Four Text Types

Text Types Resource Page

Text Type	Characteristics	Examples	
Narrative	• Entertains the reader • Tells a story • Contains character(s) and a setting • Contains events • Has a problem/resolution • Contains theme that explains meaning of story • May be written in first, second, or third person • Makes sense when read from beginning to end	• Biographies • Drama • Diaries • Fables • Fantasies • Folk tales • Historical fiction • Legends • Mysteries	• Myths • Novels • Personal narratives • Plays • Poetry • Science fiction • Short stories • Tall tales, etc.
Expository	• Informs the reader • Contains facts and information • Explains, describes, discusses • May compare and contrast or present problem and solution • Includes text features such as headings, subheadings, bolded words, charts, graphs, diagrams, captions, indexes, glossaries, table of contents, etc.	• ABC books • Autobiographies • Biographies • Book reports • Brochures • Catalogs • Definitions • Essays • Interviews	• Invitations • Journals • Lists • Magazine articles • Newspaper • Recounts of an event • Research papers • Speeches, etc.

Four Text Types

Text Types Resource Page (continued)

Text Type	Characteristics	Examples	
Technical	• Nonfiction text • Gives information used to perform a task • May include explicit steps or graphics to show steps • Shortened or fragmented sentences • Numbered or bulleted lists • Organized in logical, orderly way • Focused on identified topic • Uses specific vocabulary terms • Balance of white space and text	• Brochures • Classified ads • Consumer information • Directions • Floor plans • Forms • Graphs and charts • How-to guides • Instructions • Job preparation manuals	• Maps • Menus • Questionnaires • Recipes • Regulations • Schedules • School forms • Syllabi • Transcripts • Warranties, etc.
Persuasive • Introduction only in second grade	• Nonfiction • Author intends to convince reader to take a particular opinion or perform a certain action • Attempts to solve problem through change • Uses appeal to reason, emotional appeal, or endorsement by an influential figure (bandwagon approach, glittering gereralities, testimonials, citing authority, statistics)	• Advertisements • Book reviews • Brochures • Business letters • Charitable campaign appeals • Commercials • Debates (written) • Editorials • Essays • Letters to the editor • Movie critiques • Political campaign literature • Position papers • Posters • Speeches, etc.	

Text Structures

Text Structures Resource Page

Text Type	Tells...	Signal Words		
Sequence	series or steps	• first • second • third • next	• finally • then • before • after	• now • during • while • not long after
Description	attributes, facts, and details about something	• some characteristics are • for instance	• in fact • in addition • has a	• about • is
Compare and Contrast	similarities and differences	• different from • like • same as • similar to	• resembles • both • also • too	• more than • however
Cause and Effect	reasons why something happens or exists	• so that • because of • as a result of • since	• so • in order to • for this reason	• therefore • if...then
Problem and Solution	problem, attempted solutions, and results	• problem is • solution is • have solved this problem by		

Fact or Opinion?

Fact or Opinion Resource Page

It is important to be aware of the difference between facts and opinions, so that when something is read, its meaning can be evaluated.

Text Type	Characteristics	Examples
Fact	• A statement that can be proved to be true or false • Can be proved with evidence (from expert, encyclopedia, your own eyes or ears, etc.)	• Jogging is a form of exercising. • My dog is brown. • The man was driving over the speed limit.
Opinion	• What someone believes or thinks • Cannot be proven true or false • How someone feels	Words that can express how someone feels give you clues that a statement is an opinion. feel, believe, always, never none, most, least, best worst, think, like, good should, probably, favorite, terrible beautiful, bad, ugly, smart better, wonderful, lovely, disgusting great, seems, all, might guess • Jogging is the best exercise. • My dog should win the contest. • I think the man was driving too fast.

Comprehension Activities and Lessons

Metacognitive Awareness Shared Read Aloud

Fly Away Home

by Eve Bunting

Materials:
- ***Fly Away Home*** by Eve Bunting
- **Metacognitive Awareness Poster Cards:** Display and refer to the appropriate cards during the shared read aloud.

Metacognitive Awareness Comprehension Lessons may be used during interactive read alouds (trade books) or shared reading (Big Books, overhead transparencies, or englarged texts).

Text Page	Structure	Metacognitive Strategies Teacher Think Aloud
Cover	Timed Pair Share	**Questioning:** What do I wonder about? (possible questions) • Why are the boy and his father at the airport? • Why do they look sad? • Why aren't they standing by the window? (share questions with partner)
5	Teacher Think Aloud	Answer questions raised from the cover. **Questioning:** What do I wonder about? (teacher think aloud for questions not raised by students) • Why don't they have a home? • Where is the boy's mother? • How is the airport better than the streets?
	Timed Pair Share	**Predicting:** How do you think they will avoid being caught?
6–13	Teacher Think Aloud	Read. Respond to predictions about ways to avoid being caught.
14–15	Timed Pair Share	**Understanding Character's Feelings:** How do you think the boy and his dad feel about their home in the airport? What makes you think that?
16–17	Teacher Think Aloud	**Making Connections:** (text to self, text to text, text to world) Read first paragraph and talk about how birds act when they get inside a building (garage, house, store). Birds will keep trying to get out of the building because they belong out in the open where they can fly. Their home is the sky. (make a connection)
	Timed Pair Share	**Visualizing:** What is the picture in my mind? "Listen and visualize (think about the picture in your head) as I reread this paragraph and finish the rest of the page." Share the picture your mind made of the bird trying to get out.
	Timed Pair Share	**Understanding the Character's Feelings:** Why do you think the boy said, "Nothing made me as happy as that bird"?

COMPREHENSION **Lesson**

Metacognitive Awareness Shared Read Aloud (continued)

Fly Away Home

Text Page	Structure	Metacognitive Strategies Teacher Think Aloud
18–25	**Teacher Think Aloud/Group Discussion**	Read and discuss answers to questions raised from page 5.
26–29	**Teacher Think Aloud**	Read.
30-31	**Timed Pair Share**	**Understanding Character's Feelings:** • How is Andrew feeling right now? Explain your thoughts. • In what ways is the airport a hard place for them to live?
32	**Timed Pair Share**	Read. **Connecting:** (text to self, text to text, text to world) Connect pages 16 and 32. (possible connecting questions) • Why is Andrew remembering the bird? • What door needs to open for Andrew and his dad to be free like the bird?

Comprehension Showdown

Teams play Showdown to master text types, text features, and fact or opinion.

Activity Steps

1. Each team receives a Team Set of cards and every student receives a Student Set of cards.
2. The Team Set is placed facedown in the middle of the team. Students hold their Student Set in their hands.
3. The teacher selects one student to be the Showdown Captain for the first round.
4. The Showdown Captain selects the top card from the middle and reads it aloud.
5. Working alone, students individually identify an answer from their card set.
6. When finished, teammates signal they are ready.
7. The Showdown Captain calls, "Showdown!"
8. Teammates show their answers at the same time.
9. The Showdown Captain leads checking.
10. If correct, the team celebrates. If not, the teammates coach, then celebrate.
11. The person to the left of the Showdown Captain becomes the Showdown Captain for the next round.

STRUCTURE
Showdown

Blacklines

Text Types—Narrative, Expository, Technical

Showdown (Team Set)

Instructions: Copy one set of cards for each team. Cut apart.

Text Types—Narrative, Expository, Technical	Text Types—Narrative, Expository, Technical
Which text type? a book about how to take care of a pet	Which text type? a drawing with labels showing where to attach bolts to a ladder
Which text type? the story about Jack and the Beanstalk	Which text type? a story about a hen, who planted wheat and made bread
Which text type? directions and steps on how to put a bicycle together	Which text type? a recipe for making cookies

Text Types—Narrative, Expository, Technical

Showdown (Team Set)

Instructions: Copy one set of cards for each team. Cut apart.

Text Types—Narrative, Expository, Technical

Which text type?

a story about a monkey fooling a crocodile

Text Types—Narrative, Expository, Technical

Which text type?

a direction sheet that came with a new TV

Text Types—Narrative, Expository, Technical

Which text type?

a report about snakes

Text Types—Narrative, Expository, Technical

Which text type?

a book about Japan

Text Types—Narrative, Expository, Technical

Which text type?

a book about different kinds of birds

Text Types—Narrative, Expository, Technical

Which text type?

a story about a man, who used logs as toothpicks

Text Types—Narrative, Expository, Technical

Showdown (Team Set)

Instructions: Copy one set of cards for each team. Cut apart.

Text Types—Narrative, Expository, Technical

Which text type?

a story about a giant who lived on top of a mountain

Text Types—Narrative, Expository, Technical

Which text type?

an article about the steps to plant a tree

Text Types—Narrative, Expository, Technical

Which text type?

a page in a magazine telling how to make a paper airplane

Text Types—Narrative, Expository, Technical

Which text type?

a book with steps and pictures for making crafts

Text Types—Narrative, Expository, Technical

Which text type?

a chapter in a book describing the weather in South America

Text Types—Narrative, Expository, Technical

Which text type?

a story about how a mouse family made a quilt

Text Types—Narrative, Expository, Technical

Showdown (Team Set)

Instructions: Copy one set of cards for each team. Cut apart.

Text Types—Narrative, Expository, Technical Which text type? an article in *Ranger Rick* about lions	**Text Types—Narrative, Expository, Technical** Which text type? the story about Cinderella
Text Types—Narrative, Expository, Technical Which text type? a story about a frog and a toad, who were best friends	**Text Types—Narrative, Expository, Technical** Which text type? a book about amazing animal facts
Text Types—Narrative, Expository, Technical Which text type? a book about animal homes	**Text Types—Narrative, Expository, Technical** Which text type? a story about twins, who traded names

Text Types—Narrative, Expository, Technical

Showdown (Team Set)

Instructions: Copy one set of cards for each team. Cut apart.

Text Types—Narrative, Expository, Technical	Text Types—Narrative, Expository, Technical
Which text type? a book about famous Americans	Which text type? a how-to book about building a bird house
Text Types—Narrative, Expository, Technical Which text type? a mystery story about a missing book	**Text Types—Narrative, Expository, Technical** Which text type? a book about extinct dinosaurs
Text Types—Narrative, Expository, Technical Which text type? directions on how to get from one city to another	**Text Types—Narrative, Expository, Technical** Which text type? a play about a little girl and a family of bears

Text Types—Narrative, Expository, Technical

Showdown (Student Set)

Note: This page has cards for two students. Copy, cut apart, and give each student one set of cards.

Text Types	Text Types	Text Types
Narrative	Expository	Technical
Text Types	**Text Types**	**Text Types**
Narrative	Expository	Technical

Text Features—Heading, Table of Contents, Glossary, Index, Caption

Showdown (Team Set)

Instructions: Copy one set of cards for each team. Cut apart.

Text Features—Heading, Table of Contents, Glossary, Index, Caption

eating, 2, 10, 17, 23
egg, 28, 29
egg tooth, 31
eyes, 15
fossils, 4, 20

Text Features—Heading, Table of Contents, Glossary, Index, Caption

Prehistoric Crocodiles

Text Features—Heading, Table of Contents, Glossary, Index, Caption

➔ Crocodiles are survivors from the dinosaur age

Text Features—Heading, Table of Contents, Glossary, Index, Caption

fossils—remains of plants and animals left in rocks

hatchling—animal that just came out of its egg

poacher—people who hunt and trap animals protected by law

Text Features—Heading, Table of Contents, Glossary, Index, Caption

Survivors 2
Keeping Cool 6
Eating 8
Squeaking Eggs 10

Text Features—Heading, Table of Contents, Glossary, Index, Caption

nest 11, 31
parents 22, 6
poacher 15, 29,
prehistoric 9, 41

Text Features—Heading, Table of Contents, Glossary, Index, Caption

Showdown (Team Set)

Instructions: Copy one set of cards for each team. Cut apart.

Text Features—Heading, Table of Contents, Glossary, Index, Caption

Tricks	3
Helping	6
Kinds	8
Breathing	12
Swimming	15

Text Features—Heading, Table of Contents, Glossary, Index, Caption

➔ Dolphin Tricks!

Dolphins preform shows at marine parks, theme parks, and aquariums. They wave with their flippers and leap high out of the water.

Text Features—Heading, Table of Contents, Glossary, Index, Caption

➔ Dolphins must come to the surface to breath air.

Text Features—Heading, Table of Contents, Glossary, Index, Caption

blowhole	hole on top of dolphin's head used for breathing
flipper	a wide, flat limb used for swimming
fluke	tail moved up and down in a wavy motion for swimming

Text Features—Heading, Table of Contents, Glossary, Index, Caption

blowholes 2, 5
fish 25
flippers 3, 9, 19
mammals 1, 15, 20
Pacific Coast 10
porpoises 3, 16
seals 13
snouts 3, 5
tails 5, 17
whales 27

Text Features—Heading, Table of Contents, Glossary, Index, Caption

dolphins—members of the whale family with long, pointy snouts

porpoises—members of the whale family with rounded snouts

"Dolphin Safe"—label on tuna meaning that fishing crews are careful not to harm dolphins

Text Features—Heading, Table of Contents, Glossary, Index, Caption

Showdown (Team Set)

Instructions: Copy one set of cards for each team. Cut apart.

Text Features—Heading, Table of Contents, Glossary, Index, Caption

Text Features—Heading, Table of Contents, Glossary, Index, Caption

➔ Bird Behavior

Have you ever looked closely at how birds behave? Have you noticed if they walk or hop? What are their flight patterns? Have you listened to their songs?

Text Features—Heading, Table of Contents, Glossary, Index, Caption

➔ Some birds spend most of their time in the water.

Text Features—Heading, Table of Contents, Glossary, Index, Caption

down feathers: soft feathers next to the bird's skin providing insulation

flight feathers: wing and tail feathers used for flying

plumage: all of a bird's feathers

Text Features—Heading, Table of Contents, Glossary, Index, Caption

Text Features—Heading, Table of Contents, Glossary, Index, Caption

<u>Bird Migration</u>

Text Features—Heading, Table of Contents, Glossary, Index, Caption

Showdown (Student Set)

Note: Copy, cut apart, and give each student one set of cards.

Text Features—Heading, Table of Contents, Glossary, Index, Caption	Text Features—Heading, Table of Contents, Glossary, Index, Caption	Text Features—Heading, Table of Contents, Glossary, Index, Caption
table of contents	index	
Text Features—Heading, Table of Contents, Glossary, Index, Caption	**Text Features—Heading, Table of Contents, Glossary, Index, Caption**	**Text Features—Heading, Table of Contents, Glossary, Index, Caption**
heading	glossary	caption

Text Features—Map, Chart, Diagram, Timeline, Graph

Showdown (Team Set)

Instructions: Copy one set of cards for each team. Cut apart.

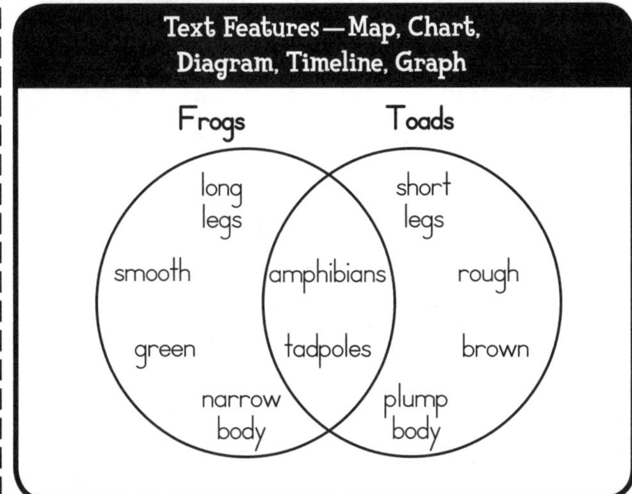

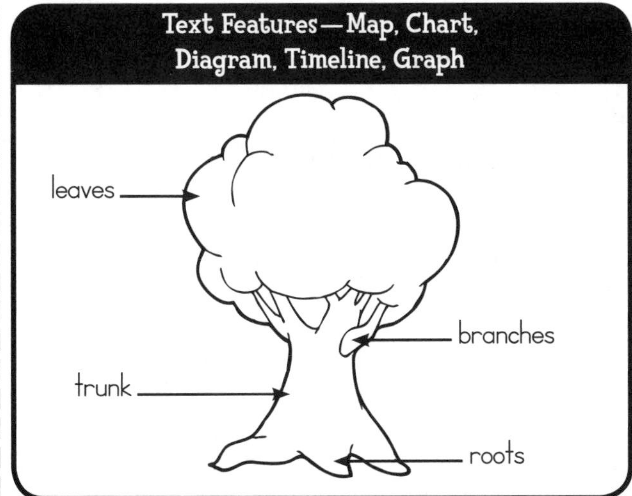

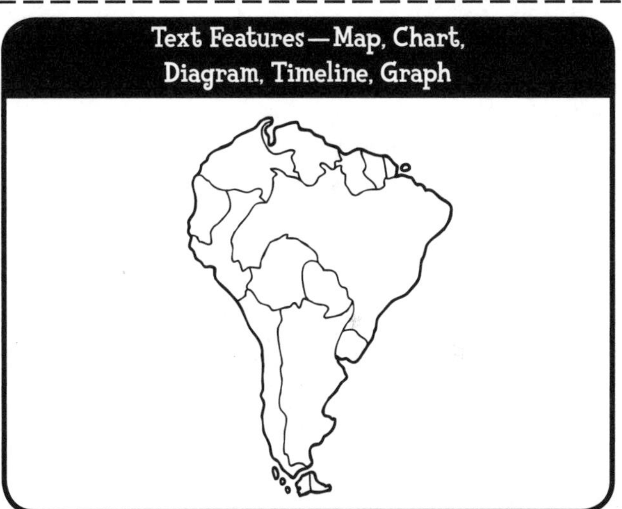

Text Features—Map, Chart, Diagram, Timeline, Graph

___at	___it
cat	lit
mat	sit
splat	split
bat	fit
fat	hit

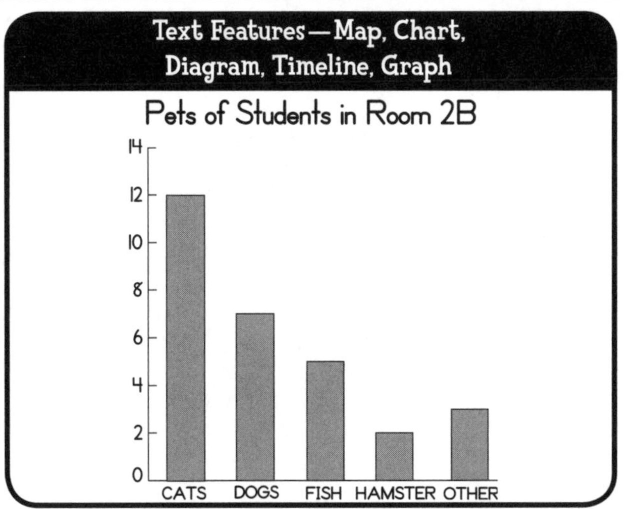

Text Features—Map, Chart, Diagram, Timeline, Graph

Showdown (Team Set)

Instructions: Copy one set of cards for each team. Cut apart.

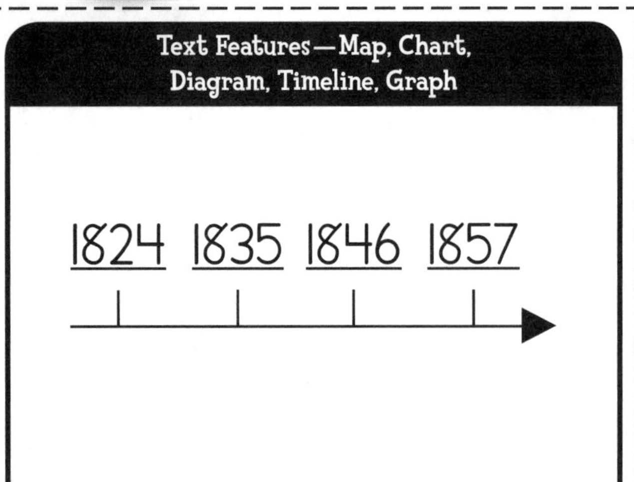

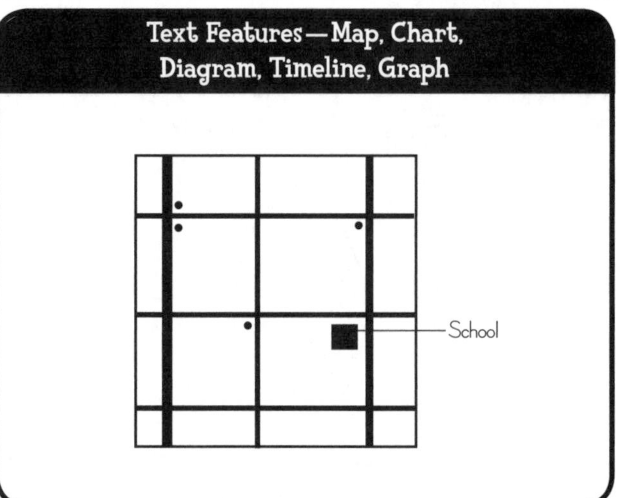

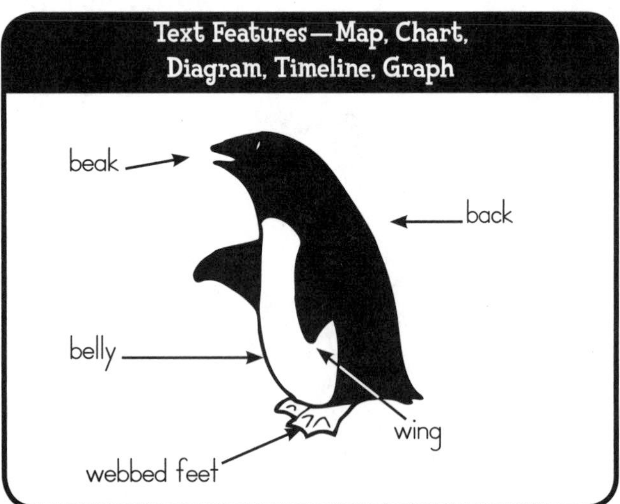

Text Features—Map, Chart, Diagram, Timeline, Graph

Carnival Tickets Sold

	Monday	Tuesday	Wednesday
Jim	23	10	15
Brett	9	11	6
Amy	14	3	17

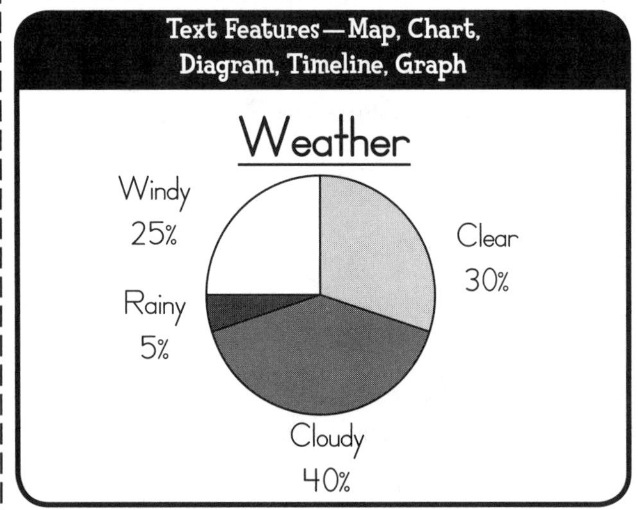

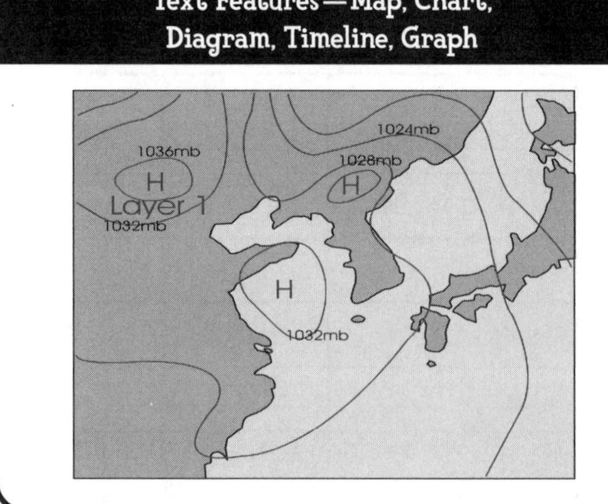

Text Features—Map, Chart, Diagram, Timeline, Graph

Showdown (Team Set)

Instructions: Copy one set of cards for each team. Cut apart.

Text Features—Map, Chart, Diagram, Timeline, Graph

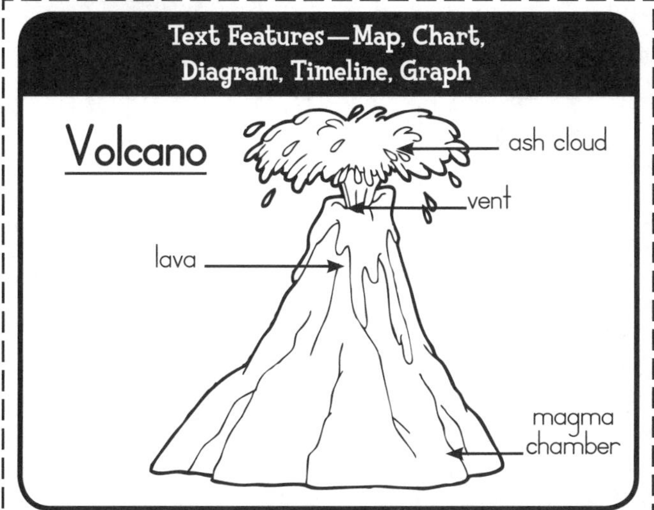

Text Features—Map, Chart, Diagram, Timeline, Graph

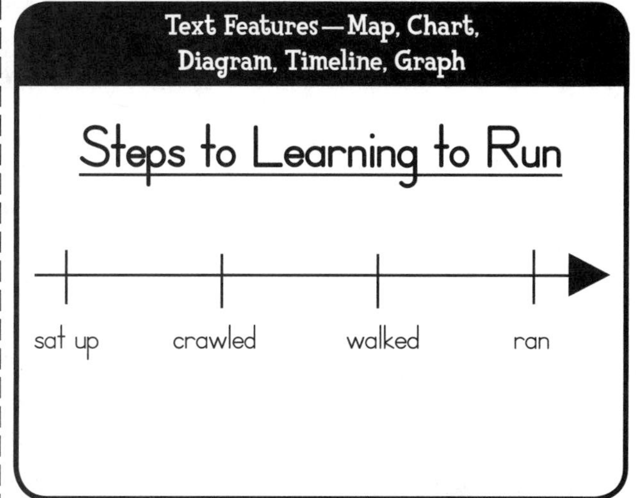

Text Features—Map, Chart, Diagram, Timeline, Graph

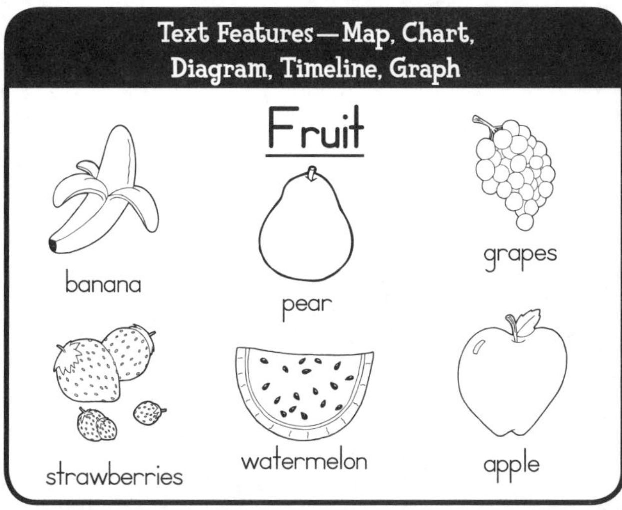

Text Features—Map, Chart, Diagram, Timeline, Graph

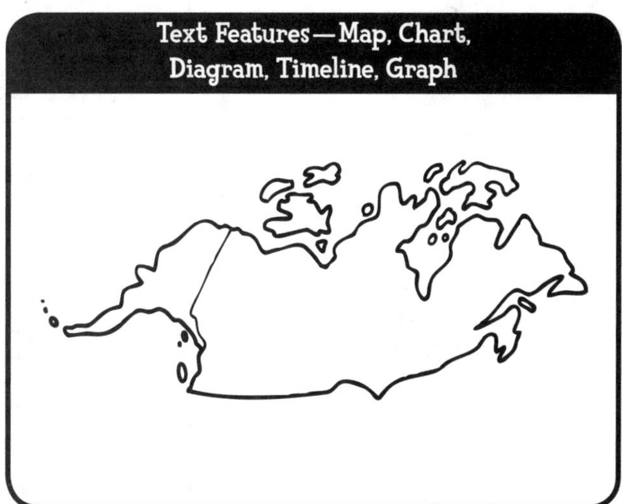

Text Features—Map, Chart, Diagram, Timeline, Graph

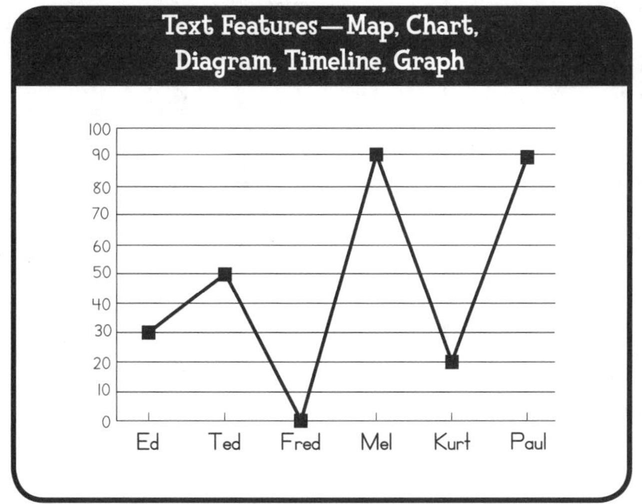

Text Features—Map, Chart, Diagram, Timeline, Graph

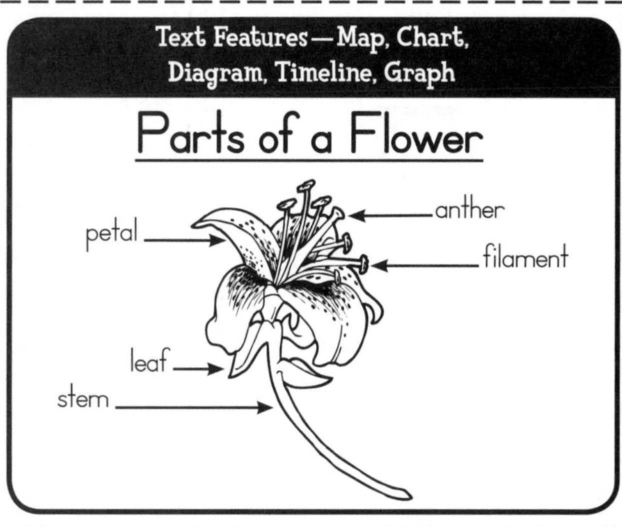

Text Features—Map, Chart, Diagram, Timeline, Graph

Showdown (Student Set)

Instructions: Copy, cut apart, and give each student one set of cards.

Text Features—Map, Chart, Diagram, Timeline, Graph	Text Features—Map, Chart, Diagram, Timeline, Graph	Text Features—Map, Chart, Diagram, Timeline, Graph
chart	timeline	

Text Features—Map, Chart, Diagram, Timeline, Graph	Text Features—Map, Chart, Diagram, Timeline, Graph	Text Features—Map, Chart, Diagram, Timeline, Graph
map	diagram	graph

Fact or Opinion?

Showdown (Team Set)

Instructions: Copy one set of cards for each team. Cut apart.

Fact or Opinion?	Fact or Opinion?
Taking a nap on an airplane is relaxing.	Steve spilled the bowl of popcorn.

Fact or Opinion?	Fact or Opinion?
It is best to read in a quiet room.	Soccer is a very entertaining game.

Fact or Opinion?	Fact or Opinion?
I think Kate should be a cheerleader because she can do a backflip.	The wind blew Abby's hat off.

Fact or Opinion?	Fact or Opinion?
Basketball was invented in 1891.	The best parties have at least ten people.

Fact or Opinion?	Fact or Opinion?
Kyle called his grandmother to tell her his team won the game.	Today is John's seventh birthday.

Fact or Opinion?

Showdown (Team Set)

Instructions: Copy one set of cards for each team. Cut apart.

Fact or Opinion?	Fact or Opinion?
Rainy days aren't fun.	Some spiders spin webs.

Fact or Opinion?	Fact or Opinion?
Sliding down a snowy hill is the most fun ever.	Mike was unhappy that his team lost.

Fact or Opinion?	Fact or Opinion?
There are many flavors of ice cream.	The perfume smells strong.

Fact or Opinion?	Fact or Opinion?
Spiders have eight legs.	Corey tells the funniest jokes.

Fact or Opinion?	Fact or Opinion?
Blue is the best color for the balloons at the party.	Subtracting is harder than adding.

Fact or Opinion?

Showdown (Team Set)

Instructions: Copy one set of cards for each team. Cut apart.

Fact or Opinion?	Fact or Opinion?
Tigger had four kittens, and they are adorable.	Turtles have hard shells.
Fact or Opinion?	**Fact or Opinion?**
Saturn is the most beautiful planet with its colorful rings.	Jazz is a gray, striped cat with green eyes.
Fact or Opinion?	**Fact or Opinion?**
Today is Monday.	It is easiest to travel by airplane.
Fact or Opinion?	**Fact or Opinion?**
Australia is an interesting place to visit.	Kansas is south of Nebraska.
Fact or Opinion?	**Fact or Opinion?**
There are four seasons in a year.	Pizza is the best food.

Fact or Opinion?

Showdown (Team Set)

Instructions: Copy one set of cards for each team. Cut apart.

Fact or Opinion?	Fact or Opinion?
My sister looks best in green.	The game was the most exciting one of the season.
Fact or Opinion?	**Fact or Opinion?**
The baseball game will be at Grasshopper Field.	Pat had a temperature of 101 degrees last evening.
Fact or Opinion?	**Fact or Opinion?**
Girls are better at soccer than boys.	This is the best book you'll ever read.
Fact or Opinion?	**Fact or Opinion?**
Japan is a beautiful country.	A red traffic light means STOP in America.
Fact or Opinion?	**Fact or Opinion?**
Chocolate candy is the most delicious.	Carrots and corn are vegetables.

Fact or Opinion?

Showdown (Student Set)

Instructions: This page has cards for three students. Copy, cut apart, and give each student one set of cards.

Fact or Opinion?	Fact or Opinion?	Fact or Opinion?
Fact	Fact	Fact

Fact or Opinion?	Fact or Opinion?	Fact or Opinion?
Opinion	Opinion	Opinion

Comprehension Quizzes

Teams play Quiz-Quiz-Trade for repeated practice on cause-effect, emotions, action words—verbs, homophone sentences, and homophones.

Activity Steps

1. Each student receives a card with a question on the front and an answer on the back.
2. Students stand up, put a hand up, and pair up with another student.
3. Partner A quizzes Partner B using the card.
4. Partner B answers the question.
5. Partner A praises if the answer is correct or provides the correct answer.
6. Partner B now quizzes Partner A, Partner A answers, and Partner B praises or provides the correct answer.
7. Partners trade cards and find a new partner to quiz. The activity continues for multiple rounds, allowing students to quiz and get quizzed multiple times.

STRUCTURE

Quiz-Quiz-Trade

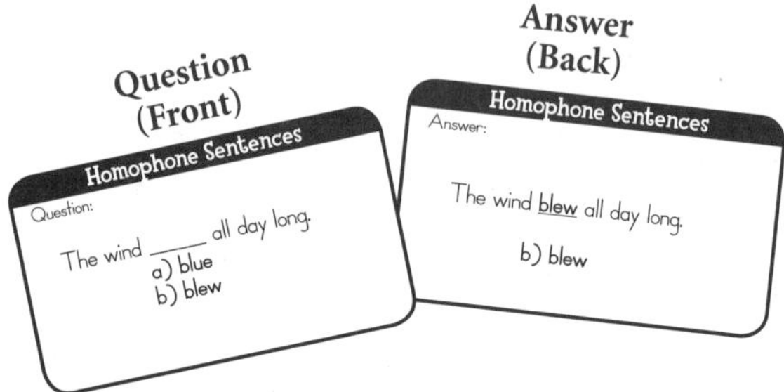

Blacklines

Cause–Effect

Quiz-Quiz-Trade

Instructions: Copy enough cards so each student has one card. Cut on dotted lines and fold in half.

Cause–Effect	Cause–Effect
Question: Which is the **cause**? Which is the **effect**? The book was so interesting. I couldn't quit reading.	Answer: Cause: The book was so interesting. Effect: I couldn't quit reading.

Cause–Effect	Cause–Effect
Question: Which is the **cause**? Which is the **effect**? The policeman put the robber in jail. The man robbed the bank.	Answer: Cause: The man robbed the bank. Effect: The policeman put the robber in jail.

Cause–Effect	Cause–Effect
Question: Which is the **cause**? Which is the **effect**? School was canceled. There were seven inches of snow on the ground this morning.	Answer: Cause: There were seven inches of snow on the ground this morning. Effect: School was canceled.

Cause–Effect	Cause–Effect
Question: Which is the **cause**? Which is the **effect**? I forgot to water my plant. The plant died.	Answer: Cause: I forgot to water my plant. Effect: The plant died.

Cause–Effect	Cause–Effect
Question: Which is the **cause**? Which is the **effect**? The tire on Alex's bike is flat. Alex rode his bike over a nail.	Answer: Cause: Alex rode his bike over a nail. Effect: The tire on Alex's bike is flat.

Cause–Effect

Quiz-Quiz-Trade

Instructions: Copy enough cards so each student has one card. Cut on dotted lines and fold in half.

Cause–Effect	Cause–Effect
Question: Which is the **cause**? Which is the **effect**? I have a sunburn. I didn't put on suntan lotion when I went to the beach.	Answer: Cause: I didn't put on suntan lotion when I went to the beach. Effect: I have a sunburn.
Cause–Effect	**Cause–Effect**
Question: Which is the **cause**? Which is the **effect**? Firemen came to put out a grass fire. A boy was playing with matches in his backyard.	Answer: Cause: A boy was playing with matches in his backyard. Effect: Firemen came to put out a grass fire.
Cause–Effect	**Cause–Effect**
Question: Which is the **cause**? Which is the **effect**? Grandma called 911. The ambulance came to Grandma's house.	Answer: Cause: Grandma called 911. Effect: The ambulance came to Grandma's house.
Cause–Effect	**Cause–Effect**
Question: Which is the **cause**? Which is the **effect**? My sand castle crumbled. The waves came crashing up on the beach.	Answer: Cause: The waves came crashing up on the beach. Effect: My sand castle crumbled.
Cause–Effect	**Cause–Effect**
Question: Which is the **cause**? Which is the **effect**? I overslept. I forgot to set my alarm clock.	Answer: Cause: I forgot to set my alarm clock. Effect: I overslept.

Cause–Effect

Quiz-Quiz-Trade

Instructions: Copy enough cards so each student has one card. Cut on dotted lines and fold in half.

Cause–Effect

Question: Which is the **cause**? Which is the **effect**?

I ate a snack.

I was hungry.

Cause–Effect

Answer:

Cause: I was hungry.

Effect: I ate a snack.

Cause–Effect

Question: Which is the **cause**? Which is the **effect**?

Sara cleaned up the sticky juice from the kitchen floor.

The carton of orange juice fell out of the refrigerator.

Cause–Effect

Answer:

Cause: The carton of orange juice fell out of the refrigerator.

Effect: Sara cleaned up the sticky juice from the kitchen floor.

Cause–Effect

Question: Which is the **cause**? Which is the **effect**?

The piano repairman came to fix the piano.

Three keys on the piano did not play.

Cause–Effect

Answer:

Cause: Three keys on the piano did not play.

Effect: The piano repairman came to fix the piano.

Cause–Effect

Question: Which is the **cause**? Which is the **effect**?

The milk jug was empty.

Chris went to the grocery store to buy milk.

Cause–Effect

Answer:

Cause: The milk jug was empty.

Effect: Chris went to the grocery store to buy milk.

Cause–Effect

Question: Which is the **cause**? Which is the **effect**?

The trash can in the garage was overflowing.

Mike put the trash in a large black trash bag and took it to the curb.

Cause–Effect

Answer:

Cause: The trash can in the garage was overflowing.

Effect: Mike put the trash in a large black trash bag and took it to the curb.

Cause–Effect

Quiz-Quiz-Trade

Instructions: Copy enough cards so each student has one card. Cut on dotted lines and fold in half.

Cause–Effect

Question: Which is the **cause**? Which is the **effect**?

Tina fell down at recess while playing soccer.

Tina went to the nurse's office for a bandage.

Cause–Effect

Answer:

Cause: Tina fell down at recess while playing soccer.

Effect: Tina went to the nurse's office for a bandage.

Cause–Effect

Question: Which is the **cause**? Which is the **effect**?

Mark locked his car keys in his sports car.

Mark walked two miles to get home after work.

Cause–Effect

Answer:

Cause: Mark locked his car keys in his sports car.

Effect: Mark walked two miles to get home after work.

Cause–Effect

Question: Which is the **cause**? Which is the **effect**?

The road crew fixed the street.

The street had many potholes and cracks.

Cause–Effect

Answer:

Cause: The street had many potholes and cracks.

Effect: The road crew fixed the street.

Cause–Effect

Question: Which is the **cause**? Which is the **effect**?

Chloe's story was published in the school newspaper.

Chloe worked carefully writing a story about her cat, Sophie.

Cause–Effect

Answer:

Cause: Chloe worked carefully writing a story about her cat, Sophie.

Effect: Chloe's story was published in the school newspaper.

Cause–Effect

Question: Which is the **cause**? Which is the **effect**?

Hannah was chosen for the lead role in the play.

Hannah tried out for the school play after practicing her lines.

Cause–Effect

Answer:

Cause: Hannah tried out for the school play after practicing her lines.

Effect: Hannah was chosen for the lead role in the play.

Cause–Effect

Quiz-Quiz-Trade

Instructions: Copy enough cards so each student has one card. Cut on dotted lines and fold in half.

Cause–Effect	Cause–Effect
Question: Which is the **cause**? Which is the **effect**? Parker cleaned the garage and found his tools. Parker couldn't find the tools in his garage to fix his bike.	Answer: Cause: Parker couldn't find the tools in his garage to fix his bike. Effect: Parker cleaned the garage and found his tools.
Cause–Effect	**Cause–Effect**
Question: Which is the **cause**? Which is the **effect**? We caught our limit of fish. The fish in the lake were extremely hungry this evening.	Answer: Cause: The fish in the lake were extremely hungry this evening. Effect: We caught our limit of fish.
Cause–Effect	**Cause–Effect**
Question: Which is the **cause**? Which is the **effect**? Three extra people came for lunch. We ran out of food.	Answer: Cause: Three extra people came for lunch. Effect: We ran out of food.
Cause–Effect	**Cause–Effect**
Question: Which is the **cause**? Which is the **effect**? The snow fell for three hours. We needed to shovel the snow from our sidewalk.	Answer: Cause: The snow fell for three hours. Effect: We needed to shovel the snow from our sidewalk.
Cause–Effect	**Cause–Effect**
Question: Which is the **cause**? Which is the **effect**? We were unable to get a drink of water. The city turned off the water for several hours, so repairs could be made to the water line.	Answer: Cause: The city turned off the water for several hours, so repairs could be made to the water line. Effect: We were unable to get a drink of water.

Emotions

Quiz-Quiz-Trade

Instructions: Copy enough cards so each student has one card. Cut on dotted lines and fold in half.

Emotions	Emotions
Say the word. Act it out. **happy**	Say the word. Act it out. **happy**
Say the word. Act it out. **excited**	Say the word. Act it out. **excited**
Say the word. Act it out. **angry**	Say the word. Act it out. **angry**
Say the word. Act it out. **ashamed**	Say the word. Act it out. **ashamed**

Emotions

Quiz-Quiz-Trade

Instructions: Copy enough cards so each student has one card. Cut on dotted lines and fold in half.

Emotions	Emotions
Say the word. Act it out. worried	Say the word. Act it out. worried
Say the word. Act it out. scared	Say the word. Act it out. scared
Say the word. Act it out. embarrassed	Say the word. Act it out. embarrassed
Say the word. Act it out. proud	Say the word. Act it out. proud

Emotions

Quiz-Quiz-Trade

Instructions: Copy enough cards so each student has one card. Cut on dotted lines and fold in half.

Emotions	Emotions
Say the word. Act it out. shocked	Say the word. Act it out. shocked
Say the word. Act it out. interested	Say the word. Act it out. interested
Say the word. Act it out. exhausted	Say the word. Act it out. exhausted
Say the word. Act it out. shy	Say the word. Act it out. shy

Emotions

Quiz-Quiz-Trade

Instructions: Copy enough cards so each student has one card. Cut on dotted lines and fold in half.

Emotions	Emotions
Say the word. Act it out. stubborn	Say the word. Act it out. stubborn
Say the word. Act it out. tired	Say the word. Act it out. tired
Say the word. Act it out. angry	Say the word. Act it out. angry
Say the word. Act it out. terrified	Say the word. Act it out. terrified

Emotions

Quiz-Quiz-Trade

Instructions: Copy enough cards so each student has one card. Cut on dotted lines and fold in half.

Emotions	Emotions
Say the word. Act it out. **relaxed**	Say the word. Act it out. **relaxed**
Say the word. Act it out. **afraid**	Say the word. Act it out. **afraid**
Say the word. Act it out. **jealous**	Say the word. Act it out. **jealous**
Say the word. Act it out. **disgusted**	Say the word. Act it out. **disgusted**

Emotions

Quiz-Quiz-Trade

Instructions: Copy enough cards so each student has one card. Cut on dotted lines and fold in half.

Emotions	Emotions
Say the word. Act it out. **lonely**	Say the word. Act it out. **lonely**
Say the word. Act it out. **undecided**	Say the word. Act it out. **undecided**
Say the word. Act it out. **curious**	Say the word. Act it out. **curious**
Say the word. Act it out. **hurt**	Say the word. Act it out. **hurt**

Emotions

Quiz-Quiz-Trade

Instructions: Copy enough cards so each student has one card. Cut on dotted lines and fold in half.

Emotions	Emotions
Say the word. Act it out. **sad**	Say the word. Act it out. **sad**
Say the word. Act it out. **determined**	Say the word. Act it out. **determined**
Say the word. Act it out. **frustrated**	Say the word. Act it out. **frustrated**
Say the word. Act it out. **mad**	Say the word. Act it out. **mad**

Action Words—Verbs

Quiz-Quiz-Trade

Instructions: Copy enough cards so each student has one card. Cut on dotted lines and fold in half.

Action Words—Verbs

Say the word. Act it out.

snort

Action Words—Verbs

Say the word. Act it out.

snort

Action Words—Verbs

Say the word. Act it out.

complain

Action Words—Verbs

Say the word. Act it out.

complain

Action Words—Verbs

Say the word. Act it out.

shriek

Action Words—Verbs

Say the word. Act it out.

shriek

Action Words—Verbs

Say the word. Act it out.

weep

Action Words—Verbs

Say the word. Act it out.

weep

Action Words—Verbs

Quiz-Quiz-Trade

Instructions: Copy enough cards so each student has one card. Cut on dotted lines and fold in half.

Action Words—Verbs	Action Words—Verbs
Say the word. Act it out. protest	Say the word. Act it out. protest
Action Words—Verbs Say the word. Act it out. agree	**Action Words—Verbs** Say the word. Act it out. agree
Action Words—Verbs Say the word. Act it out. howl	**Action Words—Verbs** Say the word. Act it out. howl
Action Words—Verbs Say the word. Act it out. snarl	**Action Words—Verbs** Say the word. Act it out. snarl

Action Words—Verbs

Quiz-Quiz-Trade

Instructions: Copy enough cards so each student has one card. Cut on dotted lines and fold in half.

Action Words—Verbs	Action Words—Verbs
Say the word. Act it out. **lecture**	Say the word. Act it out. **lecture**

Action Words—Verbs	Action Words—Verbs
Say the word. Act it out. **moan**	Say the word. Act it out. **moan**

Action Words—Verbs	Action Words—Verbs
Say the word. Act it out. **sniff**	Say the word. Act it out. **sniff**

Action Words—Verbs	Action Words—Verbs
Say the word. Act it out. **hoot**	Say the word. Act it out. **hoot**

Action Words—Verbs

Quiz-Quiz-Trade

Instructions: Copy enough cards so each student has one card. Cut on dotted lines and fold in half.

Action Words—Verbs	Action Words—Verbs
Say the word. Act it out. gasp	Say the word. Act it out. gasp
Action Words—Verbs Say the word. Act it out. bawl	Action Words—Verbs Say the word. Act it out. bawl
Action Words—Verbs Say the word. Act it out. brag	Action Words—Verbs Say the word. Act it out. brag
Action Words—Verbs Say the word. Act it out. chuckle	Action Words—Verbs Say the word. Act it out. chuckle

Action Words—Verbs

Quiz-Quiz-Trade

Instructions: Copy enough cards so each student has one card. Cut on dotted lines and fold in half.

Action Words—Verbs	Action Words—Verbs
Say the word. Act it out. coax	Say the word. Act it out. coax
Action Words—Verbs	Action Words—Verbs
Say the word. Act it out. stutter	Say the word. Act it out. stutter
Action Words—Verbs	Action Words—Verbs
Say the word. Act it out. blurt	Say the word. Act it out. blurt
Action Words—Verbs	Action Words—Verbs
Say the word. Act it out. echo	Say the word. Act it out. echo

Action Words—Verbs

Quiz-Quiz-Trade

Instructions: Copy enough cards so each student has one card. Cut on dotted lines and fold in half.

Action Words—Verbs	Action Words—Verbs
Say the word. Act it out. frolic	Say the word. Act it out. frolic
Action Words—Verbs	Action Words—Verbs
Say the word. Act it out. nibble	Say the word. Act it out. nibble
Action Words—Verbs	Action Words—Verbs
Say the word. Act it out. swoop	Say the word. Act it out. swoop
Action Words—Verbs	Action Words—Verbs
Say the word. Act it out. slither	Say the word. Act it out. slither

Action Words—Verbs

Quiz-Quiz-Trade

Instructions: Copy enough cards so each student has one card. Cut on dotted lines and fold in half.

Action Words—Verbs	Action Words—Verbs
Say the word. Act it out. tiptoe	Say the word. Act it out. tiptoe
Action Words—Verbs	Action Words—Verbs
Say the word. Act it out. glance	Say the word. Act it out. glance
Action Words—Verbs	Action Words—Verbs
Say the word. Act it out. collapse	Say the word. Act it out. collapse
Action Words—Verbs	Action Words—Verbs
Say the word. Act it out. trudge	Say the word. Act it out. trudge

Action Words—Verbs

Quiz-Quiz-Trade

Instructions: Copy enough cards so each student has one card. Cut on dotted lines and fold in half.

Action Words—Verbs	Action Words—Verbs
Say the word. Act it out. snicker	Say the word. Act it out. snicker
Say the word. Act it out. tumble	Say the word. Act it out. tumble
Say the word. Act it out. whirl	Say the word. Act it out. whirl
Say the word. Act it out. sprint	Say the word. Act it out. sprint

Homophone Sentences

Quiz-Quiz-Trade

Instructions: Copy enough cards so each student has one card. Cut on dotted lines and fold in half.

Homophone Sentences	Homophone Sentences
Question: Jim _____ a card for his mom. a) made b) maid	Answer: Jim made a card for his mom. a) made
Question: Our _____ cleaned the kitchen. a) made b) maid	Answer: Our maid cleaned the kitchen. b) maid
Question: One _____ crawled on my arm. a) aunt b) ant	Answer: One ant crawled on my arm. b) ant
Question: Sharon's _____ came to visit. a) aunt b) ant	Answer: Sharon's aunt came to visit. a) aunt

Homophone Sentences

Quiz-Quiz-Trade

Instructions: Copy enough cards so each student has one card. Cut on dotted lines and fold in half.

Homophone Sentences	Homophone Sentences
Question: We saw _____ rabbit hop in the grass. a) one b) won	Answer: We saw one rabbit hop in the grass. a) one
Question: The team _____ the game. a) one b) won	Answer: The team won the game. b) won
Question: We baked _____ cookies. a) ate b) eight	Answer: We baked eight cookies. b) eight
Question: The children _____ lunch. a) ate b) eight	Answer: The children ate lunch. a) ate

Homophone Sentences

Quiz-Quiz-Trade

Instructions: Copy enough cards so each student has one card. Cut on dotted lines and fold in half.

Homophone Sentences	Homophone Sentences
Question: The ship sailed on the _____. a) sea b) see	Answer: The ship sailed on the <u>sea</u>. a) sea
Question: From the deck we could _____ the lake. a) sea b) see	Answer: From the deck we could <u>see</u> the lake. b) see
Question: After being sick Joe was _____. a) week b) weak	Answer: After being sick Joe was <u>weak</u>. b) weak
Question: It has been one _____ since I saw you. a) week b) weak	Answer: It has been one <u>week</u> since I saw you. a) week

Homophone Sentences

Quiz-Quiz-Trade

Instructions: Copy enough cards so each student has one card. Cut on dotted lines and fold in half.

Homophone Sentences	Homophone Sentences
Question: Today _____ will go to school. a) I b) eye	Answer: Today I will go to school. a) I
Question: Dust blew into my _____. a) I b) eye	Answer: Dust blew into my eye. b) eye
Question: The bright _____ warmed us. a) son b) sun	Answer: The bright sun warmed us. b) sun
Question: Cole is Kay's _____. a) son b) sun	Answer: Cole is Kay's son. a) son

Homophone Sentences

Quiz-Quiz-Trade

Instructions: Copy enough cards so each student has one card. Cut on dotted lines and fold in half.

Homophone Sentences	Homophone Sentences
Question: The rope had a large _____ . a) knot b) not	Answer: The rope had a large knot. a) knot
Question: We will _____ be going to the zoo today. a) knot b) not	Answer: We will not be going to the zoo today. b) not
Question: The wind _____ all day long. a) blue b) blew	Answer: The wind blew all day long. b) blew
Question: His shirt was light _____ . a) blue b) blew	Answer: His shirt was light blue. a) blue

Homophone Sentences

Quiz-Quiz-Trade

Instructions: Copy enough cards so each student has one card. Cut on dotted lines and fold in half.

Homophone Sentences	Homophone Sentences
Question: The dog's _____ wagged when you came. a) tail b) tale	Answer: The dog's tail wagged when you came. a) tail
Question: The boy read the _____ to the class. a) tail b) tale	Answer: The boy read the tale to the class. b) tale
Question: The box was _____ in the mail. a) sent b) cent	Answer: The box was sent in the mail. a) sent
Question: A penny is one _____. a) sent b) cent	Answer: A penny is one cent. b) cent

Homophone Sentences

Quiz-Quiz-Trade

Instructions: Copy enough cards so each student has one card. Cut on dotted lines and fold in half.

Homophone Sentences	Homophone Sentences
Question: The store had a _____ on pants. a) sale b) sail	Answer: The store had a <u>sale</u> on pants. a) sale
Question: The wind blew the _____ on the ship. a) sale b) sail	Answer: The wind blew the <u>sail</u> on the ship. b) sail
Question: Where will you _____ at two o'clock? a) be b) bee	Answer: Where will you <u>be</u> at two o'clock? a) be
Question: The _____ buzzed as it flew to the hive. a) be b) bee	Answer: The <u>bee</u> buzzed as it flew to the hive. b) bee

Homophones Sentences

Quiz-Quiz-Trade

Instructions: Copy enough cards so each student has one card. Cut on dotted lines and fold in half.

Homophone Sentences	Homophone Sentences
Question: Kim watched _____ birds fly. a) four b) for	Answer: Kim watched four birds fly. a) four
Question: The gift is _____ you. a) four b) for	Answer: The gift is for you. b) for
Question: Amy left _____ chips on her plate. a) two b) to	Answer: Amy left two chips on her plate. a) two
Question: May we go _____ the store? a) two b) to	Answer: May we go to the store? b) to

Homophones (it's, its)

Quiz-Quiz-Trade

Instructions: Copy enough cards so each student has one card. Cut on dotted lines and fold in half.

Homophones (it's, its)	Homophones (it's, its)
Question: Choose the correct spelling for the missing word. _____ going to be a long day. a) It's b) Its	Answer: It's going to be a long day. a) It's
Question: Choose the correct spelling for the missing word. _____ tail was wagging. a) It's b) Its	Answer: Its tail was wagging. b) Its
Question: Choose the correct spelling for the missing word. Jed thinks _____ Monday. a) it's b) its	Answer: Jed thinks it's Monday. a) it's
Question: Choose the correct spelling for the missing word. I don't know _____ name. a) it's b) its	Answer: I don't know its name. b) its

Homophones (it's, its)

Quiz-Quiz-Trade

Instructions: Copy enough cards so each student has one card. Cut on dotted lines and fold in half.

Homophones (it's, its)

Question: Choose the correct spelling for the missing word.

_____ time for school.

a) It's

b) Its

Homophones (it's, its)

Answer:

It's time for school.

a) It's

Homophones (it's, its)

Question: Choose the correct spelling for the missing word.

The dog buried _____ bone.

a) it's

b) its

Homophones (it's, its)

Answer:

The dog buried its bone.

b) its

Homophones (it's, its)

Question: Choose the correct spelling for the missing word.

_____ up to you.

a) It's

b) Its

Homophones (it's, its)

Answer:

It's up to you.

a) It's

Homophones (it's, its)

Question: Choose the correct spelling for the missing word.

The cat sharpened _____ claws on the tree trunk.

a) it's

b) its

Homophones (it's, its)

Answer:

The cat sharpened its claws on the tree trunk.

a) its

Homophones (it's, its)

Quiz-Quiz-Trade

Instructions: Copy enough cards so each student has one card. Cut on dotted lines and fold in half.

Homophones (it's, its) Question: Choose the correct spelling for the missing word. _____ been enjoyable to spend time with you. a) It's b) Its	**Homophones (it's, its)** Answer: It's been enjoyable to spend time with you. b) It's
Homophones (it's, its) Question: Choose the correct spelling for the missing word. I wasn't sure about _____ color. a) it's b) its	**Homophones (it's, its)** Answer: I wasn't sure about its color. b) its
Homophones (it's, its) Question: Choose the correct spelling for the missing word. I think _____ going to snow today. a) it's b) its	**Homophones (it's, its)** Answer: I think it's going to snow today. a) it's
Homophones (it's, its) Question: Choose the correct spelling for the missing word. The tree lost _____ leaves in the fall. a) it's b) its	**Homophones (it's, its)** Answer: The tree lost its leaves in the fall. b) its

Homophones (it's, its)

Quiz-Quiz-Trade

Instructions: Copy enough cards so each student has one card. Cut on dotted lines and fold in half.

Homophones (it's, its)

Question: Choose the correct spelling for the missing word.

_____ a huge lion!

a) It's

b) Its

Homophones (it's, its)

Answer:

It's a huge lion!

a) It's

Homophones (it's, its)

Question: Choose the correct spelling for the missing word.

The bear hid _____ cubs.

a) it's

b) its

Homophones (it's, its)

Answer:

The bear hid its cubs.

b) its

Homophones (it's, its)

Question: Choose the correct spelling for the missing word.

_____ fun to visit the zoo.

a) It's

b) Its

Homophones (it's, its)

Answer:

It's fun to visit the zoo.

a) It's

Homophones (it's, its)

Question: Choose the correct spelling for the missing word.

A zebra can't change _____ stripes.

a) it's

b) its

Homophones (it's, its)

Answer:

A zebra can't change its stripes.

b) its

Homophones (it's, its)

Quiz-Quiz-Trade

Instructions: Copy enough cards so each student has one card. Cut on dotted lines and fold in half.

Homophones (it's, its)	Homophones (it's, its)
Question: Choose the correct spelling for the missing word. _____ important to do your best. a) It's b) Its	Answer: It's important to do your best. a) It's
Question: Choose the correct spelling for the missing word. The cat lost _____ collar. a) it's b) its	Answer: The cat lost its collar. b) its
Question: Choose the correct spelling for the missing word. _____ a true statement. a) It's b) Its	Answer: It's a true statement. a) It's
Question: Choose the correct spelling for the missing word. Each state has _____ own flag. a) it's b) its	Answer: Each state has its own flag. b) its

Homophones (it's, its)

Quiz-Quiz-Trade

Instructions: Copy enough cards so each student has one card. Cut on dotted lines and fold in half.

Homophones (it's, its)	Homophones (it's, its)
Question: Choose the correct spelling for the missing word. I hope _____ what you needed. a) it's b) its	Answer: I hope it's what you needed. a) it's
Question: Choose the correct spelling for the missing word. The ship has a hole in _____ hull. a) it's b) its	Answer: The ship has a hole in its hull. b) its
Question: Choose the correct spelling for the missing word. I am so thankful _____ going to be a sunny day. a) it's b) its	Answer: I am so thankful it's going to be a sunny day. a) it's
Question: Choose the correct spelling for the missing word. The monkey bumped _____ head on a broken branch. a) it's b) its	Answer: The monkey bumped its head on a broken branch. b) its

Homophones (it's, its)

Quiz-Quiz-Trade

Instructions: Copy enough cards so each student has one card. Cut on dotted lines and fold in half.

Homophones (it's, its)

Question: Choose the correct spelling for the missing word.

_____ time for us to board the plane.

a) It's

b) Its

Homophones (it's, its)

Answer:

It's time for us to board the plane.

a) It's

Homophones (it's, its)

Question: Choose the correct spelling for the missing word.

_____ long neck is very useful for reaching leaves.

a) It's

b) Its

Homophones (it's, its)

Answer:

Its long neck is very useful for reaching leaves.

b) Its

Homophones (it's, its)

Question: Choose the correct spelling for the missing word.

_____ two o'clock.

a) It's

b) Its

Homophones (it's, its)

Answer:

It's two o'clock.

a) It's

Homophones (it's, its)

Question: Choose the correct spelling for the missing word.

_____ teeth were extremely sharp.

a) It's

b) Its

Homophones (it's, its)

Answer:

Its teeth were extremely sharp.

b) Its

Homophones (they're, there, their)

Quiz-Quiz-Trade

Instructions: Copy enough cards so each student has one card. Cut on dotted lines and fold in half.

Homophones (they're, there, their)

Question: Choose the correct spelling for the missing word.

_____ running on the track.

a) They're
b) There
c) Their

Homophones (they're, there, their)

Answer:

They're running on the track.

a) They're

Homophones (they're, there, their)

Question: Choose the correct spelling for the missing word.

We will move the boxes over _____.

a) they're
b) there
c) their

Homophones (they're, there, their)

Answer:

We will move the boxes over there.

b) there

Homophones (they're, there, their)

Question: Choose the correct spelling for the missing word.

During the night _____ dog barked.

a) they're
b) there
c) their

Homophones (they're, there, their)

Answer:

During the night their dog barked.

c) their

Homophones (they're, there, their)

Question: Choose the correct spelling for the missing word.

_____ is a new store on the corner.

a) They're
b) There
c) Their

Homophones (they're, there, their)

Answer:

There is a new store on the corner.

b) There

Homophones (they're, there, their)

Quiz-Quiz-Trade

Instructions: Copy enough cards so each student has one card. Cut on dotted lines and fold in half.

Homophones (they're, there, their)

Question: Choose the correct spelling for the missing word.

_____ walking quickly.

a) They're c) Their
b) There

Homophones (they're, there, their)

Answer:

They're walking quickly.

a) They're

Homophones (they're, there, their)

Question: Choose the correct spelling for the missing word.

_____ is a red light at the corner.

a) They're c) Their
b) There

Homophones (they're, there, their)

Answer:

There is a red light at the corner.

b) There

Homophones (they're, there, their)

Question: Choose the correct spelling for the missing word.

They finished _____ project.

a) they're c) their
b) there

Homophones (they're, there, their)

Answer:

They finished their project.

c) their

Homophones (they're, there, their)

Question: Choose the correct spelling for the missing word.

_____ goes the ball!

a) They're c) Their
b) There

Homophones (they're, there, their)

Answer:

There goes the ball!

b) There

Homophones (they're, there, their)

Quiz-Quiz-Trade

Instructions: Copy enough cards so each student has one card. Cut on dotted lines and fold in half.

Homophones (they're, there, their)

Question: Choose the correct spelling for the missing word.

_____over by the tree.

a) They're c) Their
b) There

Homophones (they're, there, their)

Answer:

They're over by the tree.

a) They're

Homophones (they're, there, their)

Question: Choose the correct spelling for the missing word.

_____is no soap by the sink.

a) They're c) Their
b) There

Homophones (they're, there, their)

Answer:

There is no soap by the sink.

b) There

Homophones (they're, there, their)

Question: Choose the correct spelling for the missing word.

Do you know _____phone number?

a) they're c) their
b) there

Homophones (they're, there, their)

Answer:

Do you know their phone number?

c) their

Homophones (they're, there, their)

Question: Choose the correct spelling for the missing word.

They can't make up _____ minds.

a) they're c) their
b) there

Homophones (they're, there, their)

Answer:

They can't make up their minds.

c) their

Homophones (they're, there, their)

Quiz-Quiz-Trade

Instructions: Copy enough cards so each student has one card. Cut on dotted lines and fold in half.

Homophones (they're, there, their)

Question: Choose the correct spelling for the missing word.

_____ are several mistakes on the paper.

a) They're c) Their
b) There

Homophones (they're, there, their)

Answer:

There are several mistakes on the paper.

b) There

Homophones (they're, there, their)

Question: Choose the correct spelling for the missing word.

Ed and Kris are over _____.

a) they're c) their
b) there

Homophones (they're, there, their)

Answer:

Ed and Kris are over there.

b) there

Homophones (they're, there, their)

Question: Choose the correct spelling for the missing word.

_____new address is 914 Pine Street.

a) They're c) Their
b) There

Homophones (they're, there, their)

Answer:

Their new address is 914 Pine Street.

c) Their

Homophones (they're, there, their)

Question: Choose the correct spelling for the missing word.

I don't think _____ coming.

a) they're c) their
b) there

Homophones (they're, there, their)

Answer:

I don't think they're coming.

a) they're

Homophones (they're, there, their)

Quiz-Quiz-Trade

Instructions: Copy enough cards so each student has one card. Cut on dotted lines and fold in half.

Homophones (they're, there, their)

Question: Choose the correct spelling for the missing word.

_____arriving from New York City.

a) They're c) Their
b) There

Homophones (they're, there, their)

Answer:

They're arriving from New York City.

a) They're

Homophones (they're, there, their)

Question: Choose the correct spelling for the missing word.

_____is my coat.

a) They're c) Their
b) There

Homophones (they're, there, their)

Answer:

There is my coat.

b) There

Homophones (they're, there, their)

Question: Choose the correct spelling for the missing word.

That vehicle is _____ car.

a) they're c) their
b) there

Homophones (they're, there, their)

Answer:

That vehicle is their car.

c) their

Homophones (they're, there, their)

Question: Choose the correct spelling for the missing word.

_____are many choices to consider.

a) They're c) Their
b) There

Homophones (they're, there, their)

Answer:

There are many choices to consider.

b) There

Homophones (they're, there, their)

Quiz-Quiz-Trade

Instructions: Copy enough cards so each student has one card. Cut on dotted lines and fold in half.

Homophones (they're, there, their)

Question: Choose the correct spelling for the missing word.

_____ very hungry.

a) They're
b) There
c) Their

Homophones (they're, there, their)

Answer:

They're very hungry.

a) They're

Homophones (they're, there, their)

Question: Choose the correct spelling for the missing word.

If you look over _____, you will see the lake.

a) they're
b) there
c) their

Homophones (they're, there, their)

Answer:

If you look over there, you will see the lake.

b) there

Homophones (they're, there, their)

Question: Choose the correct spelling for the missing word.

They are taking _____ children to the fair.

a) they're
b) there
c) their

Homophones (they're, there, their)

Answer:

They are taking their children to the fair.

c) their

Homophones (they're, there, their)

Question: Choose the correct spelling for the missing word.

Where is _____ horse stable?

a) they're
b) there
c) their

Homophones (they're, there, their)

Answer:

Where is their horse stable?

c) their

Homophones (they're, there, their)

Quiz-Quiz-Trade

Instructions: Copy enough cards so each student has one card. Cut on dotted lines and fold in half.

Homophones (they're, there, their)

Question: Choose the correct spelling for the missing word.

Do you think _____ done reading the book?

a) they're c) their
b) there

Homophones (they're, there, their)

Answer:

Do you think they're done reading the book?

a) they're

Homophones (they're, there, their)

Question: Choose the correct spelling for the missing word.

_____ once was a bird named Dodo.

a) They're c) Their
b) There

Homophones (they're, there, their)

Answer:

There once was a bird named Dodo.

b) There

Homophones (they're, there, their)

Question: Choose the correct spelling for the missing word.

Look at the smiles on _____ faces.

a) they're c) their
b) there

Homophones (they're, there, their)

Answer:

Look at the smiles on their faces.

c) their

Homophones (they're, there, their)

Question: Choose the correct spelling for the missing word.

I don't know _____ names.

a) they're c) their
b) there

Homophones (they're, there, their)

Answer:

I don't know their names.

c) their

Homophones (are, our, hour)

Quiz-Quiz-Trade

Instructions: Copy enough cards so each student has one card. Cut on dotted lines and fold in half.

Homophones (are, our, hour)

Question: Choose the correct spelling for the missing word.

The _____ hand on the clock broke.

a) are c) our
b) hour

Homophones (are, our, hour)

Answer:

The hour hand on the clock broke.

b) hour

Homophones (are, our, hour)

Question: Choose the correct spelling for the missing word.

_____ you going to eat lunch?

a) Are c) Our
b) Hour

Homophones (are, our, hour)

Answer:

Are you going to eat lunch?

a) Are

Homophones (are, our, hour)

Question: Choose the correct spelling for the missing word.

_____ dog is barking.

a) Are c) Our
b) Hour

Homophones (are, our, hour)

Answer:

Our dog is barking.

c) Our

Homophones (are, our, hour)

Question: Choose the correct spelling for the missing word.

What song _____ they singing?

a) are c) our
b) hour

Homophones (are, our, hour)

Answer:

What song are they singing?

a) are

Homophones (are, our, hour)

Quiz-Quiz-Trade

Instructions: Copy enough cards so each student has one card. Cut on dotted lines and fold in half.

Homophones (are, our, hour)

Question: Choose the correct spelling for the missing word.

Where _____ the books?

a) are c) our
b) hour

Homophones (are, our, hour)

Answer:

Where are the books?

a) are

Homophones (are, our, hour)

Question: Choose the correct spelling for the missing word.

Let's go to _____ house.

a) are c) our
b) hour

Homophones (are, our, hour)

Answer:

Let's go to our house.

c) our

Homophones (are, our, hour)

Question: Choose the correct spelling for the missing word.

We will be one _____ late.

a) are c) our
b) hour

Homophones (are, our, hour)

Answer:

We will be one hour late.

b) hour

Homophones (are, our, hour)

Question: Choose the correct spelling for the missing word.

When will _____ mom come home?

a) are c) our
b) hour

Homophones (are, our, hour)

Answer:

When will our mom come home?

c) our

Homophones (are, our, hour)

Quiz-Quiz-Trade

Instructions: Copy enough cards so each student has one card. Cut on dotted lines and fold in half.

Homophones (are, our, hour)

Question: Choose the correct spelling for the missing word.

_____ clock needed to be reset.

a) Are c) Our

b) Hour

Homophones (are, our, hour)

Answer:

Our clock needed to be reset.

c) Our

Homophones (are, our, hour)

Question: Choose the correct spelling for the missing word.

We _____ so excited about the surprise.

a) are c) our

b) hour

Homophones (are, our, hour)

Answer:

We are so excited about the surprise.

a) are

Homophones (are, our, hour)

Question: Choose the correct spelling for the missing word.

Where did _____ cat go?

a) are c) our

b) hour

Homophones (are, our, hour)

Answer:

Where did our cat go?

c) our

Homophones (are, our, hour)

Question: Choose the correct spelling for the missing word.

They _____ leaving on vacation.

a) are c) our

b) hour

Homophones (are, our, hour)

Answer:

They are leaving on vacation.

a) are

Homophones (are, our, hour)

Quiz-Quiz-Trade

Instructions: Copy enough cards so each student has one card. Cut on dotted lines and fold in half.

Homophones (are, our, hour)

Question: Choose the correct spelling for the missing word.

Pete put _____ books on the table.

a) are c) our
b) hour

Homophones (are, our, hour)

Answer:

Pete put our books on the table.

c) our

Homophones (are, our, hour)

Question: Choose the correct spelling for the missing word.

Ted and Max _____ hiking to the lake tomorrow.

a) are c) our
b) hour

Homophones (are, our, hour)

Answer:

Ted and Max are hiking to the lake tomorrow.

a) are

Homophones (are, our, hour)

Question: Choose the correct spelling for the missing word.

The _____ passed quickly.

a) are c) our
b) hour

Homophones (are, our, hour)

Answer:

The hour passed quickly.

b) hour

Homophones (are, our, hour)

Question: Choose the correct spelling for the missing word.

The airplane will leave in one _____.

a) are c) our
b) hour

Homophones (are, our, hour)

Answer:

The airplane will leave in one hour.

b) hour

Homophones (are, our, hour)

Quiz-Quiz-Trade

Instructions: Copy enough cards so each student has one card. Cut on dotted lines and fold in half.

Homophones (are, our, hour)	Homophones (are, our, hour)
Question: Choose the correct spelling for the missing word. It will soon be _____ bedtime. a) are c) our b) hour	Answer: It will soon be our bedtime. c) our
Question: Choose the correct spelling for the missing word. It took exactly one _____ to take the test. a) are c) our b) hour	Answer: It took exactly one hour to take the test. b) hour
Question: Choose the correct spelling for the missing word. The cheetahs _____ hunting. a) are c) our b) hour	Answer: The cheetahs are hunting. a) are
Question: Choose the correct spelling for the missing word. An _____ is a short time. a) are c) our b) hour	Answer: An hour is a short time. b) hour

Homophones (are, our, hour)

Quiz-Quiz-Trade

Instructions: Copy enough cards so each student has one card. Cut on dotted lines and fold in half.

Homophones (are, our, hour)

Question: Choose the correct spelling for the missing word.

We will make _____ beds in the morning.

a) are
c) our
b) hour

Homophones (are, our, hour)

Answer:

We will make our beds in the morning.

c) our

Homophones (are, our, hour)

Question: Choose the correct spelling for the missing word.

The bus was one _____ ahead of schedule.

a) are
c) our
b) hour

Homophones (are, our, hour)

Answer:

The bus was one hour ahead of schedule.

b) hour

Homophones (are, our, hour)

Question: Choose the correct spelling for the missing word.

Where _____ we going after the movie?

a) are
c) our
b) hour

Homophones (are, our, hour)

Answer:

Where are we going after the movie?

a) are

Homophones (are, our, hour)

Question: Choose the correct spelling for the missing word.

Kate and Chad will meet us in an_____.

a) are
c) our
b) hour

Homophones (are, our, hour)

Answer:

Kate and Chad will meet us in an hour.

b) hour

Homophones (are, our, hour)

Quiz-Quiz-Trade

Instructions: Copy enough cards so each student has one card. Cut on dotted lines and fold in half.

Homophones (are, our, hour)	Homophones (are, our, hour)
Question: Choose the correct spelling for the missing word. Where will _____ new house be located? a) are c) our b) hour	Answer: Where will our new house be located? c) our
Homophones (are, our, hour)	**Homophones (are, our, hour)**
Question: Choose the correct spelling for the missing word. Sid will be ready in one _____. a) are c) our b) hour	Answer: Sid will be ready in one hour. b) hour
Homophones (are, our, hour)	**Homophones (are, our, hour)**
Question: Choose the correct spelling for the missing word. The clock will tell us when we _____ leaving. a) are c) our b) hour	Answer: The clock will tell us when we are leaving. a) are
Homophones (are, our, hour)	**Homophones (are, our, hour)**
Question: Choose the correct spelling for the missing word. When _____ you practicing piano? a) are c) our b) hour	Answer: When are you practicing piano? a) are

Pick A Card, Any Card

Using a Fan-N-Pick Mat and question cards, students play Fan-N-Pick to identify text features, answer story element questions, and preview nonfiction.

Activity Steps

1. Each team receives the Fan-N-Pick Mat, an identical text for each student on the team, and a set of cards.
2. The Fan-N-Pick Mat is placed in the center of the team table, with each corner pointing to a student.
3. Student #1 (Fan) holds question cards in a fan and says, "Pick a card, any card!"
4. Student #2 (Pick and Read) picks a card, reads the question aloud, and allows think time.
5. Student #3 (Answer) responds orally and/or shows the answer.
6. Student #4 (Check and Praise) responds to the answer by tutoring or praising.
7. The Fan-N-Pick Mat is rotated one person clockwise for each new round, indicating each student's new role.

STRUCTURE
Fan-N-Pick

Blacklines

Fan-N-Pick Mat

Instructions: Cut out this mat and place it in the center of the team. Each corner points to a student, indicating his/her role for that round of Fan-N-Pick. For each new round rotate the mat clockwise one position indicating each student's new role for that round.

Fan

Pick and Read

Fan-N-Pick Mat

Check and Praise

Answer

Text Features

Fan-N-Pick

Instructions: Copy one set of cards for each team. Cut apart. Use with Fan-N-Pick Mat.

Text Features
Find and show this text feature:
heading

Text Features
Find and show this text feature:
table of contents

Text Features
Find and show this text feature:
glossary

Text Features
Find and show this text feature:
index

Text Features
Find and show this text feature:
caption

Text Features
Find and show this text feature:
bold, italicized, stylized, or colored word

Text Features

Fan-N-Pick

Instructions: Copy one set of cards for each team. Cut apart. Use with Fan-N-Pick Mat.

Text Features	Text Features	Text Features
Find and show this text feature: bulleted list	Find and show this text feature: map	Find and show this text feature: diagram
Find and show this text feature: photograph	Find and show this text feature: boxed item or sidebar	Find and show this text feature: chart or graph or timeline

Story Elements (Fiction)

Fan-N-Pick

Instructions: Copy one set of cards for each team. Cut apart. Use with Fan-N-Pick Mat.

Story Elements (Fiction)	Story Elements (Fiction)	Story Elements (Fiction)
What is the title?	Who is the author?	Who is the illustrator?

Story Elements (Fiction)	Story Elements (Fiction)	Story Elements (Fiction)
What is the setting? • Where? • When?	Who are the main characters?	What is the problem?

Story Elements (Fiction)

Fan-N-Pick

Instructions: Copy one set of cards for each team. Cut apart. Use with Fan-N-Pick Mat.

Story Elements (Fiction)	Story Elements (Fiction)	Story Elements (Fiction)
What is the solution?	What happened in the beginning?	What happened in the middle?

Story Elements (Fiction)	Story Elements (Fiction)	Story Elements (Fiction)
What happened at the end?	What did you learn from the story?	Tell about one of the characters.

Previewing Before Reading (Nonfiction)

Fan-N-Pick

Instructions: Copy one set of cards for each team. Cut apart. Use with Fan-N-Pick Mat.

Previewing Before Reading (Nonfiction)	Previewing Before Reading (Nonfiction)	Previewing Before Reading (Nonfiction)
Show a text feature in your text and name it.	Show the text feature that you think will be most helpful to you when you read, and tell why.	Choose one type of text feature used, and count the number of times it is used.

Previewing Before Reading (Nonfiction)	Previewing Before Reading (Nonfiction)	Previewing Before Reading (Nonfiction)
Which table of contents item looks the most interesting? Why?	Find a word that is new to you. Tell some strategies that you could use to help learn about the word.	Why do you think the author wrote this text?

Previewing Before Reading (Nonfiction)

Fan-N-Pick

Instructions: Copy one set of cards for each team. Cut apart. Use with Fan-N-Pick Mat.

Previewing Before Reading (Nonfiction)	Previewing Before Reading (Nonfiction)	Previewing Before Reading (Nonfiction)
What would you like to learn from this text?	What do you think this text is mainly about?	How many <u>different</u> text features did the author use?
Previewing Before Reading (Nonfiction)	**Previewing Before Reading (Nonfiction)**	**Previewing Before Reading (Nonfiction)**
Tell what you already know about the topic of the text.	Ask a question you would like the text to answer. Start your question with Why. . . ?	Which text feature will you spend the most time studying? Why?

Comprehension Cubes

Teammates roll a comprehension cube to ask and answer questions relating to a selected text. For some cubes students may respond in any order, but they must place their Talking Chip in the center of the team table to indicate they've participated.

Activity Steps

1. Each team receives one cube and a text selection. Each teammate receives one Talking Chip (any chip or token will work).
2. Student #1 rolls the comprehension cube and reads the question or formulates a question.
3. All students take turns responding to the question, placing their chip in the center when talking.
4. When all chips are used, teammates each collect their chips.
5. Student #2 rolls the cube and repeats from Step 2.

STRUCTURE

Talking Chips

Note:
The Talking Chips structure can be used with cube activities on pages 119–122.

BlacKlines

Comprehension Story Element Cube

Instructions: Copy the cube pattern on cardstock. Cut out, fold, and tape together to form a cube. Students take turns rolling the cube. The student rolling the cube identifies the story element from the assigned reading passage.

characters

setting

problem

solution

main idea

events

COMPREHENSION **BlacKline**

Comprehension Question Cube (Story Elements)

Instructions: Copy the cube pattern on cardstock. Cut out, fold, and tape together to form a cube. Students take turns rolling the cube. The student rolling the cube answers the question about the assigned reading passage.

Who is the illustrator?

Who is the author?

What is the setting? (where? and when?)

What is the problem?

What is the solution?

Who are the characters?

Comprehension Question Cube (Before Reading)

Talking Chips

Instructions: Copy the cube pattern on cardstock. Cut out, fold, and tape together to form a cube. Students take turns rolling the cube. The student rolling the cube reads the question. All students take turns responding to the question, placing their chip in the center before talking.

What do you think the author wants us to learn from this text?

What do you already know about the topic of this text?

What type of text do you think this will be (fiction or nonfiction)? Why?

What does the cover or first page tell you?

What is one text feature that you think will be helpful? Why?

What would you expect to find out from reading this text?

Comprehension Question Cube (After Reading)

Talking Chips

Instructions: Copy the cube pattern on cardstock. Cut out, fold, and tape together to form a cube. Students take turns rolling the cube. The student rolling the cube reads the question. All students take turns responding to the question, placing their chip in the center before talking.

What would you like to know more about?

What did you learn that you did not know before?

Why do you think the author wrote this text?

Why do you think the information in this text is important?

What is one question you would like to ask the author?

What connection can you make to this text?

- Text to self
- Text to text
- Text to world

Comprehension Question Cube (Reflection)

Talking Chips

Instructions: Copy the cube pattern on cardstock. Cut out, fold, and tape together to form a cube. Students take turns rolling the cube. The student rolling the cube reads the question. All students take turns responding to the question, placing their chip in the center before talking.

What part of the text would you have changed? How and why?

What was your favorite part? Why?

What are you reminded of by the text?

What is something in the text, that you don't think could really happen? Why?

What was something in the text that could really happen? Why?

What was a tricky word? How did you figure it out?

Questioning Cube

Talking Chips

Instructions: Copy the cube pattern on cardstock. Cut out, fold, and tape together to form a cube. Students take turns rolling the cube. The student rolling the cube formulates a question beginning with the word rolled. All students take turns responding to the question, placing their chip in the center before talking. Students are encouraged to celebrate/add to previous students' responses.

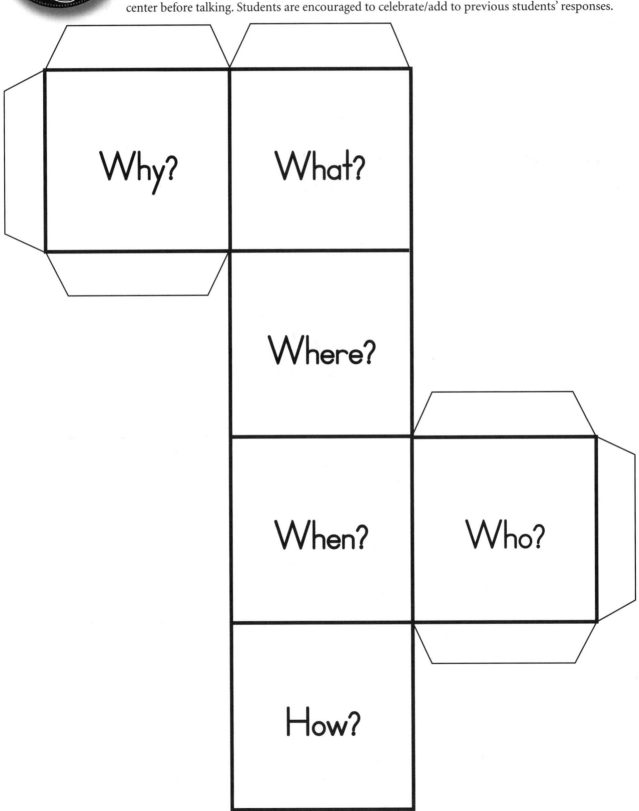

Why?

What?

Where?

When?

Who?

How?

Spinning Vocabulary

Teammates use vocabulary cards and a spinner to learn vocabulary. This is a great way to examine vocabulary words from guided reading texts, teacher read-aloud texts, and content areas (social studies, science, math).

STRUCTURE

RoundTable Consensus

Activity Steps

1. Each team receives a set of Sentence Cards and a Vocabulary Spinner (next page) on cardstock with a plastic or metal spinner arrow (if not available, use a pencil and a paperclip). Every student needs a dictionary.
2. Student #1 picks a sentence card from the pile and reads it.
3. All students look up the underlined vocabulary word in the dictionary and read the definitions silently.
4. Student #2 selects the appropriate definition for the context, reads it, and states the reason for the choice.
5. Student #2 checks for consensus.
6. Teammates show agreement or lack of agreement with thumbs up or down.
7. If there is agreement, the students celebrate and Student #2 spins the spinner. Student #3 responds to the spinner's prompt and checks for consensus.
8. Student #4 begins the next rotation by picking up a sentence card from the pile and reading it.
9. The process continues until time's up or the team has completed their vocabulary words.

Blacklines

Vocabulary Spinner

RoundTable Consensus

Instructions: Copy a spinner on cardstock for each team. Add a plastic/metal spinner in the middle or use a spinner made from a paper clip and a pencil. (To make a paper clip spinner: Place a paper clip over the center of the spinner. Place the pencil point on the center point of the spinner through the paper clip. Using the other hand, spin the paper clip around the pencil point.) Students take turns spinning the spinner and following the directions.

What is another word that means about the same as your word? (synonym)	Paraphrase the sentence.
Discuss the word: • Visual clues • Letter patterns • Tricky parts	Use the word in a new sentence.

Sentence Cards for Vocabulary Spinner

RoundTable Consensus

Instructions: Copy one set of cards per team. Cut apart.

Sentence Cards for Vocabulary Spinner	Sentence Cards for Vocabulary Spinner	Sentence Cards for Vocabulary Spinner
The two basketball teams were <u>rivals</u> for the championship game.	My dad has a long <u>commute</u> from our house to work each day.	The scouts could only carry a <u>meager</u> amount of food with them on their camping trip in the mountains.

Sentence Cards for Vocabulary Spinner	Sentence Cards for Vocabulary Spinner	Sentence Cards for Vocabulary Spinner
Andrew was always thinking of a <u>prank</u> he could play that would make people laugh.	The president had a quality <u>campaign</u> that he followed to help him win the election.	The drink of water was what I needed to <u>quench</u> my thirst.

Blank Sentence Cards for Vocabulary Spinner

RoundTable Consensus

Instructions: Use blank cards to create sentence cards.

Blank Sentence Cards for Vocabulary Spinner	Blank Sentence Cards for Vocabulary Spinner	Blank Sentence Cards for Vocabulary Spinner
Blank Sentence Cards for Vocabulary Spinner	Blank Sentence Cards for Vocabulary Spinner	Blank Sentence Cards for Vocabulary Spinner

Comprehension Puzzles

After teammates have read the same text, teammates place puzzle pieces on a puzzle mat. Each puzzle piece has a prompt for students to review the reading. Three different puzzles blacklines are provided: 1) retelling fiction, 2) retelling nonfiction, and 3) nonfiction text features.

STRUCTURE
RoundTable Consensus

Activity Steps

1. Each team receives a set of puzzle pieces and a puzzle mat. The puzzle pieces are mixed up and placed facedown in the center of team (except for the Retelling [Fiction] puzzle pieces, which need to be selected in the order of their numbers 1–8).
2. Student #1 selects one puzzle piece, reads the prompt, and gives an answer. For example, if the puzzle piece is "Title" the student states the title. The student checks for consensus.
3. Teammates show agreement or lack of agreement with thumbs up or down.
4. If there is agreement, the student places the puzzle piece on the matching section on the puzzle mat. If not, teammates discuss the response until there is agreement. If no agreement is reached, the puzzle piece is set aside to be discussed later.
5. The next student selects the next puzzle piece and the process is continued until the team completes the puzzle.

BlacKlines

Retelling (Fiction) Puzzle Pieces

RoundTable Consensus

Instructions: Cut puzzle pieces apart.

2. Characters

Retelling (Fiction)

4. Problem

Retelling (Fiction)

8. Solution

Retelling (Fiction)

3. Setting

Retelling (Fiction)

7. Event

Retelling (Fiction)

1. Title

Retelling (Fiction)

5. Event

Retelling (Fiction)

6. Event

Retelling (Fiction)

Retelling (Fiction) Puzzle Mat

RoundTable Consensus

Instructions: Copy one puzzle mat for each team.

2

4

8

3

7

1

5

6

Retelling (Nonfiction) Puzzle Pieces

RoundTable Consensus

Instructions: Cut puzzle pieces apart.

Detail

Retelling (Nonfiction)

Detail

Retelling (Nonfiction)

Text Feature

Retelling (Nonfiction)

Detail

Retelling (Nonfiction)

Information from Picture

Retelling (Nonfiction)

Heading (Main Idea)

Retelling (Nonfiction)

Text Feature

Retelling (Nonfiction)

Key Vocabulary Words

Retelling (Nonfiction)

Retelling (Nonfiction) Puzzle Pieces

RoundTable Consensus

Instructions: Copy one puzzle mat for each team.

Text Feature (Nonfiction) Puzzle Pieces

RoundTable Consensus

Instructions: Cut puzzle pieces apart.

Word
(Bolded, Italicized, Colored, or Stylized)
Text Feature (Nonfiction)

Table of Contents
Text Feature (Nonfiction)

Timeline
Text Feature (Nonfiction)

Heading
Text Feature (Nonfiction)

Index
Text Feature (Nonfiction)

Map
Text Feature (Nonfiction)

Photograph with Caption
Text Feature (Nonfiction)

Glossary
Text Feature (Nonfiction)

Label
Text Feature (Nonfiction)

Bullets
Text Feature (Nonfiction)

Boxed Item or Sidebar
Text Feature (Nonfiction)

Graph or Diagram
Text Feature (Nonfiction)

Text Feature (Nonfiction) Puzzle Mat

RoundTable Consensus

Instructions: Copy one puzzle mat for each team.

Anticipation Guide

Before reading a text, individuals mark "true" or "false" predictions on an Anticipation Guide Form. Students read the text independently and mark their answers and page number where the answer was found on the "after reading" section. Partners then take turns sharing their answers and proving them from the text. Students are allowed to adjust answers after discussion with partner.

Activity Steps

1. Using an Anticipation Guide Student Form, the teacher fills in statements relating to the reading, some true and some false. (See the Anticipation Guide Sample on page 135.)
2. Individuals receive an Anticipation Guide Form and a book or article to read.
3. Before reading the text, each individual marks true or false predictions for each statement on the form by checking the "true" or "false" box in the "Before Reading" column.
4. Students read the assigned article or book independently.
5. After reading the text, individuals read the statements on the Anticipation Guide, finding and recording the related text page.
6. Partners take turns sharing their answers and proving them from the text. Students are allowed to adjust their answers after discussion with partner.
7. Partners alternate roles for each statement.

STRUCTURE
Solo & RallyCoach

BlacKlines

Anticipation Guide Student Form

Solo and RallyCoach

Solo Before Reading		"Platypus" *Ranger Rick* March 2005 pp. 28-31	RallyCoach After Reading		
Yes	No		Pg.	Yes	No
		1. The platypus lives along rivers, creeks, and lakes in North America.			
		2. The platypus is a mammal that is furry like a beaver and has a bill like a duck.			
		3. The male platypus has a poison gland on each hind leg.			
		4. When on land the platypus can fold back the webbing on its feet.			
		5. The bill of a platypus is designed to help it dig up plants to eat.			
		6. The platypus lays eggs.			
		7. A platypus baby is only as big as a kidney bean when it is born.			
		8. The platypus makes its home in the tall reeds near the water's edge.			
		9. The platypus lives off the fat in its belly during the cold winter.			
		10. The platypus can see and hear under water just as well as when he is on land.			

What is a question you would like to ask your partner?

Anticipation Guide Answer Form

Solo and RallyCoach

Solo Before Reading		"Platypus" *Ranger Rick* March 2005 pp. 28-31	RallyCoach After Reading		
Yes	No		Pg.	Yes	No
✓		1. The platypus lives along rivers, creeks, and lakes in North America.	28		✓
✓		2. The platypus is a mammal that is furry like a beaver and has a bill like a duck.	28	✓	
	✓	3. The male platypus has a poison gland on each hind leg.	28	✓	
✓		4. When on land the platypus can fold back the webbing on its feet.	29	✓	
✓		5. The bill of a platypus is designed to help it dig up plants to eat	29		✓
	✓	6. The platypus lays eggs.	30	✓	
	✓	7. A platypus baby is only as big as a kidney bean when it is born.	31	✓	
✓		8. The platypus makes its home in the tall reeds near the water's edge.	30–31		✓
✓		9. The platypus lives off the fat in its belly during the cold winter.	28		✓
	✓	10. The platypus can see and hear under water just as well as when he is on land.	29		✓

What is a question you would like to ask your partner?

Anticipation Guide Blank Student Form

Solo and RallyCoach

Solo Before Reading		Student Name ______ Title ______ Date______ Pages ______	RallyCoach After Reading		
Yes	No		Page	Yes	No
		1.			
		2.			
		3.			
		4.			
		5.			
		6.			
		7.			
		8.			
		9.			
		10.			

What is a question you would like to ask your partner?

LISTEN-SKETECH-DRAFT

Activity

Sketching for Comprehension

Students listen to the teacher, sketch the important details, share their sketches, then draft a main idea of the statement.

Activity Steps

1. Each student is given the Listen-Sketch-Draft form.
2. The teacher presents the first chunk of information while students listen carefully.
3. The teacher stops presenting and calls for each student to sketch the most important details in the first "sketch" box.
4. Students share their sketches using RoundRobin or Timed Pair Share.
5. Students draft a main idea statement in the first "draft" box.
6. The process is repeated for additional chunks of information.
7. When all chunks of information have been presented, students draft a summary in the bottom box.
8. Students compare their summaries with a partner or teammate.

STRUCTURE

Listen-Sketch-Draft

Blacklines

Listen-Sketch-Draft Sample

Important to Remember (Sketch)	Main Idea (Draft)
fangs eyes	The tarantula is a spider.
	It jumps on its food.
	It can grow as big as a man's hand.

Summary Statement:

The tarantula is a spider with eight eyes and eight legs. It doesn't spin a web. It bites bugs with its fangs and poisons them. It can grow as big as a man's hand.

Listen-SKetch-Draft Form

Instructions: Copy for each student.

Important to Remember (SKetch)	Main Idea (Draft)

Summary Statement:

Story Predictions

Students manipulate cards with possible characters, settings, problems, and solutions to the text on the prediction mat. They confirm or adjust their predictions during reading and after reading the selection. Partners take timed turns listening and sharing about their Prediction Mats.

Activity Steps

STRUCTURE
Timed Pair Share

1. The teacher creates Story Element Cards corresponding to the story the class will read. (One sample set is provided.)
2. Each student receives a Prediction Mat and a set of story cards.
3. As the story is read, students are stopped periodically and given time to make story predictions by manipulating their Story Cards on their Prediction Mats. Stories can be read using:
   - Teacher read aloud
   - RallyRobin reading (partners take turns)
   - Independent reading
4. After each prediction adjustment, students are each given one minute to share their prediction with a partner.

Blacklines

Prediction Mat

Timed Pair Share

Instructions: Copy for each student.

Characters	Setting

Problem	Solution

Important Words

Blank Story Element Cards for Prediction Mat

Timed Pair Share

Instructions: Teacher writes possible story elements in these boxes and makes copies for each student.

Blank Story Element Cards	Blank Story Element Cards	Blank Story Element Cards	Blank Story Element Cards
Blank Story Element Cards	Blank Story Element Cards	Blank Story Element Cards	Blank Story Element Cards
Blank Story Element Cards	Blank Story Element Cards	Blank Story Element Cards	Blank Story Element Cards
Blank Story Element Cards	Blank Story Element Cards	Blank Story Element Cards	Blank Story Element Cards
Blank Story Element Cards	Blank Story Element Cards	Blank Story Element Cards	Blank Story Element Cards
Blank Story Element Cards	Blank Story Element Cards	Blank Story Element Cards	Blank Story Element Cards

Story Element Cards for Prediction Mat

Timed Pair Share

***Owl Moon by* Jane Yolen**

Instructions: Copy for each student. Cut apart.

Story Element Cards	Story Element Cards	Story Element Cards	Story Element Cards
Pa	child	quiet	waiting
Story Element Cards	Story Element Cards	Story Element Cards	Story Element Cards
winter	brave	woods	pine trees
Story Element Cards	Story Element Cards	Story Element Cards	Story Element Cards
Great Horned Owl	words	calling	moonlight
Story Element Cards	Story Element Cards	Story Element Cards	Story Element Cards
flashlight	hope	owling	listening
Story Element Cards	Story Element Cards	Story Element Cards	Story Element Cards
moon	"Whooo-whoo-whooo"	night	
Story Element Cards	Story Element Cards	Story Element Cards	Story Element Cards

Sort It Out

Teammates cover a mat with ideas about what they just read on small sticky notes. Then they sort the ideas into categories. This is a great way to promote active listening and processing of reading content.

STRUCTURE
Jot Thoughts & Sorting

Note:
Additional boxes may be added to the Sorting Mat.

Activity Steps

1. After reading a story, each team receives a Recall Mat, a Sorting Mat, four different colored pencils, and a pad of sticky notes.
2. Students recall things from the story, write the idea or event on a sticky note, and announce it as they place the sticky note on the Recall Mat. Each student uses a different color pencil.
3. After students have numerous sticky notes on the Recall Mat, they pull out their Sorting Mat.
4. Teams discuss possible categories for their Sorting Mat. Once they reach consensus on the category names, they write them on the Sorting Mat. (Teacher may previously written category headings on the sorting mat.)
5. Students take turns reading each sticky note and placing it on the Sorting Mat.

Blacklines

Recall Mat

Jot Thoughts

Instructions: Copy one mat per team. Use to generate ideas for Sorting Mat.

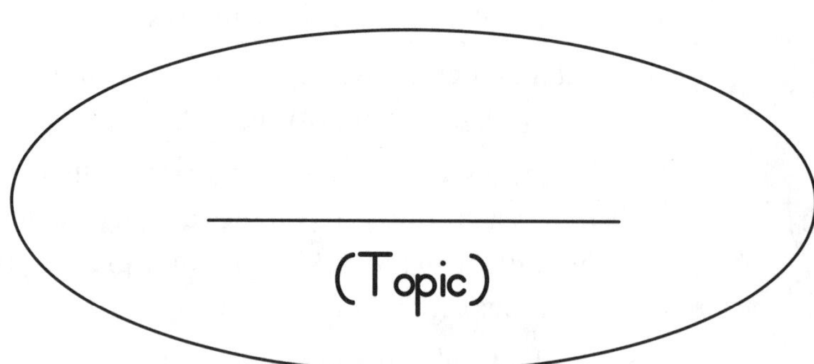

Sorting Mat

Jot Thoughts

Instructions: Copy one mat per team. Use to sort ideas from Recall Mat.

______________________	______________________
______________________	______________________

Coach Me

Partners take turns matching text structures, fact or opinion and idioms with their meanings.

Activity Steps

1. Each pair receives a sorting mat and a set of cards. (Two matching cards are provided for Idiom activity.) They spread out the cards so they can read them all.
2. Partner A chooses a card (or two matching cards from Idioms activity) from the cards in the middle. Partner A places the cards on the correct columns of the sorting mat.
3. Partner B watches, listens, checks, and praises.
4. Partner B chooses a card (or two matching cards from Idioms activity) from the cards in the middle. Partner B places the cards on the correct columns of the sorting mat.
5. Partner A watches, listens, checks, and praises.
6. The process is continued until the pair fills out the mat.

STRUCTURE
RallyCoach

BlacKlines

Text Structure Sorting Mat

RallyCoach

Instructions: Copy for each pair of students. Sort the cards using signal words as clues to text structures.

Cause-Effect	
Description	
Comparison	
Problem-Solution	
Sequence	

Text Structure Cards For Mat

RallyCoach

Instructions: Copy one set of cards for each pair of students. Cut apart.

Text Structure Cards	Text Structure Cards	Text Structure Cards	Text Structure Cards
First, put the cookies in the oven. Second, set the timer. Last, take the cookies out of the oven.	Our flowers were wilted, but we solved the problem by watering them.	Worker ants are strong. An ant can lift as much as 50 times its own weight.	Puffy, with flat bottoms, is a characteristic of cumulus clouds. In addition, they are low in the sky and are always changing shape.
Text Structure Cards	**Text Structure Cards**	**Text Structure Cards**	**Text Structure Cards**
If a frog has a problem with a snake trying to catch it, the frog can use its strong back legs to jump away.	Now, it is time to clean my room. Later, I will be able to go to the park.	Coral could look like the antlers on a deer or the branches of a tree.	Insects have six legs. In fact, some insects also have wings.
Text Structure Cards	**Text Structure Cards**	**Text Structure Cards**	**Text Structure Cards**
Owls listen for noises while hunting. For example, they listen for sounds of mice on the ground or moth wings in the air.	To help solve the problem of littering along roads, there are laws giving fines for littering.	First, we put on our pajamas. Then, we will brush our teeth. Finally, we will go to bed.	Starfish may be many different colors. For example, they may be orange, blue, red, brown, purple, or yellow.
Text Structure Cards	**Text Structure Cards**	**Text Structure Cards**	**Text Structure Cards**
The reason Chris was so sleepy in class was because he went to bed late last night.	As a result of eating too many cookies, Tami had a stomachache.	One solution to running out of books to read is to check out more books from the library.	Both eagles and hawks hunt during the day. Owls are different because they hunt at night.
Text Structure Cards	**Text Structure Cards**	**Text Structure Cards**	**Text Structure Cards**
If you read the story, then you will be able to tell a friend about it.	During the ballgame, we yelled for our team. Afterwards, we told them they had a GREAT game.	Since Kim ran through the water puddle, her shoes were wet.	The insect looked like a leaf. Therefore, it was able to stay hidden from the bird.

Fact or Opinion Sorting Mat

RallyCoach

Instructions: Sort the statements into the correct columns according to whether they are facts or opinions.

Fact	Opinion

Fact or Opinion Cards

RallyCoach

Instructions: Copy one set of cards for each pair of students. Cut apart.

Fact or Opinion Cards	Fact or Opinion Cards
Todd is wearing a blue shirt.	I read all the words in the story.
Ross woke up at 6:00 in the morning.	The flowers in the case look very pretty.
Cats can be pets.	Cats are the best pets.
Carrots are my favorite vegetable.	Cherries taste so good.
Bread is made from flour.	We will spend the night in Denver.
Two plus four equals six.	The Fourth of July is celebrated on July 4th.
Summer is the best season because school is out.	Houses are sometimes built with brick.
If you are over 30, you're old.	Pens are easier to write with than pencils.
Pumpkin pie is the best pie.	Flour may be made from wheat.
Meat is kept frozen in the freezer.	Everyone should run two miles a day.

Fact or Opinion Cards

RallyCoach

Instructions: Copy one set of cards for each pair of students. Cut apart.

Fact or Opinion Cards	Fact or Opinion Cards
Michael Jordan played for the Chicago Bulls.	A is the first letter of the alphabet.
Ponds are small bodies of water.	Horses have four legs.
It would be fun to swim at the lake every weekend.	I like small dogs best.
Dr. Pepper is the best pop to drink.	In basketball, each team has five players on the court at one time.
More people own white cars than pink cars.	Chocolate milk tastes better than white milk.
The lake is beautiful at sunset.	Soccer is played with a round ball.
Babe Ruth is the greatest baseball player who ever lived.	The food pyramid is a guide for choosing food.
Being a doctor is the best job in the world.	Fake rocks are used in Hollywood movies.
George Washington was the first president of the United States.	Pine Swamp should be drained.
Astronauts landed on the moon.	I love spinach.

Fact or Opinion Cards

RallyCoach

Instructions: Copy one set of cards for each pair of students. Cut apart.

Fact or Opinion Cards	Fact or Opinion Cards
Apples, bananas, and grapes are fruits.	The Super Bowl would be better if my favorite team was in it.
Fact or Opinion Cards	**Fact or Opinion Cards**
Milk comes from cows	Mice eat seeds.
Fact or Opinion Cards	**Fact or Opinion Cards**
Mrs. Case is the best principal ever.	It is easy to learn how to write your name in cursive.
Fact or Opinion Cards	**Fact or Opinion Cards**
Babies are younger than teenagers.	Mr. Phillips has one son and one daughter.
Fact or Opinion Cards	**Fact or Opinion Cards**
Many people order cheese pizza.	Cheese pizza is the best kind of pizza.
Fact or Opinion Cards	**Fact or Opinion Cards**
Computers can be used to send messages.	Everyone should try to swim at least once a week.
Fact or Opinion Cards	**Fact or Opinion Cards**
Farmers grow many different kinds of crops.	Sitting in the sun is relaxing.
Fact or Opinion Cards	**Fact or Opinion Cards**
If you drop a glass it may break.	It is harder to subtract than to add.
Fact or Opinion Cards	**Fact or Opinion Cards**
It is better to eat apples than oranges for a snack.	There are many stars in the sky.
Fact or Opinion Cards	**Fact or Opinion Cards**
Recess is a part of the school day.	Recess is the best part of the school day.

Idiom Sorting Mat

RallyCoach

Instructions: Copy for each pair of students. Sort each matching idiom and meaning card across from each other.

Idiom	Meaning

Idiom Cards

RallyCoach

Instructions: Copy one set of cards for each pair of students. Cut apart.

Idiom Cards	Idiom Cards
I'm all ears.	I am listening very carefully.
Give him a hand.	Help him.
You better shake a leg.	You need to work faster.
Get off my back!	Leave me alone and let me work.
He's a ball of fire.	He's full of energy.
Don't blow your top.	Stay calm.
I feel like a million dollars.	I feel wonderful.
Let's get the ball rolling.	Let's start work on this.
They will hit the ceiling.	They will be very upset.
She's going to hit the hay.	She's going to bed.

Idiom Cards

RallyCoach

Instructions: Copy one set of cards for each pair of students. Cut apart.

Idiom Cards	Idiom Cards
She is a peach.	She's sweet and helpful.
He's full of beans.	He's not telling the truth.
I'm nuts about you.	I really like you.
It's a piece of cake.	It's very easy.
She eats like a bird.	She eats very little.
Please don't monkey around.	Get serious and stop playing.
It's raining cats and dogs.	It is raining really hard.
My lips are sealed.	I will never tell the secret.
You get on my nerves.	What you do or say bothers me.
I've got my eye on you.	I'm watching you.

TEAM LINE-UPS

Activity

Sequencing

Teammates each receive a card and position themselves in a line so that they correctly sequence the cards.

Activity Steps

1. Each team receives one set of Jumbled Sentence Word Cards (fourteen sets are provided) or one set of Sequencing Event Cards. (Six different sets are provided.) Each student gets one card.
2. Each teammate reads his/her card using RoundRobin.
3. Student #1 states where he/she should stand in the team line-up and gets consensus from teammates (thumbs up).
4. Students #2–4 repeat Step 3.
5. Team checks the finished sequence, makes adjustments if necessary, and celebrates when correct.

STRUCTURE

Team Line-Ups

Blacklines

Jumbled Sentences

Team Line-Ups

Instructions: The numbers in the corners of the cards indicate which cards belong to each sentence.

Jumbled Sentences Cards	Jumbled Sentences Cards	Jumbled Sentences Cards	Jumbled Sentences Cards
Let's 1	go 1	to 1	school 1
The 2	cold 2	rain 2	fell 2
A 3	car 3	sped 3	by 3
We 4	will 4	go 4	home 4
Jed 5	ran 5	the 5	race 5
Ted 6	will 6	buy 6	milk 6
Sing 7	a 7	happy 7	song 7

Jumbled Sentences

Team Line-Ups

Instructions: The numbers in the corners of the cards indicate which cards belong to each sentence.

Jumbled Sentences Cards	Jumbled Sentences Cards	Jumbled Sentences Cards	Jumbled Sentences Cards
The (8)	truck (8)	drove (8)	fast (8)
Fred (9)	found (9)	two (9)	books (9)
Four (10)	dogs (10)	are (10)	barking (10)
A (11)	frog (11)	hopped (11)	away (11)
Lock (12)	the (12)	huge (12)	door (12)
Let (13)	us (13)	play (13)	outside (13)
What (14)	should (14)	we (14)	do (14)

Sequencing Events Cards

Team Line-Ups

Instructions: Copy one set of cards for each team. Cut apart.

Baseball

Sequencing Event Cards—Set 1
Baseball
I saw the baseball coming toward me.

Sequencing Event Cards—Set 1
Baseball
I scooped the ball up in my baseball mitt.

Sequencing Event Cards—Set 1
Baseball
I threw the ball to the third baseman.

Sequencing Event Cards—Set 1
Baseball
"Out!" yelled the umpire.

S'mores

Sequencing Event Cards—Set 2
S'mores
I placed half of the chocolate bar on top of a graham cracker square.

Sequencing Event Cards—Set 2
S'mores
I put a toasted marshmallow on top of the chocolate bar.

Sequencing Event Cards—Set 2
S'mores
I placed another graham cracker square on top of the marshmallow.

Sequencing Event Cards—Set 2
S'mores
I enjoyed eating the s'more.

Sequencing Events Cards

Team Line-Ups

Instructions: Copy one set of cards for each team. Cut apart.

Fishing

Sequencing Event Cards—Set 3
Fishing
The boy cast his fishing line into the lake.

Sequencing Event Cards—Set 3
Fishing
He watched his bobber go up and down.

Sequencing Event Cards—Set 3
Fishing
The tip of his fishing pole bent over as the fish struggled to get away.

Sequencing Event Cards—Set 3
Fishing
With all his strength, he reeled in the two-pound bass fish.

Movie

Sequencing Event Cards—Set 4
Movie
We waited in line to buy movie tickets.

Sequencing Event Cards—Set 4
Movie
When we got to the window the lady said, "The movie is sold out."

Sequencing Event Cards—Set 4
Movie
We walked away.

Sequencing Event Cards—Set 4
Movie
We decided to go swimming instead.

Sequencing Events Cards

Team Line-Ups

Instructions: Copy one set of cards for each team. Cut apart.

Toast

Sequencing Event Cards—Set 5 **Toast**	Sequencing Event Cards—Set 5 **Toast**
I plugged the toaster into the outlet.	I placed a piece of bread in each slot of the toaster.
Sequencing Event Cards—Set 5 **Toast**	Sequencing Event Cards—Set 5 **Toast**
I patiently waited.	Pop! Up came two pieces of warm toast.

Diving

Sequencing Event Cards—Set 6 **Diving**	Sequencing Event Cards—Set 6 **Diving**
I slowly walked to the edge of the diving board.	I kept telling myself, "Jump!"
Sequencing Event Cards—Set 6 **Diving**	Sequencing Event Cards—Set 6 **Diving**
Down, down, down, I fell.	Splash!

Balanced Literacy

Comprehension 

Word Study 

Fluency 

Writing 

Word Study

Effective word study instruction involves both decoding words and deriving meaning from words (vocabulary). Word study allows students to take words apart while reading and put word parts together while writing. Word-solving strategies help students learn important concepts related to decoding, spelling, and understanding vocabulary. As students participate in word study activities, they become aware of relationships between sounds, letters, letter combinations, and word parts. Various cooperative activities in this book provide opportunities for students to practice application of word study skills and decoding strategies for effective reading and writing.

Following the framework of balanced literacy allows the teacher to scaffold instruction through use of explicit teaching during read/write alouds and shared reading/writing to explain strategies used to decode words and understand their meanings. Scaffolding continues during guided reading/writing as the teacher monitors and provides feedback to students applying word-solving skills and strategies. Support is withdrawn as students independently apply these skills and strategies successfully.

Table of Word Study Resources

Page(s)	Resources	Balanced Literacy				
		Aloud	Shared	Guided	Independent	Literature Circles
	Word Study Descriptions and Lists					
174	Word Study Resources/ Materials Descriptions					
175	Spelling Strategies	●	●	●	●	●
176	Prefix and Suffix Word List	●	●	●	●	●
178	Contractions List	●	●	●	●	●
179	Homophone List	●	●	●	●	●
182	Compound Word List	●	●	●	●	●

Table of Word Study Activities and Lessons

		Balanced Literacy					
Page(s)	Activities/Lessons	Blacklines	Aloud	Shared	Guided	Independent	Literature Circles
194	Partner Word Study Activities		●	●	●	●	●
198	Team Word Study Activities		●	●	●	●	●
202	Class Word Study Activities		●	●	●	●	●
203	Making Words Lesson Plans						
204	Lesson 1: "Flowers"						
204	RallyCoach Activity						
204	Activity 1: Making Words	• Teacher Transparency Form • Student Form	●	●	●	●	
206	Find My Rule Activity						
206	Activity 2: Sorting	• Teacher Transparency Form • Find My Rule Mat	●	●	●	●	
207	RallyCoach Activity						
207	Activity 3: Transfer		●	●	●	●	
210	Lesson 2: "Blanket"						
210	RallyCoach Activity						
210	Activity 1: Making Words	• Teacher Transparency Form • Student Form	●	●	●	●	
211	Find My Rule Activity						
211	Activity 2: Sorting	• Teacher Transparency Form • Find My Rule Mat	●	●	●	●	
211	RallyCoach Activity						
211	Activity 3: Transfer		●	●	●	●	
214	Lesson 3: "Breaking"						

Table of Word Study Activities and Lessons (continued)

			Balanced Literacy				
Page(s)	Activities/Lessons	Blacklines	Aloud	Shared	Guided	Independent	Literature Circles
214	**RallyCoach Activity**						
214	Activity 1: Making Words	• Teacher Transparency Form • Student Form	●	●	●	●	
215	**Find My Rule Activity**						
215	Activity 2: Sorting	• Teacher Transparency Form • Find My Rule Mat	●	●	●	●	
215	**RallyCoach Activity**						
215	Activity 3: Transfer		●	●	●	●	
221	**Find Someone Who Activity**						
222	Adding ar/or, Prefixes, Antonyms, Base Words, Compound Words, Contractions, Suffixes	• Worksheet		●	●		
223	Adding er, ir, or ur, Prefixes, Adding ou/ow, Synonyms, Contractions, Word Family	• Worksheet		●	●		
224	Plurals, Sound of "C", Compound Words, Sentence Conventions	• Worksheet		●	●		
225	Find Someone Who	• Form		●	●		
226	**Quiz-Quiz-Trade Activities**						
227	Rhyming Words	• Question/Answer Cards		●	●		
234	gn, kn, wr (silent letters)	• Question/Answer Cards		●	●		
241	Letter Patterns—Long A: (ay, ai, a-e)	• Question/Answer Cards		●	●		
248	Antonyms or Synonyms?	• Question/Answer Cards		●	●		
255	Plural	• Question/Answer Cards		●	●		

Table of Word Study Activities and Lessons (continued)

		Balanced Literacy					
Page(s)	Activities/Lessons	Blacklines	Aloud	Shared	Guided	Independent	Literature Circles
	Quiz-Quiz-Trade Activities—continued						
262	Singular/Plural	• Question/Answer Cards		●	●		
270	Singular and Plural Nouns	• Question/Answer Cards		●	●		
275	Are, Is	• Question/Answer Cards		●	●		
282	Sentences With or Without Silent e	• Question/ Answer Cards		●	●		
289	Prefixes (re- and un-)	• Question/ Answer Cards		●	●		
295	Suffixes (-er, -ly, -ful, -y)	• Question/ Answer Cards		●	●		
303	**RallyCoach Activity**						
304	Onset and Rime Cubes with Worksheet (Onsets and Rimes)	• Cubes • Worksheet		●	●		
307	Onset (Blends) Cube and Worksheets	• Cube • Worksheets		●	●		
310	Cube and Worksheet (oi, oy)	• Cube • Worksheet		●	●		
312	Cube and Worksheet (ou, ow)	• Cube • Worksheet		●	●		
314	Cube and Worksheet (au, aw)	• Cube • Worksheet		●	●		
316	Cube and Worksheet (ar, or)	• Cube • Worksheet		●	●		
318	Cube and Worksheets (ea, ee)	• Cube • Worksheets		●	●		
321	Prefix Cube and Worksheet (re-, un-)	• Cube • Worksheet		●	●		
323	Suffix Cube and Worksheet (-er, -est)	• Cube • Worksheet		●	●		

Table of Word Study Activities and Lessons (continued)

Page(s)	Activities/Lessons	Balanced Literacy					
		Blacklines	Aloud	Shared	Guided	Independent	Literature Circles
	RallyCoach Activity—continued						
325	Suffix Cube and Worksheet (-ful, -ly)	• Cube • Worksheet		●	●		
327	Doubling Final Consonants Cube and Worksheet (-ed, -ing)	• Cube • Worksheet		●	●		
329	Antonym/Synonym Cube and Worksheet	• Cube • Worksheet		●	●		
331	Spinner and Worksheet (er, ir, ur)	• Spinner • Worksheet		●	●		
333	Spinner and Worksheet (aw, ew, ow)	• Spinner • Worksheet		●	●		
335	Contraction Spinner and Worksheets (not, is, will)	• Spinner • Worksheets		●	●		
338	Prefix Sorting Mat and Word Cards (re-, un-)	• Mat • Word Cards		●	●		
340	Sorting Mat and Word Cards (add -s, -es)	• Mat • Word Cards		●	●		
342	Plural Sorting Mat and Word Cards (f to v, y to i)	• Mat • Word Cards		●	●		
344	Compound Words Worksheet and Word Cards	• Worksheet • Word Cards		●	●		
346	Onset Blends (Nonsense Words) Word Cards	• Word Cards		●	●		
349	Word Cards and Letter Pattern Cards (ir, er, ur)	• Word Cards • Letter Pattern Cards		●	●		
352	Word Cards and Letter Pattern Cards (ai, aw)	• Word Cards • Letter Pattern Cards		●	●		

Table of Word Study Activities and Lessons (continued)

Page(s)	Activities/Lessons	Blacklines	Balanced Literacy: Aloud	Shared	Guided	Independent	Literature Circles
	Showdown Activity						
356	Prefixes (re- and –un)	• Team Set • Student Set		●	●		
360	Suffixes (-ly and –ful)	• Team Set • Student Set		●	●		
366	c as /s/ and /k/	• Team Set • Student Set		●	●		
369	g as /j/ and /g/	• Team Set • Student Set		●	●		
372	Compounds, Possessives, Contractions	• Team Set • Student Set		●	●		
375	**Numbered Heads Together Activity**						
376	Second Grade Word Wall List	• Word List		●	●	●	
377	Second Grade Word Wall Cards	• Word Wall Cards		●	●	●	
383	Second Grade Additional Word Wall Cards	• Word Wall Cards		●	●	●	
398	Second Grade Blank Word Wall Cards	• Blank Word Wall Cards		●	●	●	

Word Study Resources

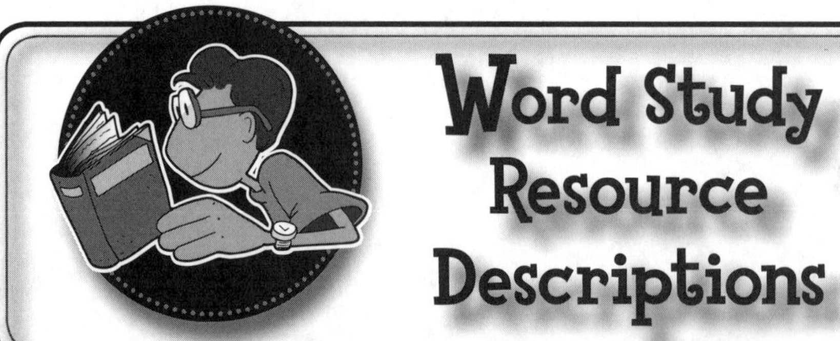

Resources/Materials Descriptions

Spelling Strategies (p. 175)
The goal of word study is to spell words correctly in everyday writing. Spelling strategies, which students should learn to use, are listed as a resource. Several of the Kagan activities in this book reinforce these spelling strategies.

Prefix and Suffix Word List (p. 176)
This resource lists several prefixes and suffixes, their meanings, and word examples.

Contractions List (p. 178)
This contraction list includes contractions made with *am, are, had, would, have, is, has, not, us,* and *will.*

Homophone List (p. 179)
Homophones are words that are spelled differently, but sound the same such as *rain, rein, reign*. This homophone list is a classroom resource for teachers and students.

Compound Word List (p. 182)
Compound words are made by combining two words. This compound word list is a resource for teachers and students.

Partner, Team, and Class Word Study Activities (p. 194)
These word study activities are arranged according to partner, team, and class activities. The Kagan cooperative learning structure, activity name, and a brief description are included.

Word Study Spelling Strategies

Visualize it. 	Try it several ways. Which way looks right? 
Stretch it out. Listen to the sounds. • Letter patterns • Endings • Prefixes	Ask a friend. 
Circle the word. Come back later. 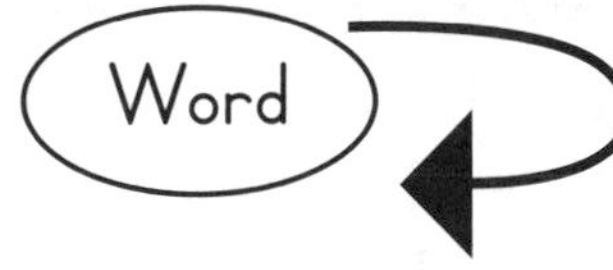	Check the Word Wall. 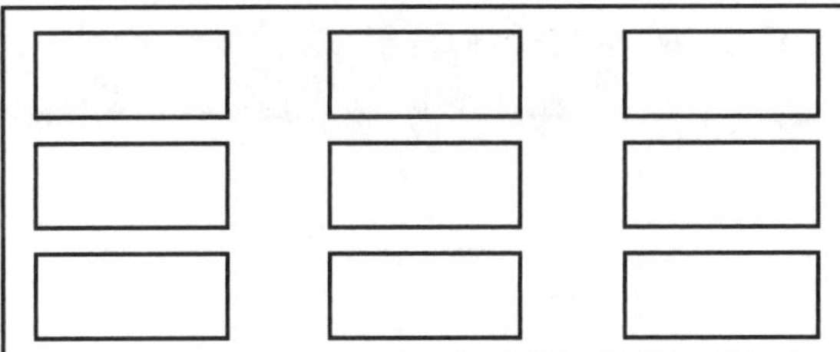
Use what you already know. (analogy) 	Use a dictionary or spell check.

Word Study Prefix and Suffix Word List

Teacher Resources

Prefixes			
	re–	"again, back"	refresh, reclaim, rejoin, reappear, recharge, recover, recondition, return, replace, refund, rewrite, refill, repaid, rebuild, recheck, recount, reopen, rearrange, reinvent, reenter, reconstruct, renew, reheat, recycle, refresh, reinforce, recreate, redirect, rewire, replay, redress, resale
	un–	"not"	unknown, unkind, unfit, unable, undo, unpack, unequal, unlikely, unlucky, unpleasant, unnecessary, untidy, unplug, uncooked, unharmed, unpaid, unpopular, unlock, unwrap, unfamiliar, unfair, unafraid, uncover, unhappy, unpredictable, uncommon, unseen, unzip, untrue, unclean, uncertain, unfasten, unborn, ungrateful
Suffixes			
	–er	"one who"	reader, writer, cutter, builder, mover, teacher, helper, cooker, printer, runner, racer, farmer, batter, eraser, programmer, player, worker, singer
	–er	"more"	taller, shorter, smarter, richer, sweeter, wiser, friendlier, safer, whiter, smaller, softer, quicker, earlier, nicer, bigger, colder, harder, slower
	–est	"most"	tallest, shortest, smartest, richest, sweetest, wisest, friendliest, safest, whitest, smallest, softest, quickest, earliest, nicest, biggest, coldest, hardest, slowest

Word Study Prefix and Suffix Word List

Teacher Resources (continued)

Suffixes			
	–ly	"every"	weekly, daily, yearly, hourly, monthly, nightly, periodically
	–ly	"like" "in that way"	happily, slowly, really, actually, highly, properly, quickly, sadly, keenly, oily, quietly, bravely, speedily, warmly, rarely, carefully, lazily, joyfully, fully, gratefully, smoothly, brightly, softly, loudly, friendly, lovely, badly, deadly, equally, fatherly, motherly, fondly, greatly, ideally, lately, lonely, newly, orderly, poorly, probably, rarely, shortly, smelly, timely, actually, barely, bubbly, clearly, curly, earthly, finally, eventually, happily, hilly, jointly, lightly, lovely, mostly, overly, possibly, properly, sickly, solely, totally, widely, beastly, certainly, costly, currently, elderly, exactly, frequently, hardly, honestly, kindly, likely, madly, quickly, normally, partly, presently, purely, rightly, simply, truly, wobbly, awfully, blindly, chilly, cowardly, surely, scaly, entirely, mainly, lively, prickly, perfectly
	–ful	"full of"	mouthful, beautiful, wonderful, colorful, wishful, cheerful, hopeful, painful, powerful, useful, grateful, meaningful, joyful, pocketful, basketful, plateful, armful, doubtful, flavorful, regretful, revengeful, spoonful, spiteful, tasteful, handful, mouthful, plentiful, thankful, useful, delightful, faithful, stressful, thoughtful, youthful, wasteful, careful, disgraceful, fearful, graceful, peaceful, sorrowful, successful, trustful

Word Study Contractions List

Teacher Resources

am
I'm

are
they're
we're
you're

had would
I'd
it'd
she'd
there'd
they'd

have
could've
I've
might've
should've
they've
we've
would've
you've

is has
here's
he's
it's
she's
that's
there's
what's
where's

not
aren't
can't
couldn't
didn't
doesn't
don't
hadn't
hasn't
haven't
isn't
mustn't
needn't
shouldn't
wouldn't

us
let's

will
he'll
I'll
it'll
she'll
that'll
they'll
we'll
you'll

Word Study Homophone List

Teacher Resources

accept/except	bough/bow	creak/creek	genes/jeans
ad/add	boy/buoy	cymbal/symbol	great/grate
affect/effect	break/brake	days/daze	groan/grown
ail/ale	brews/bruise	dear/deer	guessed/guest
aisle/I'll/isle	bridal/bridle	dew/do/due	hail/hale
all/awl	buy/by/bye	die/dye	hall/haul
aloud/allowed	capital/capitol	doe/dough	hare/hair
alter/altar	carat/caret/carrot	dual/duel	hay/hey
ant/aunt	caught/cot	earn/urn	heal/heel/he'll
arc/ark	ceiling/sealing	ewe/yew/you	hear/here
ate/eight	cell/sell	eye/I	heard/herd
aye/eye/I	cellar/seller	fair/fare	hi/high
bale/bail	cent/sent/scent	fairy/ferry	higher/hire
ball/bawl	cents/scents/sense	feat/feet	him/hymn
base/bass	cereal/serial	find/fined	hoarse/horse
be/bee	cheap/cheep	fir/fur	hole/whole
bear/bare	chews/choose	flair/flare	holy/wholly
beat/beet	chili/chilly	flea/flee	hour/our
beau/bow	choral/coral	flew/flue/flue	idle/idol
berry/bury	chord/cord	flour/flower	in/inn
billed/build	chute/shoot	foaled/fold	Jim/gym
bite/byte	cite/sight/site	for/fore/four	knead/need
blue/blew	close/clothes	foreword/forward	knew/new
boar/bore	coarse/course	forth/fourth	knight/night
board/bored	core/corps	foul/fowl	knit/nit
bold/bowled	council/counsel	gate/gait	knot/not

Word Study Homophone List
(continued)

Teacher Resources

know/no	pair/pare/pear	red/read	
knows/nose	past/passed	right/rite/write	
lead/led	patience/patients	ring/wring	
leak/leek	pause/paws	road/rode/rowed	
lessen/lesson	peace/piece	role/roll	
lie/lye	peal/peel	root/route	
links/lynx	pearl/purl	rose/rows	
load/lode	pedal/peddle	rote/wrote	
loot/lute	peek/peak	rough/ruff	
made/maid	peer/pier	rye/wry	
mail/male	pi/pie	sail/sale	
main/Maine/mane	plane/plain	scene/seen	
Mary/marry/merry	plum/plumb	sea/see	
meat/meet	pole/poll	seam/seem	
might/mite	pour/pore	sew/so/sow	
mind/mined	praise/prays/preys	shear/sheer	
missed/mist	pray/prey	shoe/shoo	
moose/mousse	presence/presents	shone/shown	
none/nun	prince/prints	side/sighed	
oar/or/ore	principal/principle	sole/soul	
oh/owe	profit/prophet	some/sum	
one/won	quarts/quartz	son/sun	
overdo/overdue	rain/reign/rein	stair/stare	
paced/paste	raise/rays/raze	stake/steak	
pail/pale	rap/wrap	stationary/stationery	
pain/pane	real/reel	steal/steel	

Word Study Homophone List
(continued)

Teacher Resources

straight/strait	wait/weight		
suite/sweet	waive/wave		
sundae/Sunday	ware/wear/where		
tacks/tax	wave/waive		
tail/tale	way/weigh/whey		
tea/tee	we/wee		
team/teem	weak/week		
teas/tease/tees	weather/whether		
their/there/they're	weave/we've		
theirs/there's	we'd/weed		
threw/through	were/whirr		
throne/thrown	which/witch		
thyme/time	whine/wine		
tide/tied	who's/whose		
to/too/two	woe/whoa		
toad/towed	wood/would		
told/tolled	worn/warn		
tow/toe	yoke/yolk		
troop/troupe	you/ewe		
vain/vane/vein	you'll/Yule		
vale/veil	your/you're		
vary/very			
vial/vile			
wade/weighed			
wail/whale			
waist/waste			

Word Study Compound Word List

Teacher Resources

aircraft	bedroom	butterfingers	corkscrew
airplane	bedspread	butterfly	cornerstone
airport	bedtime	buttermilk	cornstalk
anybody	beeline	campfire	cornstarch
anyone	bellhop	cannot	cottontail
anyplace	billboard	capsize	cottonwood
anything	birdhouse	carhop	countdown
anywhere	birthday	catfish	courthouse
applesauce	blacktop	catnip	courtyard
armchair	blockbuster	cattail	cowboy
arrowhead	bobcat	chalkboard	cowgirl
audiotape	bobtail	championship	cowpoke
backfire	bookmobile	checkmate	crabgrass
background	boxcar	checkup	crackerjack
backstroke	boyfriend	cheesecloth	crossbar
backtrack	brainstorm	chestnut	crossbones
backyard	brainwash	chopstick	crosscurrent
bagpipe	briefcase	citizenship	crossroad
ballroom	broadcast	classmate	crosswalk
bankroll	brotherhood	clockwise	crowbar
barefoot	bucktooth	clockwork	crybaby
barnyard	bulldog	cobweb	cubbyhole
baseball	bulldozer	cockpit	cupboard
bathroom	bullfrog	cookbook	cupcake
beachcomber	bullheaded	copycat	cutback
bedroll	buttercup	copyright	daredevil

Word Study Compound Word List (continued)

Teacher Resources

darkroom	dropkick	fairway	floodgate
dashboard	drugstore	falsehood	floodlight
daybreak	drumstick	fanfare	flycatcher
daydream	dugout	farewell	flypaper
daylight	dustpan	farmhouse	foghorn
daytime	earache	farmyard	folklore
deadline	earmuff	featherbed	folktale
dishwasher	earring	featherweight	foolproof
dogcatcher	earshot	feedback	football
dogsled	earthquake	fellowship	foothill
doorbell	eggplant	fiddlesticks	foothold
doorknob	elbowroom	fingernail	footlights
doormat	elsewhere	firecracker	footlocker
doorway	evergreen	firefighter	footnote
doughnut	everybody	firefly	footpath
downhill	everyone	fireproof	footprint
downpour	everything	firewood	footrest
downstairs	everywhere	fishbowl	footstep
downstream	eyeball	fisherman	footstool
downtown	eyebrow	fishhook	forecast
downwind	eyelash	flagpole	forefather
drainpipe	eyelid	flapjack	foreground
drawbridge	eyesight	flashback	foreman
drawstring	eyesore	flashlight	forenoon
dressmaker	eyestrain	flatcar	foresight
driveway	eyewitness	flatfoot	forever

Word Study Compound Word List
(continued)

Teacher Resources

fourteen	grandstand	handball	headphone
foxhole	grapefruit	handbook	headquarters
framework	grapevine	handcuff	headrest
freehand	grasshopper	handmade	headwaiter
freeman	grassland	handout	hearsay
freeway	gravestone	handsome	heartache
freshman	graveyard	handwriting	heartbreak
freshwater	greyhound	handyman	heartburn
frostbite	griddlecake	hangout	heartsick
fullback	groundwork	hardship	heavyset
gangplank	guardhouse	hardware	heavyweight
gatekeeper	guesswork	hardwood	hedgehog
girlfriend	guidebook	hayfork	heirloom
giveaway	guideline	hayloft	herself
globetrotter	guidepost	haystack	heyday
goalkeeper	gumdrop	haywire	hideaway
goldfish	hailstone	hazelnut	highlands
goldsmith	hairbrush	headache	highlight
gooseberry	haircut	headband	highway
grandchildren	hairdo	headdress	hillbilly
granddaughter	hairdresser	headfirst	hillside
grandfather	hairline	headgear	hilltop
grandma	halfback	headlight	himself
grandmother	halfway	headline	hindsight
grandpa	hamburger	headmaster	hoedown
grandson	handbag	headmistress	hogwash

Word Study Compound Word List
(continued)

Teacher Resources

hollyhock	housefly	jitterbug	letterhead
Hollywood	household	johnnycake	lifeboat
homebody	housekeeper	keepsake	lifeguard
homecoming	housewarming	keyboard	lifelong
homeland	housework	keyhole	lifetime
homemade	humankind	keynote	lightheaded
homeroom	humbug	kickoff	lighthouse
homesick	humdinger	kickstand	lightweight
homestead	hummingbird	kindhearted	likewise
homework	humpback	knapsack	limelight
honeybee	iceberg	kneecap	limestone
honeycomb	iccebox	knockout	lineman
honeydew	icebreaker	knothole	lipstick
honeymoon	inchworm	ladybug	litterbug
hookup	indoors	ladyfinger	livestock
hopscotch	infield	landholder	lockout
horseback	inkblot	landlord	logrolling
horsefly	inside	landmark	lookout
horseplay	into	landslide	loophole
horsepower	itself	lawmaker	lopsided
horseradish	jackpot	lawsuit	loudmouth
horseshoe	jawbone	layoff	lovebird
hotheaded	jawbreaker	layout	lukewarm
hourglass	jaywalk	layover	lumberjack
houseboat	jellyfish	leapfrog	lumberyard
housecoat	jigsaw	leftovers	mailbox

Word Study Compound Word List
(continued)

Teacher Resources

mailman	moonwalk	nobody	outside
mainland	motorcycle	noonday	overact
mainstream	mousetrap	noontime	overactive
makeshift	mouthpiece	notebook	overall
manhole	mouthwash	noteworthy	overcoat
mankind	muskrat	nutcracker	overexcite
manpower	myself	nuthatch	overexert
marketplace	namesake	nutshell	overextend
markup	neckline	offbeat	overfeed
masterpiece	needlepoint	offshore	overfill
matchbook	neighborhood	offspring	overflow
matchmaker	network	oncoming	overgrown
maybe	newborn	oneself	overhand
mayflower	newcomer	ongoing	overhaul
maypole	newsboy	onlooker	overhead
mealtime	newscast	otherwise	overhear
meanwhile	newsletter	ourselves	overheat
merrymaking	newspaper	outbid	overjoyed
milkman	newsprint	outburst	overnight
milkweed	necktie	outcry	overpass
millstream	nightcap	outdistance	overpay
minuteman	nightclothes	outdoors	overpopulate
mockingbird	nightgown	outfield	overripe
molehill	nightmare	outfit	overrun
monkeyshine	nightstick	outgoing	overseas
moonlight	nighttime	outsell	oversee

Word Study Compound Word List
(continued)

Teacher Resources

oversize	pigeonhole	potpie	ripcord
oversleep	piggyback	powerboat	riverside
overstuffed	pigpen	powerhouse	roadrunner
overtake	pigtail	praiseworthy	roadside
overthrow	pillbox	pressroom	roadway
overtime	pillowcase	proofread	rollerblade
overuse	pincushion	pullover	roommate
pacemaker	pineapple	pushcart	rosebud
pancake	pinhole	quarterback	roughneck
paperback	pinkeye	quicksand	roundabout
paperwork	pinpoint	racehorse	roundup
parkway	pinstripe	racetrack	rowboat
passport	pinwheel	ragtime	runaway
password	pipeline	ragweed	runoff
patchwork	plainclothes	railroad	safeguard
pathfinder	playground	railway	safekeeping
pathway	playhouse	rainbow	sagebrush
payoff	playpen	raincoat	sailboat
payroll	plaything	rainfall	salesperson
peacemaker	pocketbook	rainstorm	saltshaker
peanut	policeman	rainwater	saltwater
peephole	popcorn	rattlesnake	sandalwood
penlight	potbelly	redhead	sandbar
pitchfork	potholder	redwood	sandblast
pickax	pothole	ringleader	sandbox
pickup	potluck	ringworm	sandman

Word Study Compound Word List
(continued)

Teacher Resources

sandpaper	shellfish	sightseeing	snowflake
sandstone	shipbuilding	silkworm	snowman
sandstorm	shipshape	silversmith	snowplow
saucepan	shipwreck	silverware	snowshoes
sawdust	shipyard	singsong	snowstorm
scarecrow	shoelace	skylark	softball
scatterbrain	shoemaker	skylight	somebody
schoolboy	shopkeeper	skyline	someday
schoolgirl	shopwindow	skyrocket	somehow
schoolhouse	shorebird	skyscraper	someone
schoolteacher	shoreline	skywriting	someplace
scrapbook	shortcake	slapstick	something
screenplay	shortcoming	sleepwalking	sometime
screwdriver	shortsighted	sleepyhead	someway
seaboard	shortstop	slingshot	somewhat
seacoast	showcase	slipcover	somewhere
seafood	showoff	slipknot	songbird
searchlight	shuffleboard	smallpox	soundproof
seashell	sickbed	smokehouse	soundtrack
seashore	sideburns	smokestack	sourpuss
seasick	sidecar	snapdragon	southeast
secondhand	sidekick	snapshot	soybean
sendoff	sidesaddle	snowball	spacecraft
setback	sidestep	snowbound	spaceship
sharecropper	sidestroke	snowdrift	speedway
sheepskin	sideway	snowfall	spellbound

Word Study Compound Word List
(continued)

Teacher Resources

spendthrift	stepson	sunroom	textbook
spillway	stockpile	sunset	thanksgiving
sportswear	stopwatch	sunshine	themselves
spotlight	storehouse	sunspot	thoroughbred
springboard	storekeeper	sunstroke	threadbare
springtime	storeroom	suntan	throughout
spyglass	stovepipe	superhuman	thumbtack
stagecoach	stowaway	superman	thunderbird
staircase	straightedge	supermarket	thunderbolt
stairway	strawberry	surfboard	thunderclap
standby	streetcar	swallowtail	thundercloud
standstill	strikeout	sweepstakes	thunderstorm
starfish	stronghold	sweetheart	tidewater
starlight	sugarplum	switchboard	tightlipped
steadfast	suitcase	swordfish	tightrope
steamboat	summertime	tablecloth	timberline
steamroller	sunburn	tablespoon	timekeeper
stepbrother	Sunday	taillight	timepiece
stepchild	sundial	takeoff	timetable
stepdaughter	sundown	taproot	timeworn
stepfather	sunfish	tattletale	tinfoil
stepladder	sunflower	teammate	tiptoe
stepmother	sunglasses	teardrop	toadstool
stepparent	sunlight	teaspoon	today
steppingstone	sunlit	tenderloin	toenail
stepsister	sunrise	tenpin	tollgate

Word Study Compound Word List
(continued)

Teacher Resources

tomboy	underbrush	underweight	warlike
tombstone	undercharge	upbeat	warpath
tomcat	undercoat	upbringing	wartime
toothbrush	undercook	upcoming	washboard
toothpaste	undercover	update	washcloth
toothpick	undercurrent	upgrade	washroom
topcoat	underdeveloped	uphill	washtub
tossup	underdog	upkeep	wasteland
touchdown	underfed	uplift	watchdog
townspeople	underfoot	upon	watchman
trademark	underground	upright	waterfall
treadmill	underline	uproar	waterfowl
troublemaker	undernourished	uproot	waterfront
truckload	underpass	upset	watermelon
trustworthy	underpay	upstairs	waterproof
tryout	underprivileged	upstream	watershed
tugboat	undershirt	uptown	waterspout
tumbleweed	underside	videotape	waterway
turnabout	undersized	viewpoint	wavelength
turnover	understaffed	vineyard	wayside
turnpike	understand	volleyball	weatherman
turntable	understood	waistline	weatherproof
turtledove	undertaker	wallpaper	weekday
typewriter	undertow	wardrobe	weekend
underachieve	underwater	warehouse	weightlifting
underarm	underwear	warfare	whatever

Word Study Compound Word List
(continued)

Teacher Resources

wheelchair	within		
whenever	without		
whichever	wonderland		
whirlpool	woodcarving		
whiteboard	woodchuck		
wholesale	woodcutter		
wholesome	woodland		
widespread	woodpecker		
wildcat	woodwork		
wildfire	workbench		
wildlife	workout		
windburn	workroom		
windmill	workshop		
windowpane	worldwide		
windowsill	worthwhile		
windshield	yardstick		
windsock	yearbook		
windstorm	yourself		
wingspan			
wintergreen			
wintertime			
wiretap			
wisecrack			
wishbone			
withdraw			
withhold			

Word Study Activities and Lessons

Partner Word Study Activities

Match My Word

Structure: Match Mine

Use stand-up folders as buddy barriers. The teacher shows Partner A a slip of paper with a word study word on it. Partner A writes the word on a small dry-erase board, which Partner B cannot see. Partner A tells Partner B how to spell the word on his or her dry-erase board. The directions may include how to form the letters, but the letter names may not be said. Partners switch roles for the next word.

Big Words/Little Words

Structure: RallyCoach

The teacher makes individual letter cards for words. These are packaged in separate bags. Partners take a bag and take turns making as many different words as they can using the letters from the bag. Each word is recorded. A mystery word can be made by using all the letters in the bag.

Computer Typing

Structure: RallyCoach

Partners use a word list to take turns giving each other words to type on a word-processing program on the computer. They change the font style and sizes, so each word looks different. Print out the words to see the finished product.

Foamy Fun

Structure: RallyCoach

Partners sit side by side. The teacher squirts a heap of shaving cream on a protected surface. One at a time, the teacher calls out the word study words. The partners use their fingertips to write the word in the foam. Partners check and praise each other.

Hand Spelling

Structure: RallyCoach

Partner A traces the letters of a word in the palm of Partner B's hand. Partner A says the name of the traced word. Partners take turns tracing the word, praising, coaching, and naming the word. Partners try identifying the word while looking and then with eyes closed.

Illustrating Words

Structure: RallyCoach

Partners take turns giving each other a word from a list. Partner A gives Partner B a word. Partner B writes the word and draws a picture to represent the word. Partner B then explains the picture and spells the word aloud without looking. Partner A praises and coaches. Partner B then gives a word to Partner A. Each word has its own box on the paper.

Partner Word Study Activities (continued)

Inflatable Ball Spelling

Structure: RallyCoach

Use an inflatable ball with letters printed on it. (You may purchase one with letters already on it or make your own by printing letters with a permanent marker.) Partners take turns tossing the ball back and forth. When the catcher gets the ball, he or she lifts one hand and sees which letter is under it. As quickly as possible, he or she says a word beginning with that letter and spells it. Together partners decide if the word is correctly spelled and record it on paper.

Memory

Structure: RallyCoach

Partners work together to make two identical word cards for each word on the list. Partners check each other's word cards. The cards are mixed up and placed facedown in rows. Partner A turns over two cards, saying the words. If the cards are a match, he or she removes them, spells the word without looking, and takes another turn. If they are not a match, the cards are turned facedown, and Partner B has a turn. Partners praise and coach each other.

Letter Ladders

Structure: RallyCoach

Partners are given a set of letter cards (one of every consonant and several of every vowel). Partners take turns making new words by changing one letter at a time. The teacher begins by giving the first word (for example, *hat*). Partner A may change the *h* to *c* to make a new word (*cat*) above the first word. Partner B may then change the *t* to *n* to make *can*. Challenge partners to see how tall they can make their ladders.

Onsets and Rimes

Structure: RallyCoach

Partners use a container filled with individual onsets. They take turns adding these to rimes provided by the teacher to make new words, which are recorded on paper. Partners check then coach or praise.

On My Back

Structure: RallyCoach

Partner A sits on a chair without a back. Partner B stands in back with a list of words. Partner B "draws" the letters to spell a word on the back of Partner A. Partner A writes the word on paper. Partner B praises and coaches. Partners switch roles.

Partner Word Study Activities (continued)

Roll a Word

Structure: RallyCoach

Prepare two large dice by writing onsets on one and rimes on the other. Partners take turns rolling both dice. If a word is rolled, partners praise and both write the word. If the roll does not make a word, the partner rolls the dice again until a word is rolled.

Sit and Spell

Structure: RallyCoach

The teacher writes a word list on the chalkboard. Students sit in two lines facing one another, so that only one line of students can see the word list. Students identify their partners, who are directly across from them. Partners A, who can see the words, are the "callers." Partners B are the "spellers." A caller reads a word aloud and listens carefully as the partner spells the word. If an incorrect spelling is given, the caller repeats the word and the partners spell it together. If a correct spelling is given, the partner praises. Partners switch roles for the next word.

Spelling Takes a Hit

Structure: RallyCoach

Partner A gives Partner B a word to spell by using a flyswatter to "hit" letters printed on a shower curtain hung on a wall. Partner A praises and coaches. Partners take turns giving the word and "hitting" the letters.

Study Buddies

Structure: RallyCoach

Partners take turns giving each other words to spell. A form with three columns is used. Partner A gives a word to Partner B to write in the first column. If the word is spelled correctly the first time, Partner A gives another word, which is written in a new first column. If the word is not spelled correctly, Partner B tries again in the second column. If that word is not correct, Partner A coaches by showing the word. Partner B writes it again in the third column. At any point that the word is correctly spelled, the partner is given a smiley face by the word. Partners switch roles when the words on the list have been spelled correctly or when the teacher indicates it is time to switch roles.

Water Spelling

Structure: RallyCoach

Partner A gives Partner B a word to spell on the sidewalk using a paintbrush and a container of water. Partner A praises and coaches. Partners take turns giving the word and "painting" it. (Note: Water sticks—plastic tubes with sponges on the ends—may also be used to "paint" words on the chalkboard.)

Partner Word Study Activities (continued)

Word Search

Structure: RallyCoach

Students use graph paper to create their own word searches, including the words they are focusing on for that week. Students form partners. Using one partner's word search, partners take turns circling one hidden word at a time. Each partner has a different colored pencil. Partners coach and praise. When one word search is completed, the other one is used.

Tic-Tac-Toe—Three Words in a Row

Structure: RallyRobin

Each set of partners is given a set of word cards, a Tic-Tac-Toe worksheet, and two different colors or types of counters. Partner A picks up a card and reads it to Partner B. If Partner B correctly spells the word, he or she places a counter on any open square of the game board. If Partner B gives an incorrect response, Partner A correctly spells the word and coaches Partner B to spell the word correctly. The word card is placed at the bottom of the pile and no counter is placed on the game board. Partner A now has a turn to spell the next word. Partners try to place three counters in a row (horizontally, vertically, or diagonally). Partners celebrate.

Word Family Race

Structure: RallyTable

Partners have a letter die and a sheet of paper. Partner A rolls the die and announces the letter it lands on. Together the partners decide on a word that begins with that letter. For example, if the die lands on the letter *c*, the word *cat* could be written. Partners then take turns writing words in the word family. For example, Partner A could write *mat*. Partner B could write *flat*. Partners continue to alternate generating written words. When neither partner can think of another word belonging in the word family, the letter die is rolled again and new words are generated.

Spelling Toss

Structure: RallyToss

Partners spell a word while tossing a ball back and forth. Each partner says the next letter of the word until the word is spelled.

Word Toss Game

Structure: RallyToss

Partner A tosses a ball to Partner B at the same time as saying a word. Partner B writes the word on paper and spells it aloud to Partner A. Partner A praises or coaches. Continue by switching roles.

Team Word Study Activities

Spelling Detective

Structure: CenterPiece

Each team needs a page from a newspaper for each team member and one for the center. Each team member has a different colored pencil. The teacher calls out a word pattern and students look for a word on their newspaper page, which fits the pattern, and circle it. Students then trade their paper with the one in the center. Students continue circling words which fit the pattern until the teacher calls a new word pattern (examples: silent *e*, -ing ending, end chunk, etc.).

Add On Relay

Structure: RoundTable

A team forms a line facing the chalkboard. Teammate #1 gives a word. Teammate #2 goes to the chalkboard and writes the first letter of the word, returning to the line and handing the chalk to Teammate #3, who writes the second letter of the word. Continue in this manner, until the word is spelled. If a student sees that a team member has made a spelling error, he or she may use a turn to correct the error. Teammate #2 gives the second word. (A markerboard could also be used.)

Scrambled Word Problem Solving

Structure: Jigsaw Problem Solving

Each team is given a bag with the individual letters of a word. Teammates each take a letter or letters, until all the letters are taken. Student #1 states his or her letter and where it goes in the sequence. Teammates check, coach, and move letters. Process continues with each teammate until word is spelled correctly. When the word is spelled correctly, the team receives a new bag with a new word.

Bean Bag Word Family Game

Structure: RoundTable

Each team needs a set of laminated cards with a word family written on the top (for example: ind, ant, ine), a set of word cards, a bean bag, and a different colored transparency pen for each student. Lay out the set of word cards on the floor. Teammate #1 tosses the bean bag at the cards. He or she picks up the card that the bean bag landed on, says the word, and uses a transparency pen to write the word on the correct word family card. The word card goes in a discard pile. The other teammates take turns tossing the bean bag and writing the words on the word family cards.

Word Family Lists

Structure: Jot Thoughts

Teammates cover the table with words, belonging to a word family, written on slips of paper. Each student writes one word per slip of paper and announces the word before placing it in the middle of the table. Each added word needs to be new. (Variation: words that begin or end the same; words that were made plural by adding *es*, words ending with ing, etc.)

Team Word Study Activities
(continued)

Colorful Team Spelling

Structure: RoundTable

Each team member has a different colored pencil or marker. The teacher gives a word. The team passes a paper around the table. Each student adds one letter to spell the word and passes the paper on to the next student until the word is spelled.

Sentence Writing

Structure: RoundTable

Each student on the team has a different colored pencil. Each person adds a word to a paper, which is passed around the table. The words need to form a complete sentence. When the sentence is completed, the sentence is read to the other teams. Each weekly word study word that is used correctly in the sentence is worth one point for class goal.

Guess the Letters

Structure: Talking Chips

Use a large dry-erase board or chalkboard that all team members can see. Teammate #1 looks at a list of words and chooses one word. He or she makes a line for each letter of the word (_ _ _ _). The other team members take turns putting a talking chip in the middle of the table and guessing a letter or the word. If the word is not guessed and all the talking chips have been used, teammates pick up their talking chips and begin guessing again. When the word has been identified, Teammate #2 chooses a new word. Continue until all teammates have had an opportunity to choose a word.

Do You Know My Word?

Structure: Showdown

One teammate spells a word aloud. Once the word is spelled, teammates pick up a marker and spell the word on individual dry-erase boards. When the Showdown Captain calls, "Showdown," teammates hold up their boards and show their spellings and name the word. They then celebrate or coach.

Find the Errors

Structure: Simultaneous RoundTable

Each team has four teacher-made sentence strips with spelling errors (one for each student). Each student has a different colored pencil. The papers are passed around the table, with each student correcting one error before passing the paper to the next student. Keep passing the sentences around until all the errors have been corrected.

Word Family Web

Structure: RoundTable

Each team works together to create a word family web. A large piece of paper is placed in the center of the team with a word family written in the middle (for example: ick, ate, ip). Each student has a different colored marker. Teammates take turns adding a word to the word family web. The team needs to agree on the spelling of the word before the next person writes.

Team Word Study Activities
(continued)

Body Spelling

Structure: Team Formations

Each team receives a word on a card. Their task is to use their bodies to spell the word. Each person on the team must be part of the spelling. Other teams guess what word was spelled.

Movement Spelling

Structure: Team Formations

The teacher calls out a word. Each team decides on a repetitive movement to use with each letter. For example, one team may decide to hop on one foot for each letter of the word as they spell it. Teams spell the word for the other teams, after practicing their words and movements at least three times. (Variation: Teams may use a different movement for each letter of the word.)

Spelling Cheerleaders

Structure: Team Formations

Students in teams act out the given word with their bodies, showing the tall letters (stretching tall with hands over heads), short letters (putting arms straight out or on hips), and tail letters (squatting or touching toes). For example, "Give me a ____. Give me an ____. Give me a __."

Machine Spelling

Structure: Team Line-Ups

Each student on a team becomes one letter of the word being spelled. They line up in order. The word is spelled orally with each student saying his or her word while making a body motion. The team becomes a "word machine." Teams demonstrate their machines to the other teams.

Word Line-Ups

Structure: Team Line-Ups

Each team receives a stack of scrambled letters, which spell a word. Each teammate takes one of the letters. (Teammates may need to take more than one letter or share a letter, depending on the length of the word.) Each team tries to be the first to line up holding the letters in the correct order to spell the word. (If a team member has two letters, which are not positioned side by side in the word, the team will need to be creative in solving the problem.) Teams share their words with other teams.

Word Practice

Structure: Team-Pair-Solo

Teams work together to spell a word. Then teams divide into pairs and spell the same word. They compare with the other pair. Finally, individuals spell the word. They come back together as a team and compare. They celebrate or coach and begin the process with a new word.

Team Word Study Activities (continued)

Spelling Word Collage

Structure: Team Word-Webbing

Roll out a large piece of paper on the floor or tape one to a wall for each team. Each student has a different colored marker. In a set amount of time, each student tries to fit in as many word study words as possible on the paper to create a colorful word collage.

Pick a Letter, Any Letter

Structure: Think-Write-RoundRobin

Each team has a bag of letters. Teammate #1 chooses a letter from the bag without looking and announces the letter to the team, placing it in the middle. Each student thinks about possible words beginning with that letter and then makes a list of words beginning with that letter on individual dry-erase boards. Time is called after a preset time limit. Teammates take turns RoundRobin sharing one of the words on their lists. If a shared word is also on their lists, students may put a mark by it. Words shared aloud must be new words not previously shared. Continue sharing until all new words have been shared. If a teammate does not have a new word on the list to share, he or she may try to come up with another word.

Spelling Walk

Structure: Traveling Heads Together

Teams huddle to make sure all can spell a given word correctly. Use dry-erase boards to practice writing the word. When everyone is confident they can spell the word, the dry-erase boards are cleared and the team sits down. The teacher calls a number and the student with that number travels to a new team with his or her cleared dry-erase board and a marker. At the new team, the student shares the spelling of the word by writing it on the dry-erase board.

Spelling Toss

Structure: Turn Toss

Teammates toss a ball to each other. As each teammate catches the ball, he or she contributes a letter to the spelling of a word called out by the teacher. Teammates continue until the word is spelled. The teacher then gives a new word.

Class Word Study Activities

Add a Word to My Family

Structure: Find Someone Who

Students have bingo sheets. At the top they put a word given by the teacher. They circulate throughout the room looking for someone who can add a word to a square on their paper and sign his or her name below the added word. The word needs to belong to the same family as the given word and needs to be one that is not already on the paper.

Spell My Word

Structure: Inside-Outside Circle

Students form two circles facing each other. Each student has a word list. As either the outside or the inside circle moves one space, students face new partners. Partners take turns having their partner spell a word from the list. Rotate.

What's My Word?

Structure: Who Am I?

Students attempt to determine their secret word (taped on their back) by circulating and asking "yes/no" questions of classmates. They are allowed three questions per classmate (or unlimited questions until they receive a "no" response). They then find a new classmate to question. When the student guesses his or her word, the student becomes a consultant to give clues to those who have not yet found their identity.

Jumping Words

Structure: Take Off, Touch Down

Give each student a word card. The teacher calls out a vowel sound. If the student's word contains the vowel sound, he or she stands or jumps up. Standing students share their words simultaneously. Teacher and class check for accuracy. The teacher continues to call vowel sounds as students listen for the vowel sound in their words. Variation: The teacher calls out a word and students jump up when they hear a word that rhymes with the word on their word card.

How Many?

Structure: Mix-Freeze-Group

Students make groups with a specific number of students corresponding to answers to questions, asked by the teacher, such as:

- # of total letters in a given word
- # of vowels in a word
- # of a specific letter in a word
- # of syllables in a word

(For example, if the answer to the question is four, when the teacher calls, "Show me," students show the number 4 with their fingers on their chests, quickly form groups of four, and kneel down. Students not finding a group should meet in a predetermined part of the room in "Lost and Found.")

Making Words Lesson Plans

On the following pages are three lessons designed to help students think about the sounds they hear in words and the letter patterns that make up those sounds. They all involve making words from one longer word. The steps for the three lessons are the same. In each of the three lessons, students proceed through three activities:

- **Activity 1: Making Words** (RallyCoach)
- **Activity 2: Sorting** (Find My Rule)
- **Activity 3: Transfer** (RallyCoach)

Since the steps are the same for all three lessons, we will provide a full description of Lesson 1, then just provide the necessary substitutions for Lessons 2 and 3.

Each lesson has its own set of blacklines, but they all share the Find My Rule Mat on page 218. Also, you will find two forms to plan and create your own Making Words lessons.

- **Making Words Planning Form (p. 219)**
- **Making Words Student Form (p. 220)**

The Magic Word

When done with each lesson, challenge pairs to see if they can discover the "Magic Word." The magic word is the word made from all the letters from each set of student letters.

The magic words from each lesson are:

Lesson 1: Flowers
Lesson 2: Blanket
Lesson 3: Breaking

Helpful Hints:

- These activities may be done in one day or two days at the beginning of the week. Making Words may be done on day one and the Sorting and Transfer activities on day two.
- Mailing envelopes or plastic sandwich baggies will help students keep their materials organized and accessible.
- These activities are most beneficial when the teacher selects or designs lessons that reinforce letter patterns the students are needing to know or strengthen for their reading and writing.
- All letters on the Making Words form are put in alphabetical order with vowels first, followed by consonants.

Making Words Lessons

WORD STUDY
Lessons

Making Words Lesson 1: "Flowers"

Activity 1: Making Words

In pairs, students take turns manipulating letter cards to make words.

Activity 1 Steps

STRUCTURE
RallyCoach

1. The teacher makes a transparency of the Making Words (*Flowers*) page and cuts out the letters and words.
2. Each pair receives one set of the following letters: *e, o, f, l, r, s, w* (the letters from the word *flowers*) from the blackline.
3. The teacher asks students to make words as described in the table on page 205, Words to Make from *Flowers*. The teacher reviews the teaching points as indicated on the table.
4. Partner A makes the first word, while Partner B coaches if necessary.
5. The teacher makes the word on the overhead projector.
6. Students write the word in a box on their student form. They will use these words in Activity 2.
7. Partners take turns for each new word and the process is repeated.

Blacklines

Words to Make from *Flowers*

Directions	Word	Teaching Point
Make: *so*	so	
Make: *row*	row	Discuss two sounds for long /o/.
Make it plural.	rows	
Make the name of a flower.	rose	Homophones: rows/rose
Make: *low*	low	What letter pattern did you use to help you? (ow)
Add /er/ to make a new word.	lower	Discuss taking off endings to decode the word.
Make: *owl*	owl	Discuss two sounds for /ow/.
Make it plural.	owls	
Rearrange the letters to make a new word.	slow	Decode: Cover up from the vowel through the rest of the word and say the beginning part. Uncover the word and say the last part.
Add /er/ to make a new word.	slower	
Make: *flow*	flow	
Rearrange the letters to make a new word.	fowl	Discuss two sounds of /ow/. Tell students they should try /ow/ with both sounds to see which way makes a word.
Use all the letters to make the magic word.	flowers	Point out the two letter patterns and the blend (fl, ow, er).

Activity 2: Sorting

The teacher makes a group of words and asks the students to guess the reason the words have been grouped together. This activity draws the students' attention to visual clues and letter patterns. Students should be given opportunities to make a sort and have their partner guess their sort.

Activity 2 Steps

STRUCTURE

Find My Rule

Ideas for Rules

- plural words
- homophones
- blends
- two different sounds of /ow/
- words with endings

1. The teacher makes a transparency of the Find My Rule Mat (page 218).
2. The teacher decides on a "rule" to place words in the two different columns of the Mat. For the example below, the rule is **long /ow/ words.**

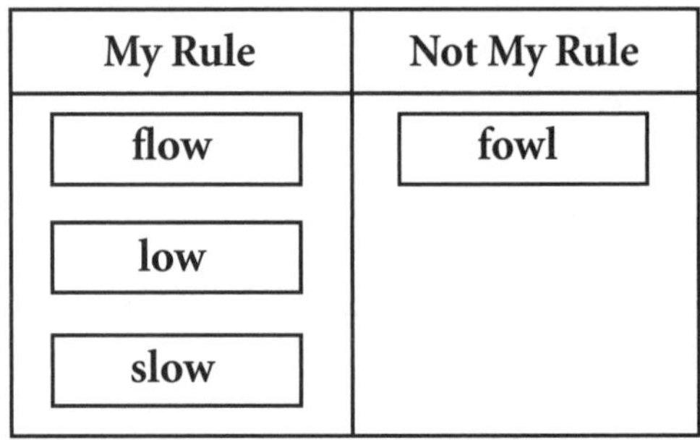

My Rule	Not My Rule
flow	fowl
low	
slow	

3. The teacher places one word in each column, and asks, "What is my rule?"
4. Students RallyRobin with their shoulder partners to determine what the rule may be.
5. The teacher adds the next two words, one in each column, and asks again, "What is my rule?"
6. Students RallyRobin again.
7. This continues until students think they know the rule. The teacher calls on students to verbalize the rule. If correct, the teacher congratulates the students, if incorrect the process continues.
8. When done, the activity may be repeated with a new rule. Other rule examples are listed at left.
9. After practice, students can cut apart their word boxes from Activity 1, step 6. They can create their own word sorts and have a partner find the rule.

BlacKlines

Activity 3: Transfer

The teacher displays a word card on the overhead projector and discusses the letter pattern. Then the teacher says, "If you can spell this word, you can also spell..." Students work in pairs to spell the new word. This activity helps students "use what they know" from one word and transfer it to a new word that they are trying to read or write.

STRUCTURE

RallyCoach

Activity 3 Steps

1. The teacher places a word card on the overhead projector.
2. The teacher states, "If you can spell this word, you can also spell…." (See the examples below.)
3. Partner A spells the word while Partner B watches, checks, and coaches as needed.
4. The teacher spells the new word for the class, and students praise their partners for correct spelling.
5. Students switch roles of Speller and Coach for each new word.

Using What You Know

If you can spell…	Then you can spell…
row	**mow, crow, below**
flower	**tower, power**
flow	**blow, glow, slow**

Making Words (*Flowers*) Teacher Transparency Form

Instructions: Make a transparency of this page. Cut out letters and words to use during Activity 1: Making Words and with Activity 2: Sorting.

e	o	f	l	r	s	w
so	row	rows	rose			
low	lower	owl	owls			
slow	slower	flow	fowl			
flowers						

Making Words (e, o, f, l, r, s, w) Student Form

Instructions: Make one copy per student. Cut apart letters to use during Activity 1: Making Words. Cut apart boxes after words are added during Activity 2: Sorting.

w

s

r

l

f

o

e

Lesson 2: "Blanket"

Activity 1: Making Words

***The steps for this activity are the same as Lesson 1, Activity 1 but substitute the following words to make from the letters in* Blanket.**

Words to Make from *Blanket*

Directions	Word	Teaching Point
Make: *tan*	tan	
Rearrange the letters and make a new word.	ant	Discuss /an/ letter pattern.
Make: *tea* *I want a cup of hot tea.*	tea	Discuss long sound of /ea/.
Move the /t/ to the end of the word.	eat	
Rearrange the letters and make a new word.	ate	Discuss silent e.
Make: *ten*	ten	Discuss /en/ letter pattern.
Rearrange the 't' and the 'n'.	net	
Replace the 'n' with an 'l'.	let	
Replace the 'l' with a 'b'.	bet	
Make: *beat.* *Beat the eggs and butter.*	beat	Discuss long sound of /ea/.
Replace the 'b' with an 'n'.	neat	
Make: *leak* *There is a leak in this pitcher.*	leak	
Add a beginning letter to make a new word.	bleak	*The weather looks bleak outside today.* Discuss familiar letter pattern.
Make: *lake*	lake	How did you know to add the silent 'e'?
Replace the 'l' with a 'b'.	bake	
Replace the 'b' with another letter.	take	Discuss /ake/ letter pattern.
Make: *tank* *The soldier was in a tank.*	tank	Discuss /ank/ letter pattern.

Directions	Word	Teaching Point
Replace the 't' and make a new word.	bank	
Add a letter and make a new word.	blank	Decode: Cover up the vowel to the end of the word. Say the beginning blend, then uncover, and say the whole word.
Use five letters and make the word 'table'.	table	How did you know how to spell this word? What letter pattern helped you?
Use five letters and spell the word 'ankle'.	ankle	How did you know how to spell this word? What letter pattern helped you?
Add one more letter to the end of 'ankle' and spell a new word.	anklet	
Use all the letters to spell the magic word.	blanket	What letter patterns helped you spell this word?

Activity 2: Sorting

The steps for this activity are the same as Lesson 1, Activity 2. Below is an example for Find My Rule using the Blanket words and additional ideas for Find My Rule.

Ideas for Rules

- **Letter patterns: /an/, /en/, /et/, /ake/, /ank/, /eat/**
- **long sound of /ea/**

My Rule	Not My Rule
lake	tank
bake	
take	

Examples: /ake/ letter patterns

Activity 3: Transfer

The steps for this activity are the same as Lesson 1, Activity 3, except use the following words to spell.

Using What You Know

If you can spell…	Then you can spell…
neat	**treat, meat, wheat**
bake	**cake, rake, wake**
blank	**crank, thank, drank**
table	**fable, stable**

Making Words (*Blanket*)
Teacher Transparency Form

Instructions: Make a transparency of this page. Cut out letters and words to use during Activity 1: Making Words and with Activity 2: Sorting.

Letters						
a	e	b	k	l	n	t

Words			
tan	ant	tea	eat
ate	ten	net	let
bet	beat	neat	leak
bleak	lake	bake	take
tank	bank	blank	table
ankle	anklet	blanket	

Making Words (a, e, b, k, l, n, t) Student Form

Instructions: Make one copy per student. Cut apart letters to use during Activity 1: Making Words. Cut apart boxes after words are added during Activity 2: Sorting.

t						
n						
l						
k						
b						
e						
a						

Lesson 3: "Breaking"

Activity 1: Making Words

The steps for this activity are the same as Lesson 1, Activity 1 but substitute the following words to make from the letters in Breaking.

Words to Make from *Breaking*

Directions	Word	Teaching Point
Make: *beg*	beg	
Replace the vowel 'e' with an 'i'.	big	
Replace the vowel with an 'a'.	bag	
Add one letter and make a new word.	brag	
Take away the 'r'. Add a new letter in a different place to make a new word.	bang	
Replace the 'g' with a 'k'.	bank	Discuss the /ank/ letter pattern.
Add the suffix /er/.	banker	Discuss the meaning of '-er'. (one who)
Make: *bear* *The bear is sleeping in a cave.*	bear	Discuss the short sound of /ea/.
Make a homophone for bear.	bare	Have a student use *bare* in a sentence. Discuss homophones (*bare, bear*).
Replace the 'r' in *bare* for a new letter.	bake	Discuss letter pattern /ake/.
Make: *baking*	baking	Discuss dropping the silent 'e' before adding suffix.
Make: *baker*	baker	What did you need to remember to spell this word?
Make: *bike*	bike	Discuss the letter pattern /ike/.
Make: *biker.*	biker	Review the suffix '-er'. Remind students that for words that end in silent 'e', you will take off the 'e' before adding the ending.
Make: *bark*	bark	Review /ar/ letter pattern.
Add an /ing/ suffix.	barking	

Directions	Word	Teaching Point
Make: *brake*	brake	What helped you know how to spell this word?
Make: *bring*	bring	What letter pattern do you see?
Make: *being*	being	What helped you spell this word?
Rearrange the letters to make a new word.	begin	
Replace one vowel with a new vowel.	began	
Make: *braking* *I was braking to a stop so I would not hit the car in front of me.*	braking	What helped you spell this word?
Magic Word: Use all the letters and spell a homophone for *braking*.	breaking	Homophones Long a sound of /ea/

Activity 2: Sorting

The steps for this activity are the same as Lesson 1, Activity 2. Below is an example for Find My Rule using the Breaking words and additional ideas for Find My Rule.

Ideas for Rules

- **/ing/ ending**
- **/ake/ letter pattern**
- **homophones (bear/ bare, break/brake)**
- **silent 'e' words**

My Rule	Not My Rule
biker	barking
banker	
baker	

Example: /-er/ ending

Activity 3: Transfer

The steps for this activity are the same as Lesson 1, Activity 3, except use the following words to spell.

Using What You Know

If you can spell…	Then you can spell…
biking	liking, hiking, spiking
bank	thank, rank, prank, blank
bark	dark, spark, lark, mark

Making Words (*BreaKing*) Teacher Transparency Form

Instructions: Make a transparency of this page. Cut out letters and words to use during Activity 1: Making Words and with Activity 2: Sorting.

a e	i b	g k	n r
beg	big	bag	brag
bang	bank	banker	bear
bare	bake	baking	baker
bike	biker	bark	barking
brake	bring	being	begin
began	braking	breaking	

Making Words (a, e, i, b, g, K, n, r)
Student Form

Instructions: Make one copy per student. Cut apart letters to use during Activity 1: Making Words. Cut apart boxes after words are added during Activity 2: Sorting.

r						
n						
k						
g						
b						
i						
e						
a						

Find My Rule Mat for Making Words

Instructions: Make a transparency of this mat for Activity 2: Sorting. Make copies for each pair of students for Activity 2: Sorting.

My Rule	Not My Rule

Making Words Planning Form

Letters: ___________________________

Magic Word: ___________________________

Part 1: Making Words (RallyCoach)

Instructions: Use this planning form to create additional Making Words lessons.

Directions	Word	Teaching Point

Part 2: Sorting (Find My Rule)	Sort For:
Part 3: Transfer (RallyCoach)	**Using What You Know**

Making Words Student Form

Instructions: Use this planning form to create the letters and words for additional Making Words lessons.

Who Knows?

Students mix about the room, finding others who can help them fill out their Find Someone Who word study worksheets.

Activity Steps

STRUCTURE
Find Someone Who

1. Every student receives a Find Someone Who worksheet.
2. Students mix around the room until they find a partner.
3. In pairs, Partner A asks a question from the worksheet. Partner B responds. Partner A records the answer on his or her worksheet.
4. Partner B checks and initials the answer.
5. Partner B asks a question from the worksheet. Partner A responds. Partner B records the answer on his or her worksheet.
6. Partner A checks and initials the answer.
7. Partners shake hands, part, and raise a hand again as they search for a new partner.
8. Students repeat the process until they complete their worksheets.
9. When their worksheets are completed, students sit down. Seated students may be approached by others as a resource.
10. In teams, students compare answers: If there is disagreement or uncertainty, they raise four hands to ask a team question.

BlacKlines

Adding ar/or, Prefixes, Antonyms, Base Words, Compound Words, Contractions, Suffixes

Find Someone Who

Name____________________________

Instructions: Copy one page per student.

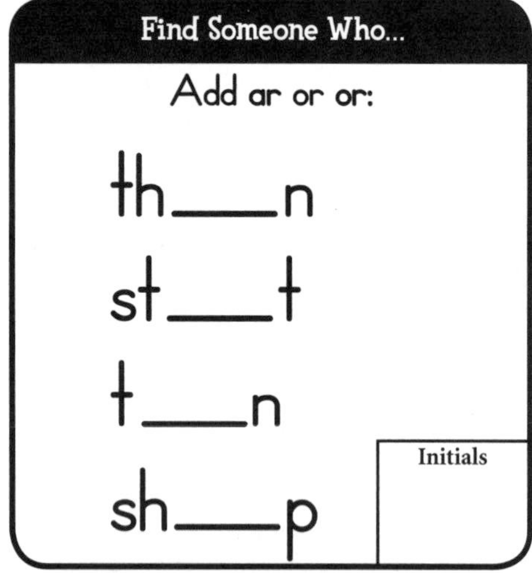

Find Someone Who...

Add ar or or:

th___n

st___t

t___n

sh___p

Initials

Find Someone Who...

Circle the base words:

running bringing tripping

Initials

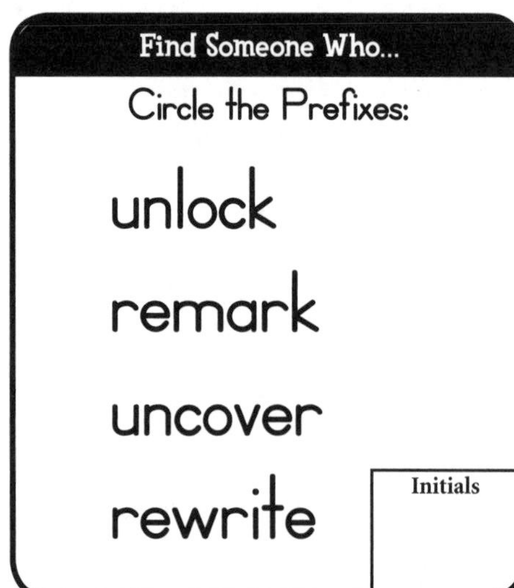

Find Someone Who...

Circle the Prefixes:

unlock

remark

uncover

rewrite

Initials

Find Someone Who...

Make Compound Words:

rain ring book ear

shelf earth drop worm

__________ __________

__________ __________

__________ __________

Initials

Find Someone Who...

Antonyms?

slow__________

down__________

short__________

Initials

Find Someone Who...

Contractions:
Add the (')

c a n t

d o n t

s h e l l

I l l

Initials

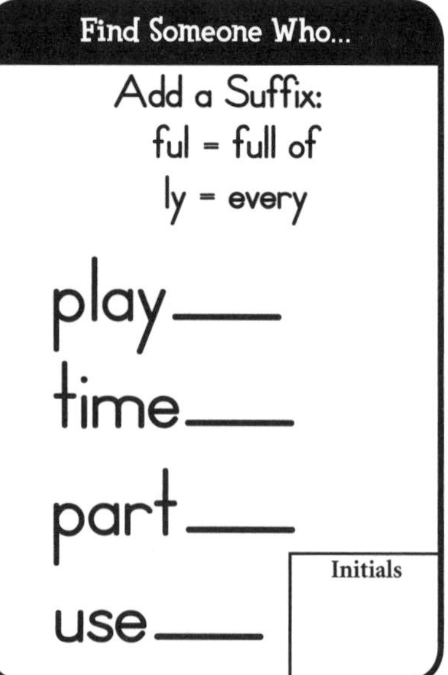

Find Someone Who...

Add a Suffix:
ful = full of
ly = every

play___

time___

part___

use___

Initials

Adding er, ir, or, ur, Prefixes, Adding ou/ow, Synonyms, Contractions, Word Family

Find Someone Who

Name______________________________

Instructions: Copy one page per student.

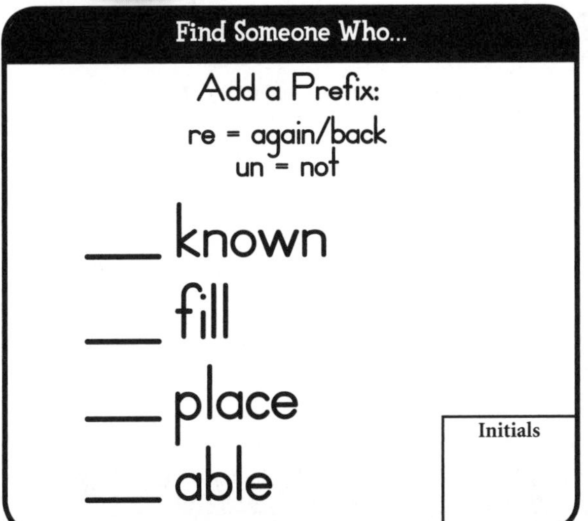

Find Someone Who...

Add a Prefix:

re = again/back
un = not

___ known
___ fill
___ place
___ able

Initials

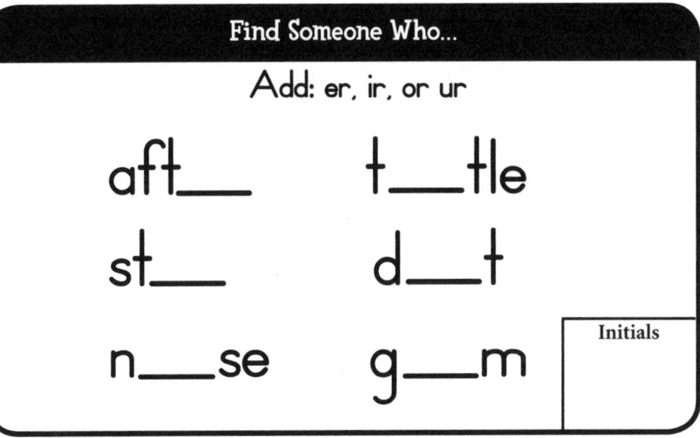

Find Someone Who...

Add: er, ir, or ur

aft___ t___tle
st___ d___t
n___se g___m

Initials

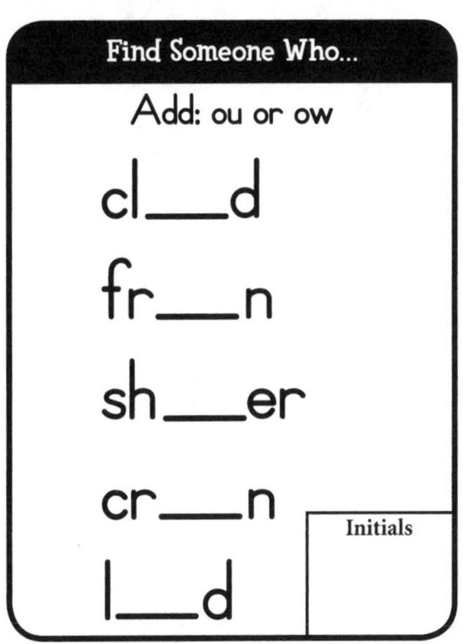

Find Someone Who...

Add: ou or ow

cl___d
fr___n
sh___er
cr___n
l___d

Initials

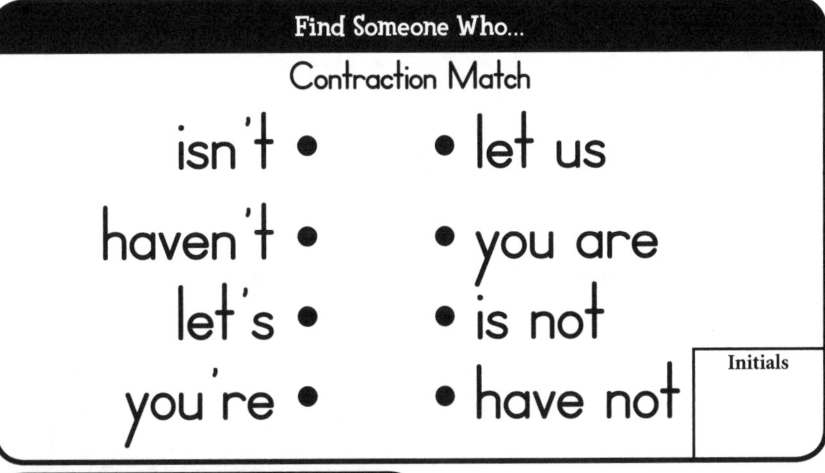

Find Someone Who...

Contraction Match

isn't •	• let us
haven't •	• you are
let's •	• is not
you're •	• have not

Initials

Find Someone Who...

Add Words to the Word Family

track
rack
____
____

Initials

Find Someone Who...

Match the Synonyms:

speak	mad
cent	see
look	talk
angry	penny

Initials

WORD STUDY BlacKline

Plurals, Sound of "C," Compound Words, Sentence Conventions

Find Someone Who

Name______________________________

Instructions: Copy one page per student.

Find Someone Who...

Make Plurals: (more than one)

dress __________

lunch __________

boy __________

bush __________

Initials

Find Someone Who...

Circle the sound made by c

color s or k	cell s or k
cent s or k	cool s or k
city s or k	

Initials

Find Someone Who...

Divide the Compound Words

footprint flashlight gumdrop

hillside songbird flagpole

Initials

Find Someone Who...

Fix the Sentence

nate and josh sprinted in the race on saturday at oak park

____

Initials

Find Someone Who...

Fix the Sentence

Thay cant wait to go two the movies with kate and sue

____

Initials

Find Someone Who Form

Instructions: Use this form to create questions for additional activities.

Initials

Initials

Initials

Initials

Initials

Initials

Initials

QUIZ-QUIZ-TRADE

Activities

Partner Word Study Practice

To practice rhyming words, plurals, antonyms, synonyms, prefixes, suffixes, and letter patterns, students quiz a partner, get quizzed by a partner, and then trade cards to repeat the process with a new partner.

Activity Steps

1. Each student receives a card with a question on the front and answer on the back.
2. All students stand up, put a hand up, and pair up.
3. Partner A quizzes Partner B.
4. Partner B answers.
5. Partner A checks the answer on back and praises or coaches.
6. Partners switch roles and quiz again.
7. After they have quizzed both ways, partners trade cards, and raise their hands to find a new partner. The partner quizzing and trading proceeds for numerous pairings.

STRUCTURE

Quiz-Quiz-Trade

Front
Silent Letters (gn, kn, wr)
Question: Say the word. Which way looks right?
a) wrestle
b) restle
Back
Silent Letters (gn, kn, wr)
Answer:
a) wrestle

Blacklines

Rhyming Words

Quiz-Quiz-Trade

Instructions: Copy enough cards so each student has one card. Cut on dotted lines and fold in half.

Rhyming Words	Rhyming Words
Say these words. Do they rhyme? pain cane	Answer: yes
Say these words. Do they rhyme? shack shake	Answer: no
Say these words. Do they rhyme? meat beet	Answer: yes
Say these words. Do they rhyme? part pants	Answer: no

Rhyming Words

Quiz-Quiz-Trade

Instructions: Copy enough cards so each student has one card. Cut on dotted lines and fold in half.

Rhyming Words	Rhyming Words
Say these words. Do they rhyme? aim / tame	Answer: yes
Say these words. Do they rhyme? seed / seal	Answer: no
Say these words. Do they rhyme? drip / dip	Answer: yes
Say these words. Do they rhyme? not / note	Answer: no

Rhyming Words

Quiz-Quiz-Trade

Instructions: Copy enough cards so each student has one card. Cut on dotted lines and fold in half.

Rhyming Words	Rhyming Words
Say these words. Do they rhyme? tail pale	Answer: yes
Say these words. Do they rhyme? kite kit	Answer: no
Say these words. Do they rhyme? high pie	Answer: yes
Say these words. Do they rhyme? land lamp	Answer: no

Rhyming Words

Quiz-Quiz-Trade

Instructions: Copy enough cards so each student has one card. Cut on dotted lines and fold in half.

Rhyming Words	Rhyming Words
Say these words. Do they rhyme? kite might	Answer: yes
Say these words. Do they rhyme? street sweep	Answer: no
Say these words. Do they rhyme? light bite	Answer: yes
Say these words. Do they rhyme? doe do	Answer: no

Rhyming Words

Quiz-Quiz-Trade

Instructions: Copy enough cards so each student has one card. Cut on dotted lines and fold in half.

Rhyming Words	Rhyming Words
Say these words. Do they rhyme? brain plane	Answer: yes
Say these words. Do they rhyme? leash reach	Answer: no
Say these words. Do they rhyme? knee sea	Answer: yes
Say these words. Do they rhyme? saw say	Answer: no

Rhyming Words

Quiz-Quiz-Trade

Instructions: Copy enough cards so each student has one card. Cut on dotted lines and fold in half.

Rhyming Words	Rhyming Words
Say these words. Do they rhyme? tax snacks	Answer: yes
Say these words. Do they rhyme? hall well	Answer: no
Say these words. Do they rhyme? eye cry	Answer: yes
Say these words. Do they rhyme? zoom moon	Answer: no

Rhyming Words

Quiz-Quiz-Trade

Instructions: Copy enough cards so each student has one card. Cut on dotted lines and fold in half.

Rhyming Words	Rhyming Words
Say these words. Do they rhyme? place ace	Answer: yes
Say these words. Do they rhyme? dream clean	Answer: no
Say these words. Do they rhyme? gate wait	Answer: yes
Say these words. Do they rhyme? less grass	Answer: no

Silent Letters (gn, Kn, wr)

Quiz-Quiz-Trade

Instructions: Copy enough cards so each student has one card. Cut on dotted lines and fold in half.

Silent Letters (gn, Kn, wr)	Silent Letters (gn, Kn, wr)
Question: Say the word. Which way looks right? a) knife b) nife	Answer: a) knife
Question: Say the word. Which way looks right? a) narl b) gnarl	Answer: b) gnarl
Question: Say the word. Which way looks right? a) doorknob b) doornob	Answer: a) doorknob
Question: Say the word. Which way looks right? a) nee b) knee	Answer: b) knee

Silent Letters (gn, Kn, wr)

Quiz-Quiz-Trade

Instructions: Copy enough cards so each student has one card. Cut on dotted lines and fold in half.

Silent Letters (gn, Kn, wr)	Silent Letters (gn, Kn, wr)
Question: Say the word. Which way looks right? a) knack b) nack	Answer: a) knack
Question: Say the word. Which way looks right? a) rerite b) rewrite	Answer: b) rewrite
Question: Say the word. Which way looks right? a) wreath b) reath	Answer: a) wreath
Question: Say the word. Which way looks right? a) nitted b) knitted	Answer: b) knitted

Silent Letters (gn, kn, wr)

Quiz-Quiz-Trade

Instructions: Copy enough cards so each student has one card. Cut on dotted lines and fold in half.

Silent Letters (gn, kn, wr)	Silent Letters (gn, kn, wr)
Question: Say the word. Which way looks right? a) knock b) nock	Answer: a) knock
Silent Letters (gn, kn, wr)	Silent Letters (gn, kn, wr)
Question: Say the word. Which way looks right? a) nat b) gnat	Answer: b) gnat
Silent Letters (gn, kn, wr)	Silent Letters (gn, kn, wr)
Question: Say the word. Which way looks right? a) gnu b) nu	Answer: a) gnu
Silent Letters (gn, kn, wr)	Silent Letters (gn, kn, wr)
Question: Say the word. Which way looks right? a) nuckle b) knuckle	Answer: b) knuckle

Silent Letters (gn, Kn, wr)

Quiz-Quiz-Trade

Instructions: Copy enough cards so each student has one card. Cut on dotted lines and fold in half.

Silent Letters (gn, Kn, wr)	Silent Letters (gn, Kn, wr)
Question: Say the word. Which way looks right? a) gnashed b) nashed	Answer: a) gnashed
Silent Letters (gn, Kn, wr) Question: Say the word. Which way looks right? a) nelt b) knelt	Silent Letters (gn, Kn, wr) Answer: b) knelt
Silent Letters (gn, Kn, wr) Question: Say the word. Which way looks right? a) knickers b) nickers	Silent Letters (gn, Kn, wr) Answer: a) knickers
Silent Letters (gn, Kn, wr) Question: Say the word. Which way looks right? a) ren b) wren	Silent Letters (gn, Kn, wr) Answer: b) wren

Silent Letters (gn, kn, wr)

Quiz-Quiz-Trade

Instructions: Copy enough cards so each student has one card. Cut on dotted lines and fold in half.

Silent Letters (gn, kn, wr)	Silent Letters (gn, kn, wr)
Question: Say the word. Which way looks right? a) wrestle b) restle	Answer: a) wrestle
Question: Say the word. Which way looks right? a) riggle b) wriggle	Answer: b) wriggle
Question: Say the word. Which way looks right? a) unknown b) unnown	Answer: a) unknown
Question: Say the word. Which way looks right? a) rinkles b) wrinkles	Answer: b) wrinkles

Silent Letters (gn, Kn, wr)

Quiz-Quiz-Trade

Instructions: Copy enough cards so each student has one card. Cut on dotted lines and fold in half.

Silent Letters (gn, Kn, wr)	Silent Letters (gn, Kn, wr)
Question: Say the word. Which way looks right? a) knapsack b) napsack	Answer: a) knapsack
Question: Say the word. Which way looks right? a) naw b) gnaw	Answer: b) gnaw
Question: Say the word. Which way looks right? a) wrong b) rong	Answer: a) wrong
Question: Say the word. Which way looks right? a) rench b) wrench	Answer: b) wrench

Silent Letters (gn, kn, wr)

Quiz-Quiz-Trade

Instructions: Copy enough cards so each student has one card. Cut on dotted lines and fold in half.

Silent Letters (gn, kn, wr)	Silent Letters (gn, kn, wr)
Question: Say the word. Which way looks right? a) wreck b) reck	Answer: a) wreck
Question: Say the word. Which way looks right? a) handritten b) handwritten	Answer: b) handwritten
Question: Say the word. Which way looks right? a) knowledge b) nowledge	Answer: a) knowledge
Question: Say the word. Which way looks right? a) rist b) wrist	Answer: b) wrist

Long A (ay, ai, a-e)

Quiz-Quiz-Trade

Instructions: Copy enough cards so each student has one card. Cut on dotted lines and fold in half.

Long A (ay, ai, a-e)	Long A (ay, ai, a-e)
Question: Say the word. Which way looks right? a) rane b) rayn c) rain	Answer: c) rain
Question: Say the word. Which way looks right? a) grain b) grane c) grayn	Answer: a) grain
Question: Say the word. Which way looks right? a) caik b) cake c) cayk	Answer: b) cake
Question: Say the word. Which way looks right? a) wait b) wayt c) wate	Answer: a) wait

Long A (ay, ai, a-e)

Quiz-Quiz-Trade

Instructions: Copy enough cards so each student has one card. Cut on dotted lines and fold in half.

Long A (ay, ai, a-e)

Question: Say the word. Which way looks right?

a) hai
b) hae
c) hay

Long A (ay, ai, a-e)

Answer:

c) hay

Long A (ay, ai, a-e)

Question: Say the word. Which way looks right?

a) spray
b) sprae
c) sprai

Long A (ay, ai, a-e)

Answer:

a) spray

Long A (ay, ai, a-e)

Question: Say the word. Which way looks right?

a) flaim
b) flame
c) flaym

Long A (ay, ai, a-e)

Answer:

b) flame

Long A (ay, ai, a-e)

Question: Say the word. Which way looks right?

a) nail
b) nale
c) nayl

Long A (ay, ai, a-e)

Answer:

a) nail

Long A (ay, ai, a-e)

Quiz-Quiz-Trade

Instructions: Copy enough cards so each student has one card. Cut on dotted lines and fold in half.

Long A (ay, ai, a-e)	Long A (ay, ai, a-e)
Question: Say the word. Which way looks right? a) paine b) payn c) pain	Answer: c) pain
Question: Say the word. Which way looks right? a) flake b) flaik c) flayk	Answer: a) flake
Question: Say the word. Which way looks right? a) faynt b) faint c) fante	Answer: b) faint
Question: Say the word. Which way looks right? a) gate b) gayt c) gaite	Answer: a) gate

Long A (ay, ai, a-e)

Quiz-Quiz-Trade

Instructions: Copy enough cards so each student has one card. Cut on dotted lines and fold in half.

Long A (ay, ai, a-e)	Long A (ay, ai, a-e)
Question: Say the word. Which way looks right? a) shayk b) shaik c) shake	Answer: c) shake
Question: Say the word. Which way looks right? a) maebe b) maibe c) maybe	Answer: c) maybe
Question: Say the word. Which way looks right? a) gaim b) game c) gaym	Answer: b) game
Question: Say the word. Which way looks right? a) clay b) clai c) clae	Answer: a) clay

Long A (ay, ai, a-e)

Quiz-Quiz-Trade

Instructions: Copy enough cards so each student has one card. Cut on dotted lines and fold in half.

Long A (ay, ai, a-e)	Long A (ay, ai, a-e)
Question: Say the word. Which way looks right? a) plae b) plai c) play	Answer: c) play
Question: Say the word. Which way looks right? a) scraip b) scrayp c) scrape	Answer: c) scrape
Question: Say the word. Which way looks right? a) strae b) stray c) strai	Answer: b) stray
Question: Say the word. Which way looks right? a) paint b) paynt c) pante	Answer: a) paint

Long A (ay, ai, a-e)

Quiz-Quiz-Trade

Instructions: Copy enough cards so each student has one card. Cut on dotted lines and fold in half.

Long A (ay, ai, a-e)	Long A (ay, ai, a-e)
Question: Say the word. Which way looks right? a) lake b) laik c) layk	Answer: a) lake
Question: Say the word. Which way looks right? a) paile b) pail c) payl	Answer: b) pail
Question: Say the word. Which way looks right? a) swae b) swai c) sway	Answer: c) sway
Question: Say the word. Which way looks right? a) plait b) plate c) playt	Answer: b) plate

Long A (ay, ai, a-e)

Quiz-Quiz-Trade

Instructions: Copy enough cards so each student has one card. Cut on dotted lines and fold in half.

Long A (ay, ai, a-e)	Long A (ay, ai, a-e)
Question: Say the word. Which way looks right? a) name b) naym c) naim	Answer: a) name
Question: Say the word. Which way looks right? a) brayn b) brain c) brane	Answer: b) brain
Question: Say the word. Which way looks right? a) grai b) grae c) gray	Answer: c) gray
Question: Say the word. Which way looks right? a) trayn b) train c) trane	Answer: b) train

Antonyms or Synonyms?

Quiz-Quiz-Trade

Instructions: Copy enough cards so each student has one card. Cut on dotted lines and fold in half.

Antonyms or Synonyms?	Antonyms or Synonyms?
Question: Antonyms or Synonyms? hot cold	Answer: antonyms
Question: Antonyms or Synonyms? gal lady	Answer: synonyms
Question: Antonyms or Synonyms? strong weak	Answer: antonyms
Question: Antonyms or Synonyms? fast speedy	Answer: synonyms

Antonyms or Synonyms?

Quiz-Quiz-Trade

Instructions: Copy enough cards so each student has one card. Cut on dotted lines and fold in half.

Antonyms or Synonyms?	Antonyms or Synonyms?
Question: Antonyms or Synonyms? day night	Answer: antonyms
Question: Antonyms or Synonyms? guy man	Answer: synonyms
Question: Antonyms or Synonyms? save spend	Answer: antonyms
Question: Antonyms or Synonyms? near close	Answer: synonyms

Antonyms or Synonyms?

Quiz-Quiz-Trade

Instructions: Copy enough cards so each student has one card. Cut on dotted lines and fold in half.

Antonyms or Synonyms?	Antonyms or Synonyms?
Question: Antonyms or Synonyms? tame wild	Answer: antonyms
Antonyms or Synonyms?	Antonyms or Synonyms?
Question: Antonyms or Synonyms? soft cuddly	Answer: synonyms
Antonyms or Synonyms?	Antonyms or Synonyms?
Question: Antonyms or Synonyms? past present	Answer: antonyms
Antonyms or Synonyms?	Antonyms or Synonyms?
Question: Antonyms or Synonyms? sick ill	Answer: synonyms

Antonyms or Synonyms?

Quiz-Quiz-Trade

Instructions: Copy enough cards so each student has one card. Cut on dotted lines and fold in half.

Antonyms or Synonyms?	**Antonyms or Synonyms?**
Question: Antonyms or Synonyms? neat messy	Answer: antonyms
Question: Antonyms or Synonyms? happy glad	Answer: synonyms
Question: Antonyms or Synonyms? yes no	Answer: antonyms
Question: Antonyms or Synonyms? kids children	Answer: synonyms

Antonyms or Synonyms?

Quiz-Quiz-Trade

Instructions: Copy enough cards so each student has one card. Cut on dotted lines and fold in half.

Antonyms or Synonyms?	Antonyms or Synonyms?
Question: Antonyms or Synonyms? never always	Answer: antonyms
Antonyms or Synonyms?	**Antonyms or Synonyms?**
Question: Antonyms or Synonyms? speak talk	Answer: synonyms
Antonyms or Synonyms?	**Antonyms or Synonyms?**
Question: Antonyms or Synonyms? pull push	Answer: antonyms
Antonyms or Synonyms?	**Antonyms or Synonyms?**
Question: Antonyms or Synonyms? tired sleepy	Answer: synonyms

Antonyms or Synonyms?

Quiz-Quiz-Trade

Instructions: Copy enough cards so each student has one card. Cut on dotted lines and fold in half.

Antonyms or Synonyms?	Antonyms or Synonyms?
Question: Antonyms or Synonyms? winter summer	Answer: antonyms

Antonyms or Synonyms?	Antonyms or Synonyms?
Question: Antonyms or Synonyms? walk hike	Answer: synonyms

Antonyms or Synonyms?	Antonyms or Synonyms?
Question: Antonyms or Synonyms? hairy bald	Answer: antonyms

Antonyms or Synonyms?	Antonyms or Synonyms?
Question: Antonyms or Synonyms? sip drink	Answer: synonyms

Antonyms or Synonyms?

Quiz-Quiz-Trade

Instructions: Copy enough cards so each student has one card. Cut on dotted lines and fold in half.

Antonyms or Synonyms?	Antonyms or Synonyms?
Question: Antonyms or Synonyms? dirty clean	Answer: antonyms
Question: Antonyms or Synonyms? silly funny	Answer: synonyms
Question: Antonyms or Synonyms? easy hard	Answer: antonyms
Question: Antonyms or Synonyms? wash scrub	Answer: synonyms

Plural

Quiz-Quiz-Trade

Instructions: Copy enough cards so each student has one card. Cut on dotted lines and fold in half.

Plural	Plural
Question: Say the word. Which way looks right? a) lunchs b) lunches	Answer: b) lunches
Plural	Plural
Question: Say the word. Which way looks right? a) keys b) keyes	Answer: a) keys
Plural	Plural
Question: Say the word. Which way looks right? a) desks b) deskes	Answer: a) desks
Plural	Plural
Question: Say the word. Which way looks right? a) dishs b) dishes	Answer: b) dishes

Plural

Quiz-Quiz-Trade

Instructions: Copy enough cards so each student has one card. Cut on dotted lines and fold in half.

Plural	Plural
Question: Say the word. Which way looks right? a) lockes b) locks	Answer: b) locks
Question: Say the word. Which way looks right? a) books b) bookes	Answer: a) books
Question: Say the word. Which way looks right? a) boxes b) boxs	Answer: a) boxes
Question: Say the word. Which way looks right? a) glassies b) glasses	Answer: b) glasses

Plural

Quiz-Quiz-Trade

Instructions: Copy enough cards so each student has one card. Cut on dotted lines and fold in half.

Plural	Plural
Question: Say the word. Which way looks right? a) churchs b) churches	Answer: b) churches
Question: Say the word. Which way looks right? a) eggs b) egges	Answer: a) eggs
Question: Say the word. Which way looks right? a) marches b) marchs	Answer: a) marches
Question: Say the word. Which way looks right? a) chaires b) chairs	Answer: b) chairs

Plural

Quiz-Quiz-Trade

Instructions: Copy enough cards so each student has one card. Cut on dotted lines and fold in half.

Plural	Plural
Question: Say the word. Which way looks right? a) taxs b) taxes	Answer: b) taxes
Question: Say the word. Which way looks right? a) teaches b) teachs	Answer: a) teaches
Question: Say the word. Which way looks right? a) mows b) mowes	Answer: a) mows
Question: Say the word. Which way looks right? a) toyes b) toys	Answer: b) toys

Plural

Quiz-Quiz-Trade

Instructions: Copy enough cards so each student has one card. Cut on dotted lines and fold in half.

Plural	Plural
Question: Say the word. Which way looks right? a) pennys b) pennies	Answer: b) pennies

Plural	Plural
Question: Say the word. Which way looks right? a) cities b) citys	Answer: a) cities

Plural	Plural
Question: Say the word. Which way looks right? a) berries b) berrys	Answer: a) berries

Plural	Plural
Question: Say the word. Which way looks right? a) babys b) babies	Answer: b) babies

Plural

Quiz-Quiz-Trade

Instructions: Copy enough cards so each student has one card. Cut on dotted lines and fold in half.

Plural	Plural
Question: Say the word. Which way looks right? a) familyes b) families	Answer: b) families
Plural	Plural
Question: Say the word. Which way looks right? a) loaves b) loafs	Answer: a) loaves
Plural	Plural
Question: Say the word. Which way looks right? a) leaves b) leafes	Answer: a) leaves
Plural	Plural
Question: Say the word. Which way looks right? a) flyes b) flies	Answer: b) flies

Plural

Quiz-Quiz-Trade

Instructions: Copy enough cards so each student has one card. Cut on dotted lines and fold in half.

Plural	Plural
Question: Say the word. Which way looks right? a) wolfes b) wolves	Answer: b) wolves
Question: Say the word. Which way looks right? a) stories b) storyies	Answer: a) stories
Question: Say the word. Which way looks right? a) spies b) spyes	Answer: a) spies
Question: Say the word. Which way looks right? a) crys b) cries	Answer: b) cries

Singular/Plural

Quiz-Quiz-Trade

Instructions: Copy enough cards so each student has one card. Cut on dotted lines and fold in half.

Singular/Plural	Singular/Plural
Question: Read the word. How Many? (one or more than one?) mice	Answer: mice (more than one)
Question: Read the word. How Many? (one or more than one?) mouse	Answer: mouse (one)
Question: Read the word. How Many? (one or more than one?) oxen	Answer: oxen (more than one)
Question: Read the word. How Many? (one or more than one?) ox	Answer: ox (one)

Singular/Plural

Quiz-Quiz-Trade

Instructions: Copy enough cards so each student has one card. Cut on dotted lines and fold in half.

Singular/Plural	Singular/Plural
Question: Read the word. How Many? (one or more than one?) people	Answer: people (more than one)
Question: Read the word. How Many? (one or more than one?) person	Answer: person (one)
Question: Read the word. How Many? (one or more than one?) geese	Answer: geese (more than one)
Question: Read the word. How Many? (one or more than one?) goose	Answer: goose (one)

Singular/Plural

Quiz-Quiz-Trade

Instructions: Copy enough cards so each student has one card. Cut on dotted lines and fold in half.

Singular/Plural	Singular/Plural
Question: Read the word. How Many? (one or more than one?) **men**	Answer: men (more than one)
Singular/Plural	**Singular/Plural**
Question: Read the word. How Many? (one or more than one?) **man**	Answer: man (one)
Singular/Plural	**Singular/Plural**
Question: Read the word. How Many? (one or more than one?) **children**	Answer: children (more than one)
Singular/Plural	**Singular/Plural**
Question: Read the word. How Many? (one or more than one?) **child**	Answer: child (one)

Singular/Plural

Quiz-Quiz-Trade

Instructions: Copy enough cards so each student has one card. Cut on dotted lines and fold in half.

Singular/Plural	Singular/Plural
Question: Read the word. How Many? (one or more than one?) **women**	Answer: **women** (more than one)
Question: Read the word. How Many? (one or more than one?) **woman**	Answer: **woman** (one)
Question: Read the word. How Many? (one or more than one?) **feet**	Answer: **feet** (more than one)
Question: Read the word. How Many? (one or more than one?) **foot**	Answer: **foot** (one)

Singular/Plural

Quiz-Quiz-Trade

Instructions: Copy enough cards so each student has one card. Cut on dotted lines and fold in half.

Singular/Plural	Singular/Plural
Question: Read the word. How Many? (one or more than one?)  teeth	Answer: teeth (more than one)
Question: Read the word. How Many? (one or more than one?)  tooth	Answer: tooth (one)
Question: Read the word. How Many? (one or more than one?) lice	Answer: lice (more than one)
Question: Read the word. How Many? (one or more than one?) louse	Answer: louse (one)

Singular/Plural

Quiz-Quiz-Trade

Instructions: Copy enough cards so each student has one card. Cut on dotted lines and fold in half.

Singular/Plural Question: Read the word. How Many? (one or more than one?) dresses	**Singular/Plural** Answer: dresses (more than one)
Singular/Plural Question: Read the word. How Many? (one or more than one?) dress	**Singular/Plural** Answer: dress (one)
Singular/Plural Question: Read the word. How Many? (one or more than one?) kisses	**Singular/Plural** Answer: kisses (more than one)
Singular/Plural Question: Read the word. How Many? (one or more than one?) kiss	**Singular/Plural** Answer: kiss (one)

Singular/Plural

Quiz-Quiz-Trade

Instructions: Copy enough cards so each student has one card. Cut on dotted lines and fold in half.

Singular/Plural	Singular/Plural
Question: Read the word. How Many? (one or more than one?) glasses	Answer: glasses (more than one)
Question: Read the word. How Many? (one or more than one?) glass	Answer: glass (one)
Question: Read the word. How Many? (one or more than one?) crosses	Answer: crosses (more than one)
Question: Read the word. How Many? (one or more than one?) cross	Answer: cross (one)

Singular/Plural

Quiz-Quiz-Trade

Instructions: Copy enough cards so each student has one card. Cut on dotted lines and fold in half.

Singular/Plural	Singular/Plural
Question: Read the word. How Many? (one or more than one?) **walruses**	Answer: walruses (more than one)
Question: Read the word. How Many? (one or more than one?) **walrus**	Answer: walrus (one)
Question: Read the word. How Many? (one or more than one?) **mattresses**	Answer: mattresses (more than one)
Question: Read the word. How Many? (one or more than one?) **mattress**	Answer: mattress (one)

Singular/Plural Nouns

Quiz-Quiz-Trade

Instructions: Copy enough cards so each student has one card. Cut on dotted lines and fold in half.

Singular/Plural Nouns

Question:

A flock of ______ were grazing in the meadow.

a) sheep
b) sheeps
c) sheepes

Singular/Plural Nouns

Answer:

A flock of sheep were grazing in the meadow.

a) sheep

Singular/Plural Nouns

Question:

We caught five ______ at the lake.

a) fishies
b) fishs
c) fish

Singular/Plural Nouns

Answer:

We caught five fish at the lake.

c) fish

Singular/Plural Nouns

Question:

A herd of ______ rested in the cool forest.

a) deer
b) deers
c) deeres

Singular/Plural Nouns

Answer:

A herd of deer rested in the cool forest.

a) deer

Singular/Plural Nouns

Question:

The ______ began their long swim upstream.

a) salmons
b) salmon
c) salmones

Singular/Plural Nouns

Answer:

The salmon began their long swim upstream.

b) salmon

Singular/Plural Nouns

Quiz-Quiz-Trade

Instructions: Copy enough cards so each student has one card. Cut on dotted lines and fold in half.

Singular/Plural Nouns

Question:
While fishing in the ocean, John reeled in two _____.

a) tunaes
b) tunas
c) tuna

Singular/Plural Nouns

Answer:
While fishing in the ocean, John reeled in two tuna.

c) tuna

Singular/Plural Nouns

Question:
The fishermen hoped to catch many _____ by noon.

a) trout
b) troutes
c) trouts

Singular/Plural Nouns

Answer:
The fishermen hoped to catch many trout by noon.

a) trout

Singular/Plural Nouns

Question:
Three _____ made a nest in the drawer.

a) mices
b) mouses
c) mice

Singular/Plural Nouns

Answer:
Three mice made a nest in the drawer.

c) mice

Singular/Plural Nouns

Question:
My _____ were sore after the long hike.

a) foots
b) feet
c) feets

Singular/Plural Nouns

Answer:
My feet were sore after the long hike.

b) feet

Singular/Plural Nouns

Quiz-Quiz-Trade

Instructions: Copy enough cards so each student has one card. Cut on dotted lines and fold in half.

Singular/Plural Nouns

Question:

The ______ played at the park all afternoon.

a) children
b) childrens
c) childs

Singular/Plural Nouns

Answer:

The children played at the park all afternoon.

a) children

Singular/Plural Nouns

Question:

I will brush my ______ before bedtime.

a) tooths
b) teeth
c) teeths

Singular/Plural Nouns

Answer:

I will brush my teeth before bedtime.

b) teeth

Singular/Plural Nouns

Question:

Five ______ flew overhead.

a) gooses
b) geeses
c) geese

Singular/Plural Nouns

Answer:

Five geese flew overhead.

c) geese

Singular/Plural Nouns

Question:

The pair of ______ pulled the covered wagon.

a) oxes
b) oxen
c) oxens

Singular/Plural Nouns

Answer:

The pair of oxen pulled the covered wagon.

b) oxen

Singular/Plural Nouns

Quiz-Quiz-Trade

Instructions: Copy enough cards so each student has one card. Cut on dotted lines and fold in half.

Singular/Plural Nouns	Singular/Plural Nouns
Question: Several ______ helped lift the heavy log. a) mens b) men c) mans	Answer: Several <u>men</u> helped lift the heavy log. b) men

Singular/Plural Nouns	Singular/Plural Nouns
Question: ______ like to live in warm places. a) Lice b) Louses c) Lices	Answer: <u>Lice</u> like to live in warm places. a) Lice

Singular/Plural Nouns	Singular/Plural Nouns
Question: Two of the ______ jogged after work. a) womans b) womens c) women	Answer: Two of the <u>women</u> jogged after work. c) women

Singular/Plural Nouns	Singular/Plural Nouns
Question: At the edge of the dock, we saw three ______ in the water. a) perches b) perch c) perchs	Answer: At the edge of the dock, we saw three <u>perch</u> in the water. b) perch

Singular/Plural Nouns

Quiz-Quiz-Trade

Instructions: Copy enough cards so each student has one card. Cut on dotted lines and fold in half.

Singular/Plural Nouns

Question:

The ______ fought the raging fire.

a) firemans
b) firemens
c) firemen

Singular/Plural Nouns

Answer:

The firemen fought the raging fire.

c) firemen

Singular/Plural Nouns

Question:

How many ______ are coming to the party?

a) peoples
b) people
c) peoplees

Singular/Plural Nouns

Answer:

How many people are coming to the party?

b) people

Singular/Plural Nouns

Question:

My ______ are sensitive to the cold.

a) teeth
b) tooths
c) teeths

Singular/Plural Nouns

Answer:

My teeth are sensitive to the cold.

a) teeth

Singular/Plural Nouns

Question:

The lion's ______ were playing in the tall grass.

a) offsprings
b) offspring
c) offspringes

Singular/Plural Nouns

Answer:

The lion's offspring were playing in the tall grass.

b) offspring

Are, Is

Quiz-Quiz-Trade

Instructions: Copy enough cards so each student has one card. Cut on dotted lines and fold in half.

Are, Is	Are, Is
Question: Choose the correct word. Read the sentence. Where ______ Tom going? a) are b) is	Answer: Where is Tom going? b) is
Question: Choose the correct word. Read the sentence. There ______ 60 people watching the movie. a) are b) is	Answer: There are 60 people watching the movie. a) are
Question: Choose the correct word. Read the sentence. There ______ some milk in the refrigerator. a) are b) is	Answer: There is some milk in the refrigerator. b) is
Question: Choose the correct word. Read the sentence. There ______ seashells washed up on the beach. a) are b) is	Answer: There are seashells washed up on the beach. a) are

Are, Is

Quiz-Quiz-Trade

Instructions: Copy enough cards so each student has one card. Cut on dotted lines and fold in half.

Are, Is

Question: Choose the correct word.

Read the sentence.

Where ______ you flying on Saturday?

a) are
b) is

Are, Is

Answer:

Where are you flying on Saturday?

a) are

Are, Is

Question: Choose the correct word.

Read the sentence.

The children ______ playing soccer.

a) are
b) is

Are, Is

Answer:

The children are playing soccer.

a) are

Are, Is

Question: Choose the correct word.

Read the sentence.

There ______ one elephant at the zoo.

a) are
b) is

Are, Is

Answer:

There is one elephant at the zoo.

b) is

Are, Is

Question: Choose the correct word.

Read the sentence.

His back ______ aching.

a) are
b) is

Are, Is

Answer:

His back is aching.

b) is

Are, Is

Quiz-Quiz-Trade

Instructions: Copy enough cards so each student has one card. Cut on dotted lines and fold in half.

Are, Is

Question: Choose the correct word.

Read the sentence.

Five hot air balloons ______ in the sky.

a) are
b) is

Are, Is

Answer:

Five hot air balloons are in the sky.

a) are

Are, Is

Question: Choose the correct word.

Read the sentence.

Her hair ______ dark brown and curly.

a) are
b) is

Are, Is

Answer:

Her hair is dark brown and curly.

b) is

Are, Is

Question: Choose the correct word.

Read the sentence.

The woman ______ washing her new red car.

a) are
b) is

Are, Is

Answer:

The woman is washing her new red car.

b) is

Are, Is

Question: Choose the correct word.

Read the sentence.

There ______ six granola bars in the box.

a) are
b) is

Are, Is

Answer:

There are six granola bars in the box.

a) are

Are, Is

Quiz-Quiz-Trade

Instructions: Copy enough cards so each student has one card. Cut on dotted lines and fold in half.

Are, Is

Question: Choose the correct word.

Read the sentence.

The bird ______ singing a song from the treetop.

a) are
b) is

Are, Is

Answer:

The bird is singing a song from the treetop.

b) is

Are, Is

Question: Choose the correct word.

Read the sentence.

The weather ______ really cold today.

a) are
b) is

Are, Is

Answer:

The weather is really cold today.

b) is

Are, Is

Question: Choose the correct word.

Read the sentence.

The apples on the tree ______ ripe.

a) are
b) is

Are, Is

Answer:

The apples on the tree are ripe.

a) are

Are, Is

Question: Choose the correct word.

Read the sentence.

A snowman in the yard ______ melting.

a) are
b) is

Are, Is

Answer:

A snowman in the yard is melting.

b) is

Are, Is

Quiz-Quiz-Trade

Instructions: Copy enough cards so each student has one card. Cut on dotted lines and fold in half.

Are, Is

Question: Choose the correct word.

Read the sentence.

People ______ arriving for the concert.

a) are
b) is

Are, Is

Answer:

People are arriving for the concert.

a) are

Are, Is

Question: Choose the correct word.

Read the sentence.

They ______ thinking about the new idea.

a) are
b) is

Are, Is

Answer:

They are thinking about the new idea.

a) are

Are, Is

Question: Choose the correct word.

Read the sentence.

Where ______ the bookmark for my book?

a) are
b) is

Are, Is

Answer:

Where is the bookmark for my book?

b) is

Are, Is

Question: Choose the correct word.

Read the sentence.

That row of trees ______ long.

a) are
b) is

Are, Is

Answer:

That row of trees is long.

b) is

Are, Is

Quiz-Quiz-Trade

Instructions: Copy enough cards so each student has one card. Cut on dotted lines and fold in half.

Are, Is	Are, Is
Question: Choose the correct word. Read the sentence. Snowflakes ______ falling from the sky. a) are b) is	Answer: Snowflakes <u>are</u> falling from the sky. a) are
Are, Is	**Are, Is**
Question: Choose the correct word. Read the sentence. Why ______ they following the tracks? a) are b) is	Answer: Why <u>are</u> they following the tracks? a) are
Are, Is	**Are, Is**
Question: Choose the correct word. Read the sentence. She ______ a talented singer. a) are b) is	Answer: She <u>is</u> a talented singer. b) is
Are, Is	**Are, Is**
Question: Choose the correct word. Read the sentence. Tomorrow ______ the first day of spring. a) are b) is	Answer: Tomorrow <u>is</u> the first day of spring. b) is

Are, Is

Quiz-Quiz-Trade

Instructions: Copy enough cards so each student has one card. Cut on dotted lines and fold in half.

Are, Is

Question: Choose the correct word.

Read the sentence.

Drawings from art class ______ on display.

a) are
b) is

Are, Is

Answer:

Drawings from art class are on display.

a) are

Are, Is

Question: Choose the correct word.

Read the sentence.

The dogs ______ barking at the cat.

a) are
b) is

Are, Is

Answer:

The dogs are barking at the cat.

a) are

Are, Is

Question: Choose the correct word.

Read the sentence.

Corbin ______ writing a mammal report.

a) are
b) is

Are, Is

Answer:

Corbin is writing a mammal report.

b) is

Are, Is

Question: Choose the correct word.

Read the sentence.

The girl ______ playing a card game with friends.

a) are
b) is

Are, Is

Answer:

The girl is playing a card game with friends.

b) is

Sentences With or Without Silent e

Quiz-Quiz-Trade

Instructions: Copy enough cards so each student has one card. Cut on dotted lines and fold in half.

Sentences With or Without Silent e

Question: Which word makes sense?
(With or Without Silent e)

Superman wears a _____ on his shoulders.

a) cap
b) cape

Sentences With or Without Silent e

Answer:

Superman wears a cape on his shoulders.

b) cape

Sentences With or Without Silent e

Question: Which word makes sense?
(With or Without Silent e)

Let's play _____ the Tail on the Donkey.

a) Pin
b) Pine

Sentences With or Without Silent e

Answer:

Let's play Pin the Tail on the Donkey.

a) Pin

Sentences With or Without Silent e

Question: Which word makes sense?
(With or Without Silent e)

Bill _____ his bicycle to school today.

a) rode
b) rod

Sentences With or Without Silent e

Answer:

Bill rode his bicycle to school today.

a) rode

Sentences With or Without Silent e

Question: Which word makes sense?
(With or Without Silent e)

The blind lady used a white_____.

a) can
b) cane

Sentences With or Without Silent e

Answer:

The blind lady used a white cane.

b) cane

Sentences With or Without Silent e

Quiz-Quiz-Trade

Instructions: Copy enough cards so each student has one card. Cut on dotted lines and fold in half.

Sentences With or Without Silent e	Sentences With or Without Silent e
Question: Which word makes sense? (With or Without Silent e) The horse had a tan colored ______. a) man b) mane	Answer: The horse had a tan colored mane. b) mane

Sentences With or Without Silent e	Sentences With or Without Silent e
Question: Which word makes sense? (With or Without Silent e) I will eat a strawberry ice cream ______. a) cone b) con	Answer: I will eat a strawberry ice cream cone. a) cone

Sentences With or Without Silent e	Sentences With or Without Silent e
Question: Which word makes sense? (With or Without Silent e) The mother bear protected her baby ______. a) cub b) cube	Answer: The mother bear protected her baby cub. b) cub

Sentences With or Without Silent e	Sentences With or Without Silent e
Question: Which word makes sense? (With or Without Silent e) We watched the bunny ______ across the yard. a) hope b) hop	Answer: We watched the bunny hop across the yard. b) hop

Sentences With or Without Silent e

Quiz-Quiz-Trade

Instructions: Copy enough cards so each student has one card. Cut on dotted lines and fold in half.

Sentences With or Without Silent e

Question: Which word makes sense?
(With or Without Silent e)

Kim ______ his mother a birthday card.

a) mad
b) made

Sentences With or Without Silent e

Answer:

Kim made his mother a birthday card.

b) made

Sentences With or Without Silent e

Question: Which word makes sense?
(With or Without Silent e)

The candy cost one ______.

a) dime
b) dim

Sentences With or Without Silent e

Answer:

The candy cost one dime.

a) dime

Sentences With or Without Silent e

Question: Which word makes sense?
(With or Without Silent e)

Roger made a ______ snowman after the storm.

a) huge
b) hug

Sentences With or Without Silent e

Answer:

Roger made a huge snowman after the storm.

a) huge

Sentences With or Without Silent e

Question: Which word makes sense?
(With or Without Silent e)

Jim hurt his ______ when he fell on the ice.

a) spin
b) spine

Sentences With or Without Silent e

Answer:

Jim hurt his spine when he fell on the ice.

b) spine

Sentences With or Without Silent e

Quiz-Quiz-Trade

Instructions: Copy enough cards so each student has one card. Cut on dotted lines and fold in half.

Sentences With or Without Silent e	Sentences With or Without Silent e
Question: Which word makes sense? (With or Without Silent e) Nancy skied down the mountain ______. a) slop b) slope	Answer: Nancy skied down the mountain <u>slope.</u> b) slope

Sentences With or Without Silent e	Sentences With or Without Silent e
Question: Which word makes sense? (With or Without Silent e) Mike and Karen will fly a ______ today. a) kite b) kit	Answer: Mike and Karen will fly a <u>kite</u> today. a) kite

Sentences With or Without Silent e	Sentences With or Without Silent e
Question: Which word makes sense? (With or Without Silent e) Never play near a building ______. a) site b) sit	Answer: Never play near a building <u>site.</u> b) site

Sentences With or Without Silent e	Sentences With or Without Silent e
Question: Which word makes sense? (With or Without Silent e) He ______ into the chewy cookie. a) bite b) bit	Answer: He <u>bit</u> into the chewy cookie. b) bit

Sentences With or Without Silent e

Quiz-Quiz-Trade

Instructions: Copy enough cards so each student has one card. Cut on dotted lines and fold in half.

Sentences With or Without Silent e	Sentences With or Without Silent e
Question: Which word makes sense? (With or Without Silent e) After playing in the dirt John took a soapy _____ . a) bathe b) bath	Answer: After playing in the dirt John took a soapy bath. b) bath

Sentences With or Without Silent e	Sentences With or Without Silent e
Question: Which word makes sense? (With or Without Silent e) We needed to _____ the ice and snow off our car. a) scrape b) scrap	Answer: We needed to scrape the ice and snow off our car. a) scrape

Sentences With or Without Silent e	Sentences With or Without Silent e
Question: Which word makes sense? (With or Without Silent e) _____ was excited about his new game. a) Pete b) Pet	Answer: Pete was excited about his new game. a) Pete

Sentences With or Without Silent e	Sentences With or Without Silent e
Question: Which word makes sense? (With or Without Silent e) Open the _____ of green beans for dinner. a) cane b) can	Answer: Open the can of green beans for dinner. b) can

Sentences With or Without Silent e

Quiz-Quiz-Trade

Instructions: Copy enough cards so each student has one card. Cut on dotted lines and fold in half.

Sentences With or Without Silent e

Question: Which word makes sense?
(With or Without Silent e)

The green _____ was slippery.

a) slim
b) slime

Sentences With or Without Silent e

Answer:

The green slime was slippery.

b) slime

Sentences With or Without Silent e

Question: Which word makes sense?
(With or Without Silent e)

We squeezed through the _____ place between the bushes.

a) slim
b) slime

Sentences With or Without Silent e

Answer:

We squeezed through the slim place between the bushes.

a) slim

Sentences With or Without Silent e

Question: Which word makes sense?
(With or Without Silent e)

Tim folded the paper into a square _____.

a) cube
b) cub

Sentences With or Without Silent e

Answer:

Tim folded the paper into a square cube.

a) cube

Sentences With or Without Silent e

Question: Which word makes sense?
(With or Without Silent e)

A _____ will protect your head from the hot sun.

a) cape
b) cap

Sentences With or Without Silent e

Answer:

A cap will protect your head form the hot sun.

b) cap

Sentences With or Without Silent e

Quiz-Quiz-Trade

Instructions: Copy enough cards so each student has one card. Cut on dotted lines and fold in half.

Sentences With or Without Silent e

Question: Which word makes sense?
(With or Without Silent e)

We will make a necklace from the _____.

a) kite
b) kit

Sentences With or Without Silent e

Answer:

We will make a necklace from the kit.

b) kit

Sentences With or Without Silent e

Question: Which word makes sense?
(With or Without Silent e)

I gave my grandpa a _____ when I saw him.

a) hug
b) huge

Sentences With or Without Silent e

Answer:

I gave my grandpa a hug when I saw him.

a) hug

Sentences With or Without Silent e

Question: Which word makes sense?
(With or Without Silent e)

Please _____ talking so loudly.

a) quit
b) quite

Sentences With or Without Silent e

Answer:

Please quit talking so loudly.

a) quit

Sentences With or Without Silent e

Question: Which word makes sense?
(With or Without Silent e)

We were _____ excited about winning the game.

a) quit
b) quite

Sentences With or Without Silent e

Answer:

We were quite excited about winning the game.

b) quite

Prefixes (re- and un-)

Quiz-Quiz-Trade

Instructions: Copy enough cards so each student has one card. Cut on dotted lines and fold in half.

Prefixes (re- and un-)	Prefixes (re- and un-)
Question: What does this word mean? reappear	Answer: to appear **again** or to be seen **again**
Question: What does this word mean? rejoin	Answer: to join **again** or to become a part of something **again**
Question: What does this word mean? unwrapped	Answer: **not** wrapped or **not** packaged
Question: What does this word mean? unzipped	Answer: **not** zipped or **not** closed

Prefixes (re- and un-)

Quiz-Quiz-Trade

Instructions: Copy enough cards so each student has one card. Cut on dotted lines and fold in half.

Prefixes (re- and un-)

Question: What does this word mean?

reopen

Prefixes (re- and un-)

Answer:

to open **again**
or
to expose **again**

Prefixes (re- and un-)

Question: What does this word mean?

recycle

Prefixes (re- and un-)

Answer:

to cycle **again**
or
to use **again**

Prefixes (re- and un-)

Question: What does this word mean?

unlocked

Prefixes (re- and un-)

Answer:

not locked
or
not closed

Prefixes (re- and un-)

Question: What does this word mean?

unseen

Prefixes (re- and un-)

Answer:

not seen
or
not in the open

Prefixes (re- and un-)

Quiz-Quiz-Trade

Instructions: Copy enough cards so each student has one card. Cut on dotted lines and fold in half.

Prefixes (re- and un-)	Prefixes (re- and un-)
Question: What does this word mean? rebuild	Answer: to build **again** or to put together **again**
Question: What does this word mean? recheck	Answer: to check **again** or to look at **again**
Question: What does this word mean? unkind	Answer: **not** kind or **not** caring
Question: What does this word mean? unafraid	Answer: **not** afraid or **not** scared

Prefixes (re- and un-)

Quiz-Quiz-Trade

Instructions: Copy enough cards so each student has one card. Cut on dotted lines and fold in half.

Prefixes (re- and un-)	Prefixes (re- and un-)
Question: What does this word mean? redress	Answer: to get dressed **again** or to put clothes on **again**
Question: What does this word mean? recount	Answer: to count **again** or to figure **again**
Question: What does this word mean? unpacked	Answer: **not** packed or to **remove** contents
Question: What does this word mean? unsaid	Answer: **not** said or **not** spoken

Prefixes (re- and un-)

Quiz-Quiz-Trade

Instructions: Copy enough cards so each student has one card. Cut on dotted lines and fold in half.

Prefixes (re- and un-)	Prefixes (re- and un-)
Question: What does this word mean? reheat	Answer: to heat **again** or make hot **again**
Question: What does this word mean? research	Answer: to search **again** or to look **again**
Question: What does this word mean? unable	Answer: **not** able or **not** capable
Question: What does this word mean? untied	Answer: **not** tied or **not** fastened

Prefixes (re- and un-)

Quiz-Quiz-Trade

Instructions: Copy enough cards so each student has one card. Cut on dotted lines and fold in half.

Prefixes (re- and un-)	Prefixes (re- and un-)
Question: What does this word mean? retake	Answer: to take **again**
Question: What does this word mean? reinvent	Answer: to invent **again**
Question: What does this word mean? untidy	Answer: **not** tidy or **not** neat
Question: What does this word mean? unhappy	Answer: **not** happy or **not** joyful

Suffixes (-er, -ly, -ful, -y)

Quiz-Quiz-Trade

Instructions: Copy enough cards so each student has one card. Cut on dotted lines and fold in half.

Suffixes (-er, -ly, -ful, -y)	Suffixes (-er, -ly, -ful, -y)
Question: What does this word mean? **reader**	Answer: someone who reads
Question: What does this word mean? **teacher**	Answer: someone who teaches
Question: What does this word mean? **farmer**	Answer: someone who farms
Question: What does this word mean? **singer**	Answer: someone who sings

Suffixes (-er, -ly, -ful, -y)

Quiz-Quiz-Trade

Instructions: Copy enough cards so each student has one card. Cut on dotted lines and fold in half.

Suffixes (-er, -ly, -ful, -y)	Suffixes (-er, -ly, -ful, -y)
Question: What does this word mean? runner	Answer: someone who runs
Question: What does this word mean? racer	Answer: someone who races
Question: What does this word mean? cooker	Answer: someone who cooks
Question: What does this word mean? helper	Answer: someone who helps

Suffixes (-er, -ly, -ful, -y)

Quiz-Quiz-Trade

Instructions: Copy enough cards so each student has one card. Cut on dotted lines and fold in half.

Suffixes (-er, -ly, -ful, -y)	Suffixes (-er, -ly, -ful, -y)
Question: What does this word mean? cloudy	Answer: full of clouds
Question: What does this word mean? fuzzy	Answer: full of fuzz
Question: What does this word mean? rocky	Answer: full of rocks
Question: What does this word mean? wordy	Answer: full of words

Suffixes (-er, -ly, -ful, -y)

Quiz-Quiz-Trade

Instructions: Copy enough cards so each student has one card. Cut on dotted lines and fold in half.

Suffixes (-er, -ly, -ful, -y)	Suffixes (-er, -ly, -ful, -y)
Question: What does this word mean? hairy	Answer: full of hair
Question: What does this word mean? lucky	Answer: full of luck
Question: What does this word mean? smelly	Answer: full of smell
Question: What does this word mean? sunny	Answer: full of sun

Suffixes (-er, -ly, -ful, -y)

Quiz-Quiz-Trade

Instructions: Copy enough cards so each student has one card. Cut on dotted lines and fold in half.

Suffixes (-er, -ly, -ful, -y)	Suffixes (-er, -ly, -ful, -y)
Question: What does this word mean? plateful	Answer: a plate **full of** something
Question: What does this word mean? pocketful	Answer: a pocket **full of** something
Question: What does this word mean? thankful	Answer: **having a lot of** thanks
Question: What does this word mean? joyful	Answer: **having a lot of** joy or **full of** joy

Suffixes (-er, -ly, -ful, -y)

Quiz-Quiz-Trade

Instructions: Copy enough cards so each student has one card. Cut on dotted lines and fold in half.

Suffixes (-er, -ly, -ful, -y)	Suffixes (-er, -ly, -ful, -y)
Question: What does this word mean? colorful	Answer: **having a lot of** color or **full of** color
Question: What does this word mean? handful	Answer: a hand **full of** something
Question: What does this word mean? fearful	Answer: **having a lot of** fear or **full of** fear
Question: What does this word mean? useful	Answer: **having a lot of** use or **full of** use

Suffixes (-er, -ly, -ful, -y)

Quiz-Quiz-Trade

Instructions: Copy enough cards so each student has one card. Cut on dotted lines and fold in half.

Suffixes (-er, -ly, -ful, -y)	Suffixes (-er, -ly, -ful, -y)
Question: What does this word mean? **loudly**	Answer: in a loud **way**
Question: What does this word mean? **warmly**	Answer: in a warm **way**
Question: What does this word mean? **smoothly**	Answer: in a smooth **way**
Question: What does this word mean? **sadly**	Answer: in a sad **way**

Suffixes (-er, -ly, -ful, -y)

Quiz-Quiz-Trade

Instructions: Copy enough cards so each student has one card. Cut on dotted lines and fold in half.

Suffixes (-er, -ly, -ful, -y)	Suffixes (-er, -ly, -ful, -y)
Question: What does this word mean?	Answer:
slowly	in a slow **way**

Suffixes (-er, -ly, -ful, -y)	Suffixes (-er, -ly, -ful, -y)
Question: What does this word mean?	Answer:
softly	in a soft **way**

Suffixes (-er, -ly, -ful, -y)	Suffixes (-er, -ly, -ful, -y)
Question: What does this word mean?	Answer:
clearly	in a clear **way**

Suffixes (-er, -ly, -ful, -y)	Suffixes (-er, -ly, -ful, -y)
Question: What does this word mean?	Answer:
slyly	in a sly **way**

RALLYCOACH Activities

Coach Me

Four different types of word study RallyCoach activities are provided: 1) cube, 2) spinner, 3) sorting mat, and 4) word cards/letter pattern cards. Using the materials provided, one partner completes the task while the other is the coach. They switch roles for each new problem.

Activity Steps

1. Depending on the activity below, each pair receives either a cube and a worksheet, a spinner and a worksheet, a sorting mat and word cards, or word cards/letter pattern cards.
2. First, Partner A completes the task.
   - Cube: Partner rolls cube and uses result to fill in worksheet.
   - Spinner: Partner spins spinner and uses result to fill in worksheet.
   - Sorting Mat: Partner picks a word card and sorts it on the mat.
   - Word Cards: Partner picks a word card and reads it (or) partner picks a word card and chooses a letter pattern card to complete the word.
3. Partner B watches and listens, checks, and praises.
4. Then, Partner B rolls the cube, spins the spinner, or selects the next word card. Partner B completes the next problem.
5. Partner A watches and listens, checks, and praises.
6. The process continues until they complete their worksheet or sort all word cards.

STRUCTURE

RallyCoach

Blacklines

Onset Cube

RallyCoach

Instructions: Copy the onset and rime cube pattern onto cardstock for each pair. Cut out, fold, and tape together to form cubes. Partners take turns rolling the cubes. If the onset and rime make a word, each partner writes the word on his/her worksheet.

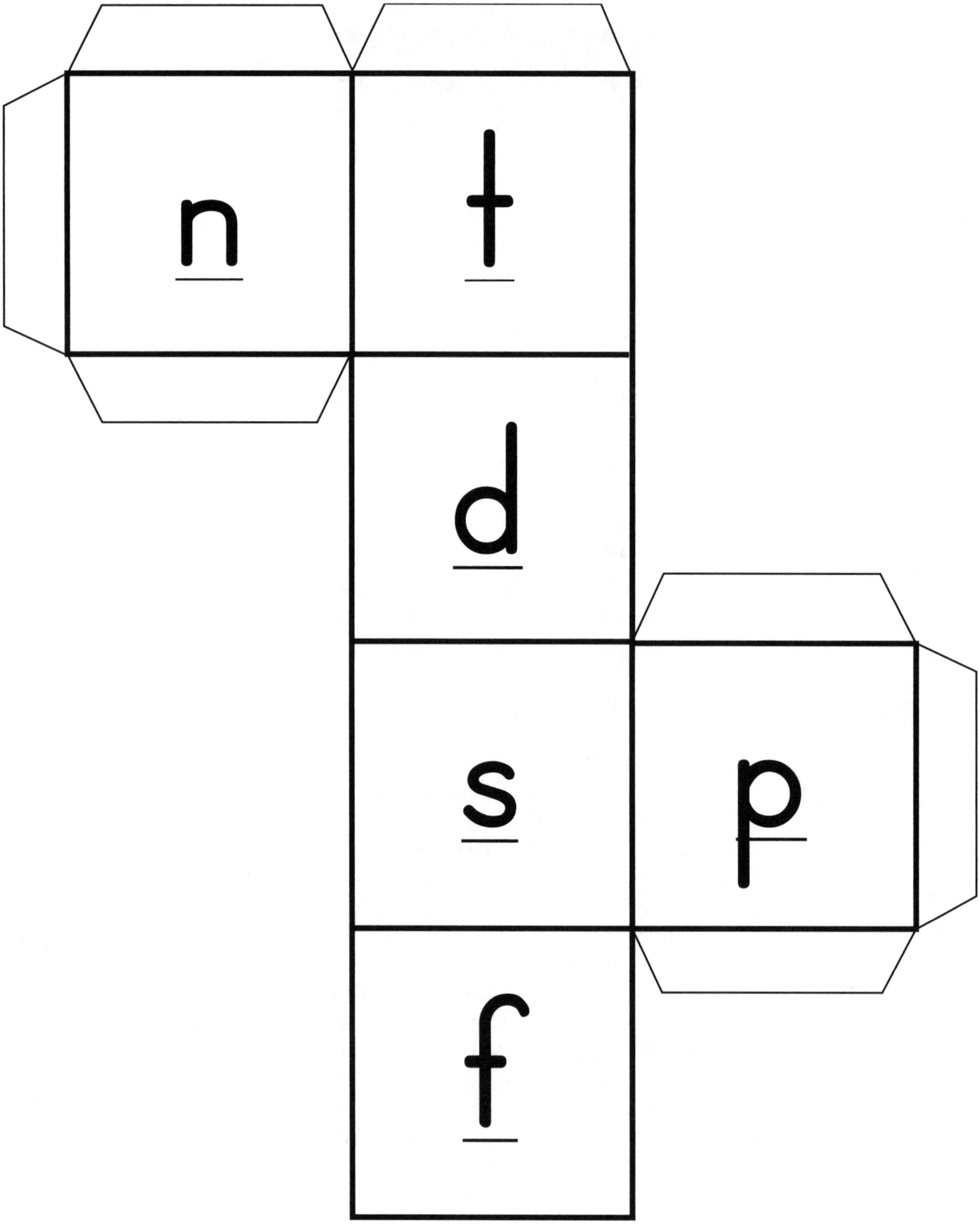

n

t

d

s

p

f

Rime Cube

RallyCoach

Instructions: Copy the onset and rime cube pattern onto cardstock for each pair. Cut out, fold, and tape together to form cubes. Partners take turns rolling the cubes. If the onset and rime make a word, each partner writes the word on his/her worksheet.

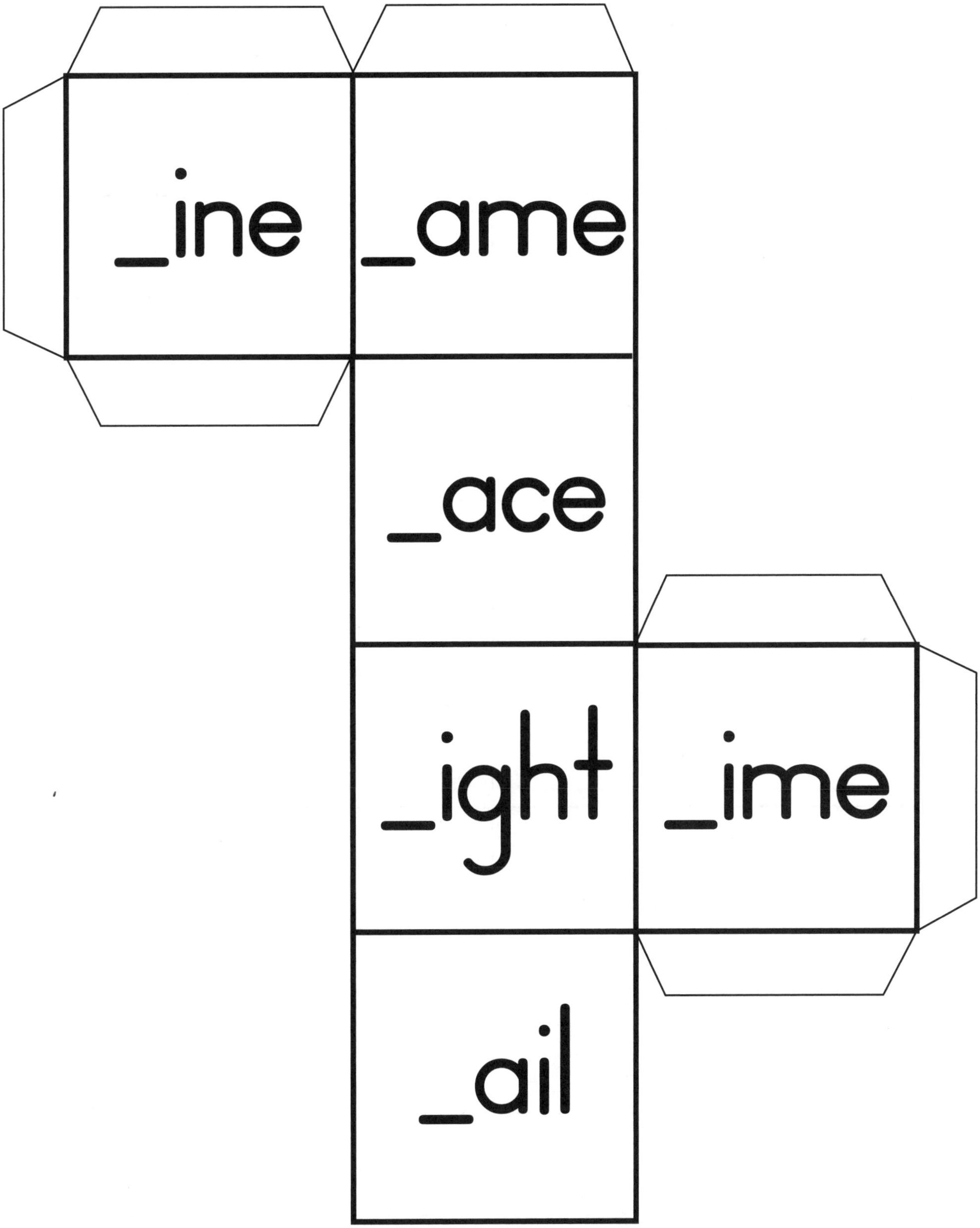

_ine

_ame

_ace

_ight

_ime

_ail

Onset and Rime Worksheet

RallyCoach

Instructions: Partners use worksheet with cubes.

Blends Cube

RallyCoach

Instructions: Copy the Blends Cube pattern onto cardstock for each pair. Cut out, fold, and tape together to form cubes. Partners take turns rolling the cube. The student rolling the cube chooses one incomplete word on the worksheet and adds the blend rolled to make a word.

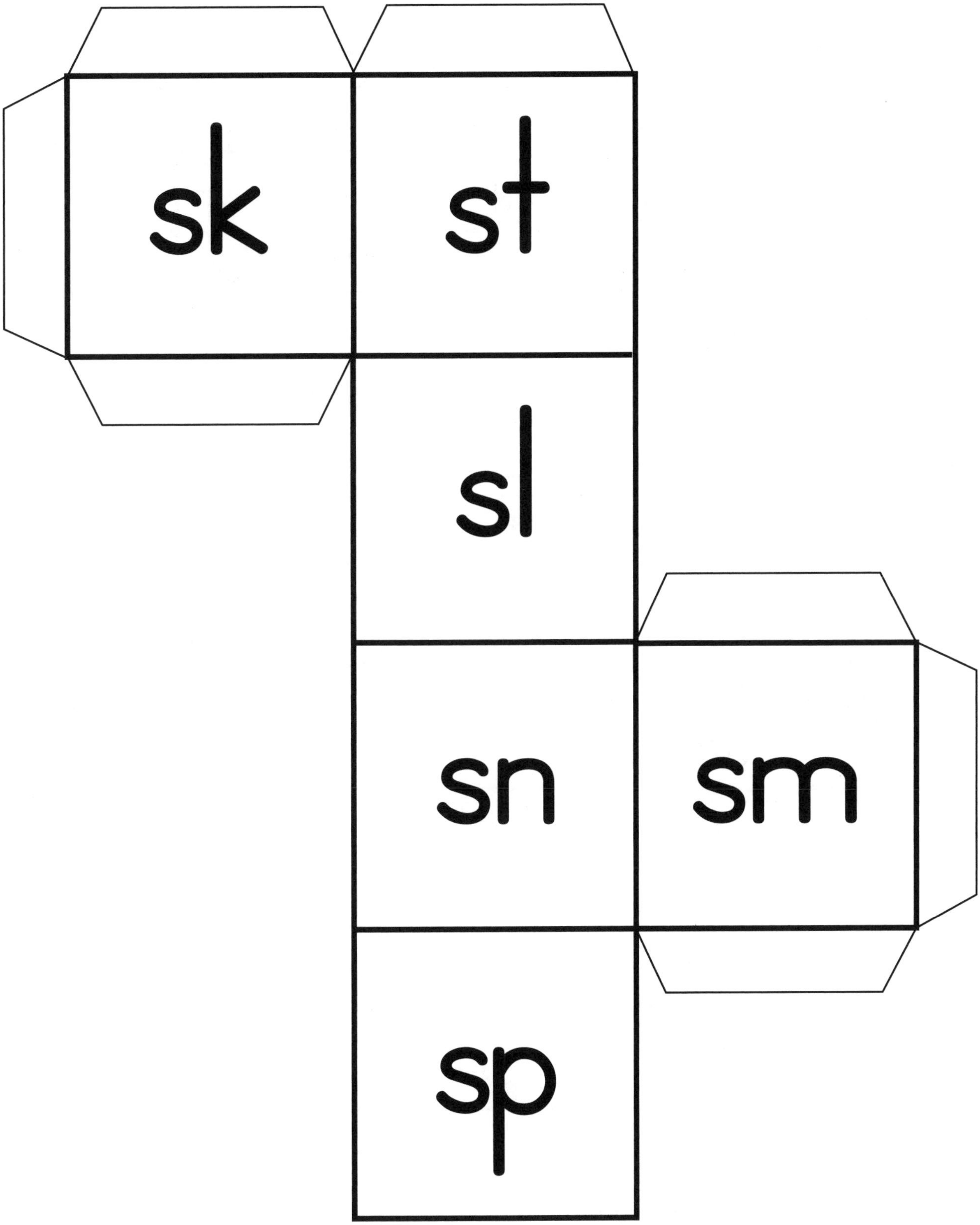

sk

st

sl

sn

sm

sp

Onset Blends Worksheet

RallyCoach

Instructions: Partners use worksheet with onset blend cube.

_____ake	_____og
_____ipper	_____amp
_____airs	_____ight
_____arl	_____ile
_____irt	_____ade
_____ar	_____oon
_____ide	_____owman
_____ate	_____ider
_____ots	_____ike
_____eakers	_____ow
_____onge	_____in
_____eep	_____ice

Onset Blends Worksheet

RallyCoach

Instructions: Partners use worksheet with onset blend cube.

_____ip	_____ick
_____ap	_____ug
_____eak	_____unk
_____ooth	_____oke
_____op	_____eleton
_____ool	_____eeze
_____all	_____ell
_____ore	_____ill
_____art	_____oil
_____eed	_____eeve
_____ore	_____y
_____inny	_____am

oi, oy Cube

RallyCoach

Instructions: Copy the cube pattern onto cardstock for each pair. Cut out, fold, and tape to form a cube. Partners take turns rolling the cube. The student rolling the cube chooses one incomplete word on the worksheet to make a word.

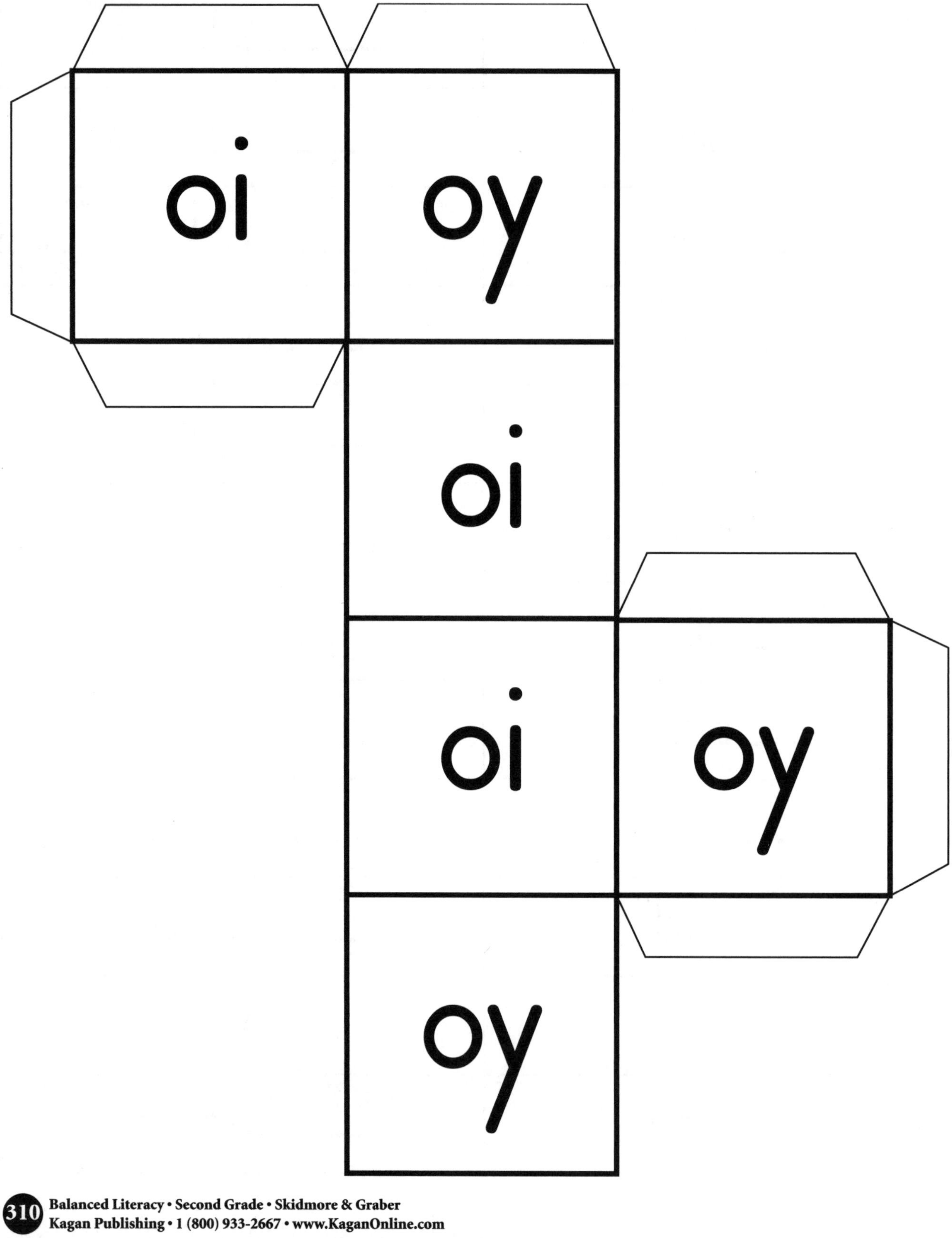

oi

oy

oi

oi

oy

oy

oi, oy Worksheet

RallyCoach

Instructions: Partners use worksheet with oi, oy cube.

j___n	b___
l___al	sp___l
f___l	c___n
j___	enj___
ch___ce	___nk
n___se	v___ce
v___age	___l
b___l	t___
c___l	r___al
t___box	p___nt
s___l	j___ful
empl___	b___friend

ou, ow Cube

RallyCoach

Instructions: Copy the cube pattern onto cardstock for each pair. Cut out, fold, and tape to form a cube. Partners take turns rolling the cube. The student rolling the cube chooses one incomplete word on the worksheet to make a word.

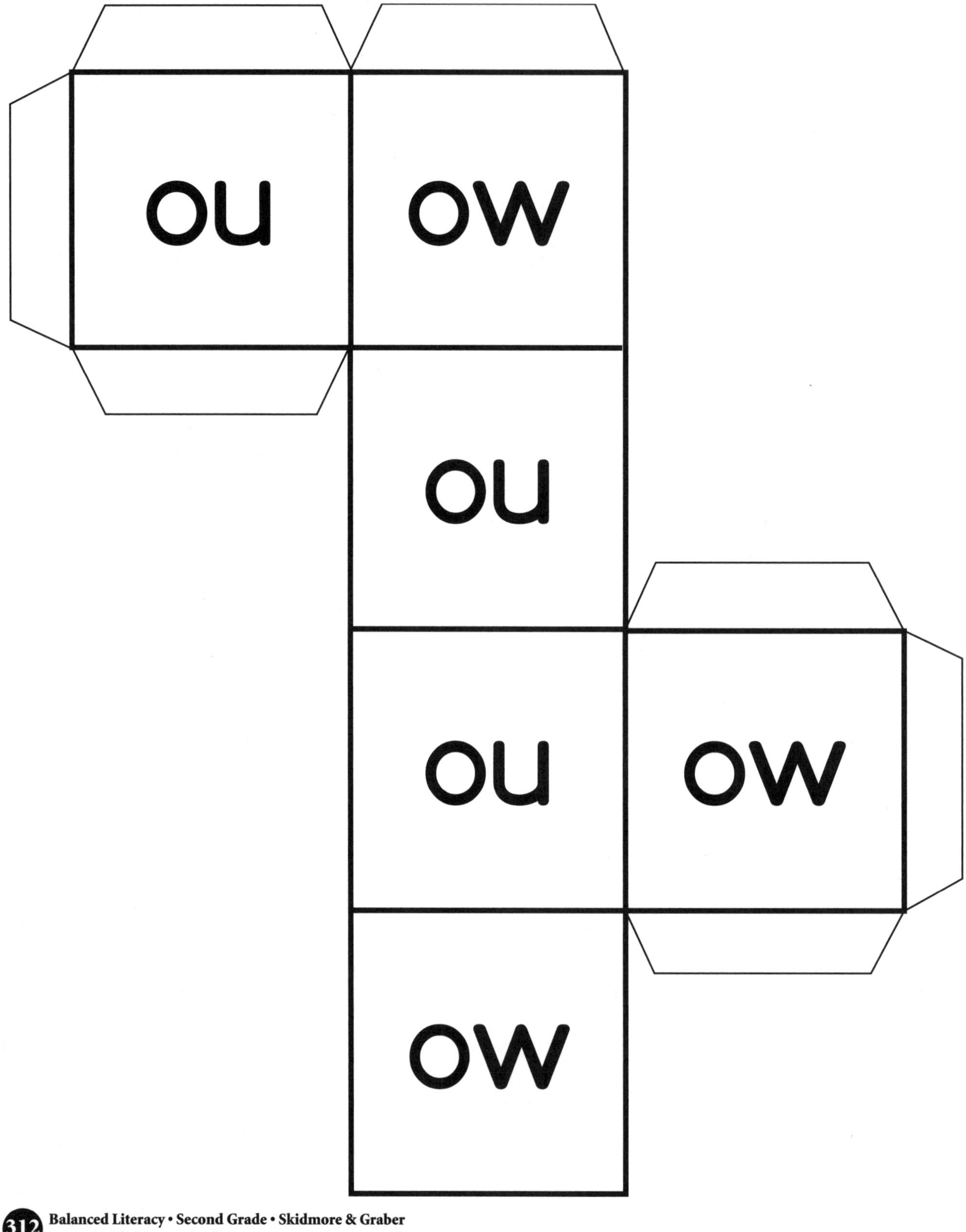

ou

ow

ou

ou

ow

ow

ou, ow WorKsheet

RallyCoach

Instructions: Partners use worksheet with ou, ow cube.

fr___n	gr___l
ab___t	ar___nd
g___n	cr___d
b___	d___n
___t	pl___
m___th	cr___n
cl___d	p___er
___l	h___se
cl___n	l___d
p___der	br___n
c___nt	t___el
sh___t	fl___er

au, aw Cube

RallyCoach

Instructions: Copy the cube pattern onto cardstock for each pair. Cut out, fold, and tape to form a cube. Partners take turns rolling the cube. The student rolling the cube chooses one incomplete word on the worksheet to make a word.

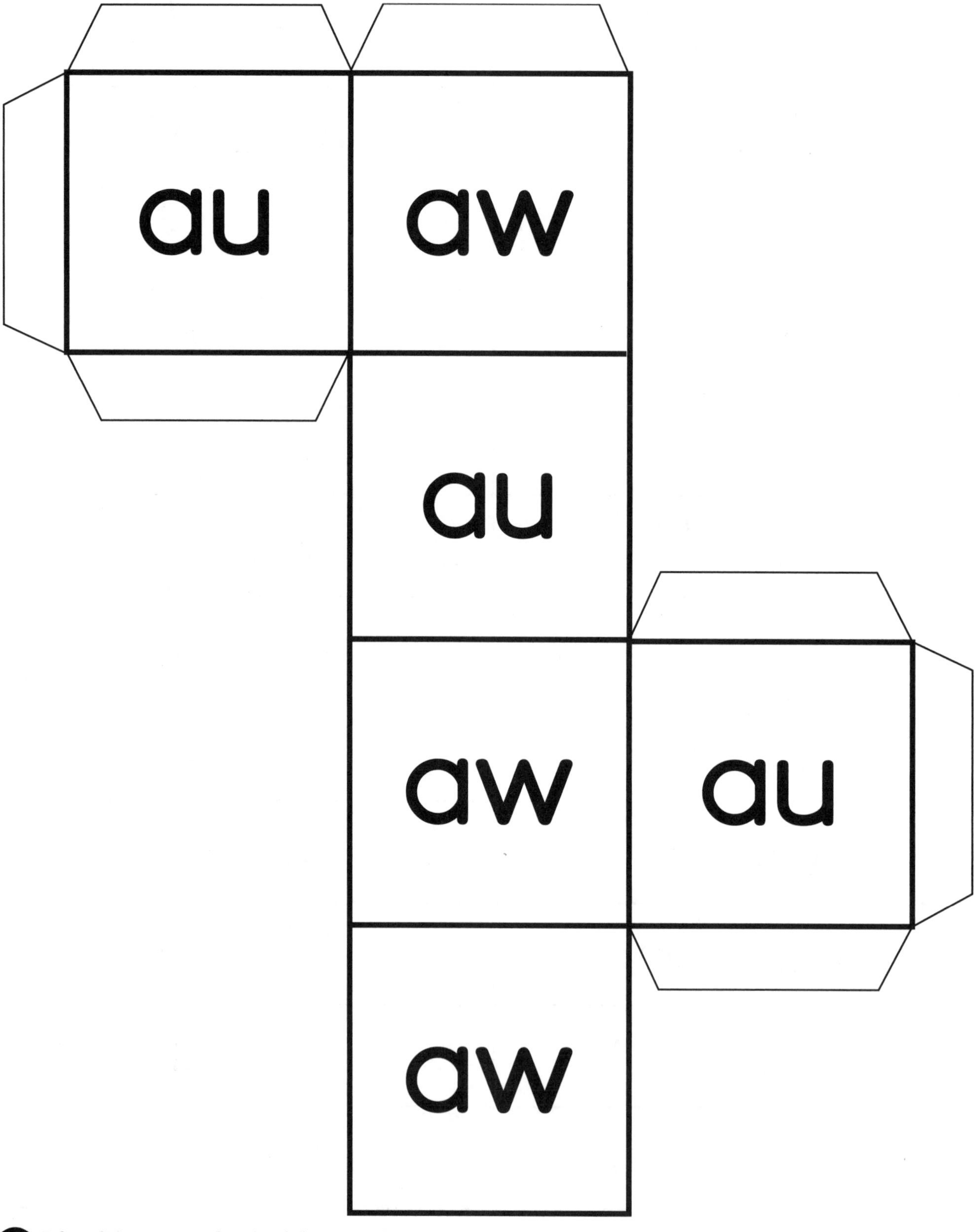

au

aw

au

aw

au

aw

au, aw Worksheet

RallyCoach

Instructions: Partners use worksheet with au, aw cube.

j___	cr___l
cl___	___gust
f___n	l___
t___ght	h___l
p___	gn___
l___n	___thor
P___l	str___
s___	th___
y___n	r___
h___k	sees___

ar, or Cube

RallyCoach

Instructions: Copy the cube pattern onto cardstock for each pair. Cut out, fold, and tape to form a cube. Partners take turns rolling the cube. The student rolling the cube chooses one incomplete word on the worksheet to make a word.

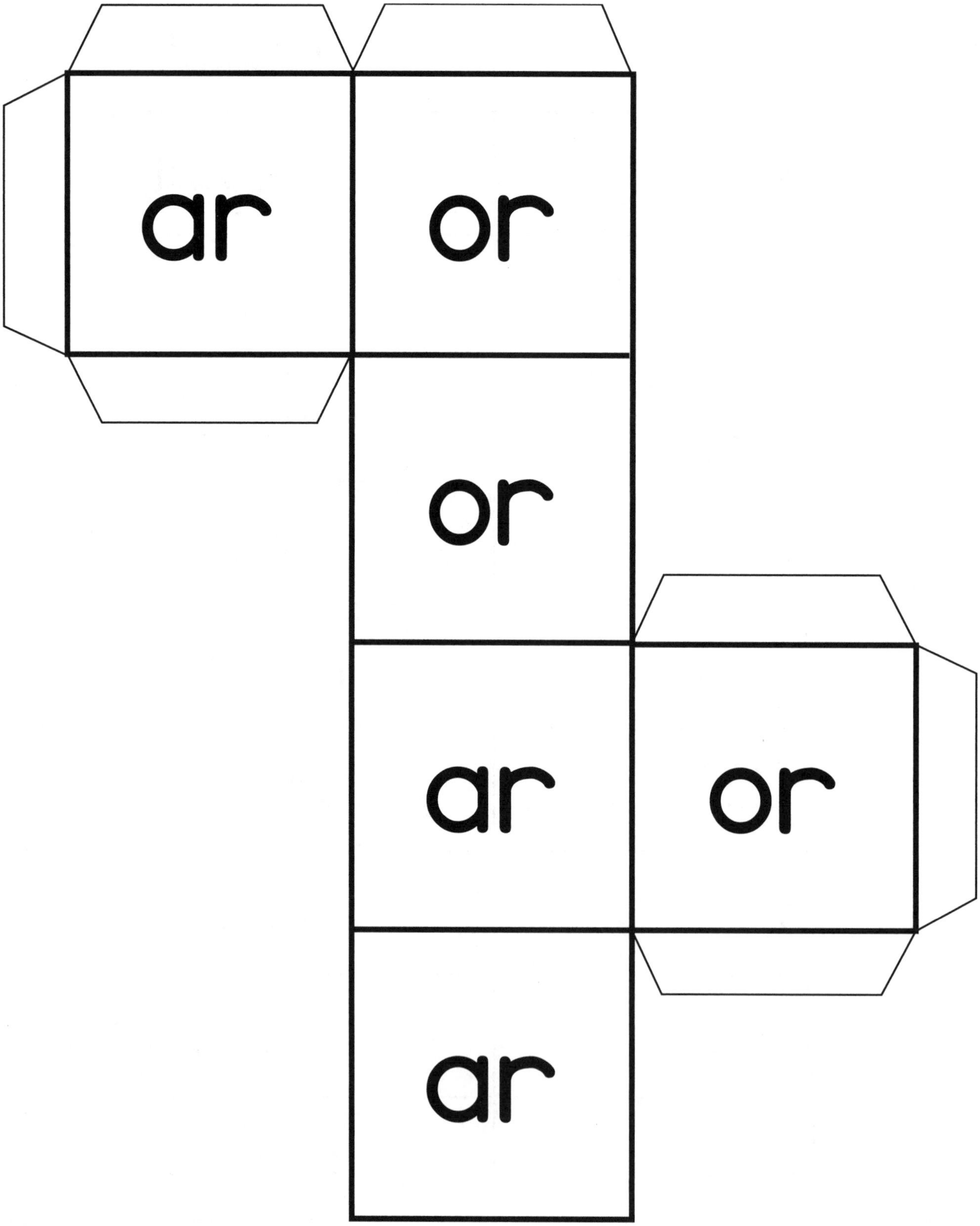

ar

or

or

ar

or

ar

ar, or WorKsheet

RallyCoach

Instructions: Partners use worksheet with ar, or cube.

ac___n	st___
h___d	h___n
sp___t	b___n
m___k	ch___t
d___k	c___n
f___m	d___t
c___k	j___
b___k	f___
t___n	h___se
f___k	c___
___t	s___t
___der	st___e

ea, ee Cube

RallyCoach

Instructions: Copy the cube pattern onto cardstock for each pair. Cut out, fold, and tape to form a cube. Partners take turns rolling the cube. The student rolling the cube chooses one incomplete word on the worksheet to make a word.

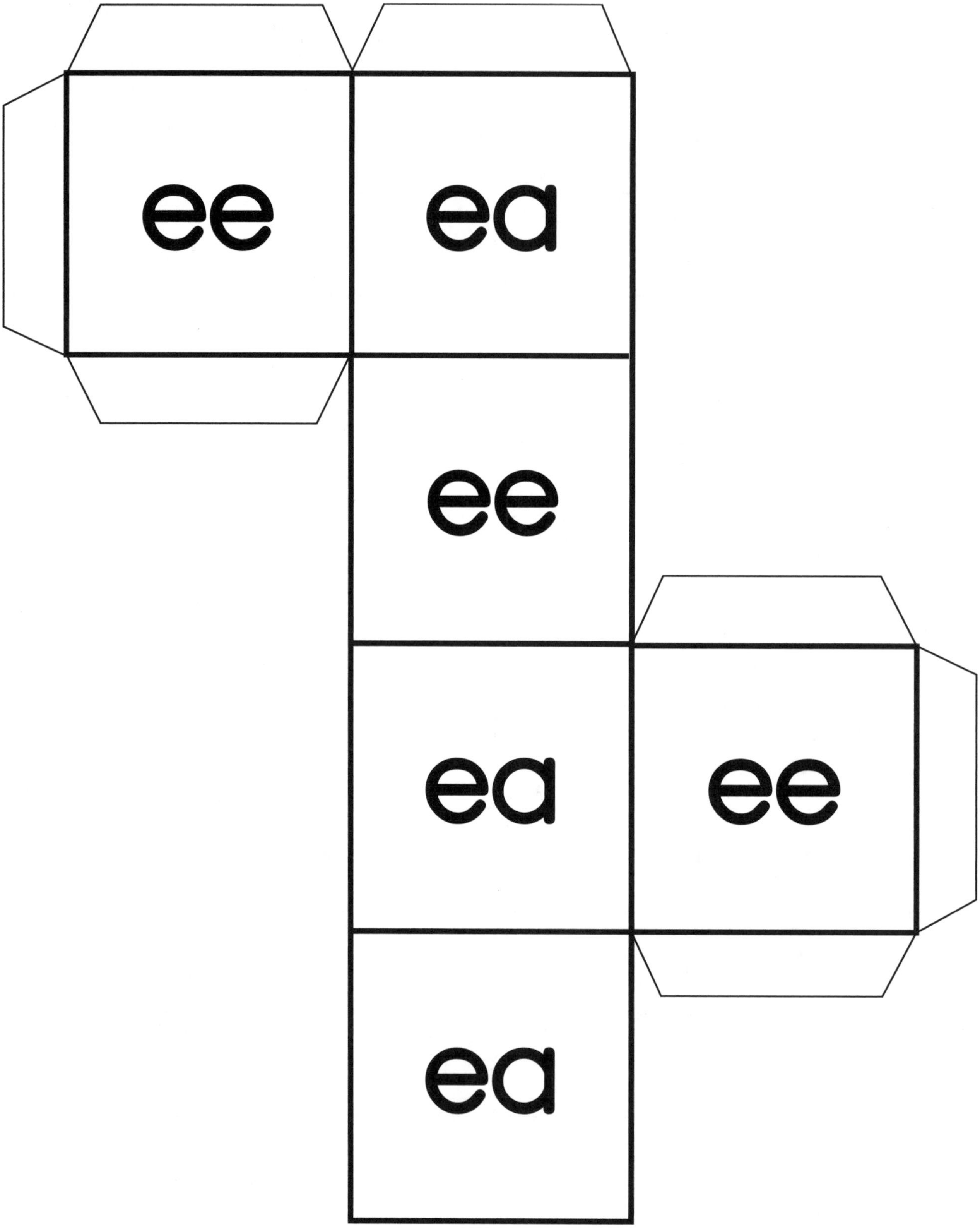

ee

ea

ee

ea

ee

ea

ea, ee Worksheet

RallyCoach

Instructions: Partners use worksheet with ea, ee cube.

tr___	gl___
w___d	n___d
s___t	fr___
d___p	m___l
b___s	sn___ze
gr___n	sp___k
br___ze	ch___se
dr___m	tw___d
p___ch	sl___p
squ___ze	___ting
s___gull	t___cher
wh___l	thr___

ea, ee Worksheet

RallyCoach

Instructions: Partners use worksheet with ea, ee cube.

sl___py	j___p
pl___se	w___
kn___l	___st
bl___d	t___th
cl___n	w___p
fr___d	fl___ing
sh___p	coff___
cr___ture	st___p
b___ch	eight___n
thirt___n	t___m
m___sles	sw___p
p___p	sevent___n

Prefix (re- and un-) Cube

RallyCoach

Instructions: Copy the cube pattern onto cardstock for each pair. Cut out, fold, and tape to form a cube. Partners take turns rolling the cube. The student rolling the cube chooses one incomplete word on the worksheet to make a word.

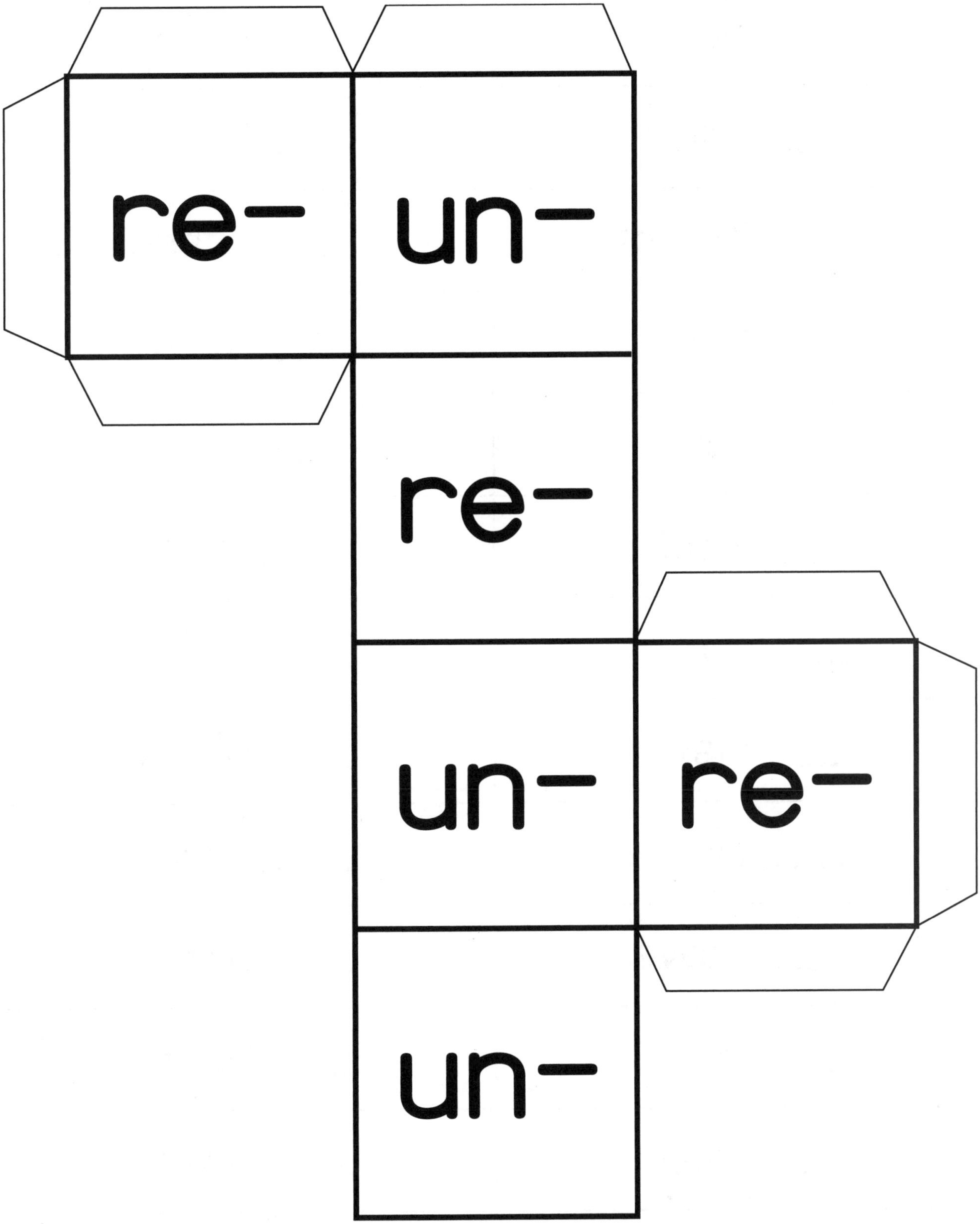

re-

un-

re-

un-

re-

un-

Prefix (re- and un-) Worksheet

RallyCoach

Instructions: Partners use worksheet with prefix cube.

____do	____able
____wind	____heat
____button	____fresh
____fair	____direct
____turn	____tie
____load	____form
____run	____roll
____view	____place
____zip	____true
____move	____mind
____join	____happy
____plug	____open

Suffix (-er and -est) Cube

RallyCoach

Instructions: Copy the cube pattern onto cardstock for each pair. Cut out, fold, and tape to form a cube. Partners take turns rolling the cube. The student rolling the cube chooses one incomplete word on the worksheet to make a word.

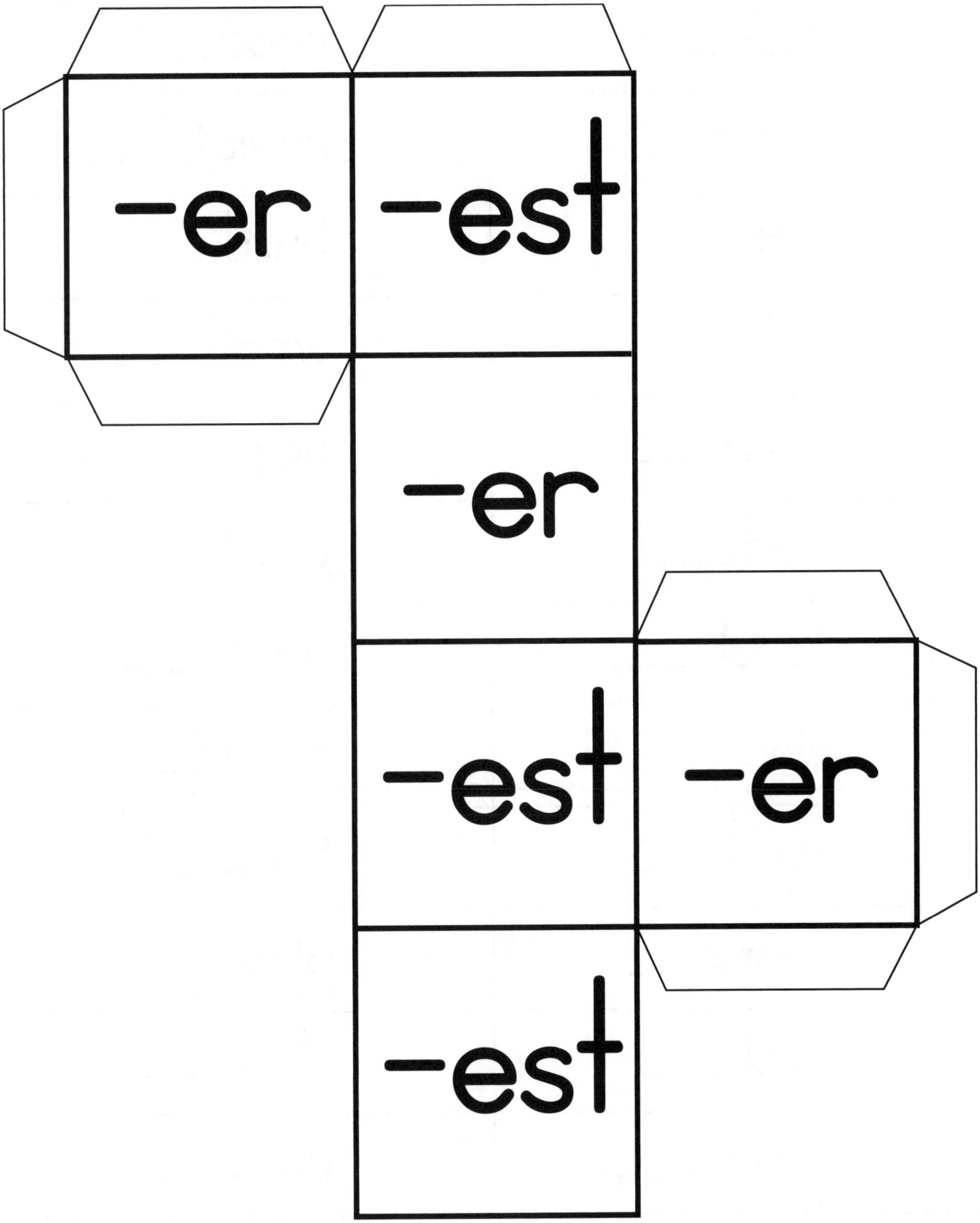

-er	-est
	-er
	-est	-er
	-est

Suffix (-er and -est) Worksheet

RallyCoach

Instructions: Partners use worksheet with suffix cube.

tall___	read___
short___	sweet___
rich___	build___
cold___	small___
farm___	help___
soft___	print___
teach___	mow___
sing___	smart___
quick___	hard___
mark___	play___
cook___	slow___
work___	dark___

Suffix (-ful and -ly) Cube

RallyCoach

Instructions: Copy the cube pattern onto cardstock for each pair. Cut out, fold, and tape to form a cube. Partners take turns rolling the cube. The student rolling the cube chooses one incomplete word on the worksheet to make a word.

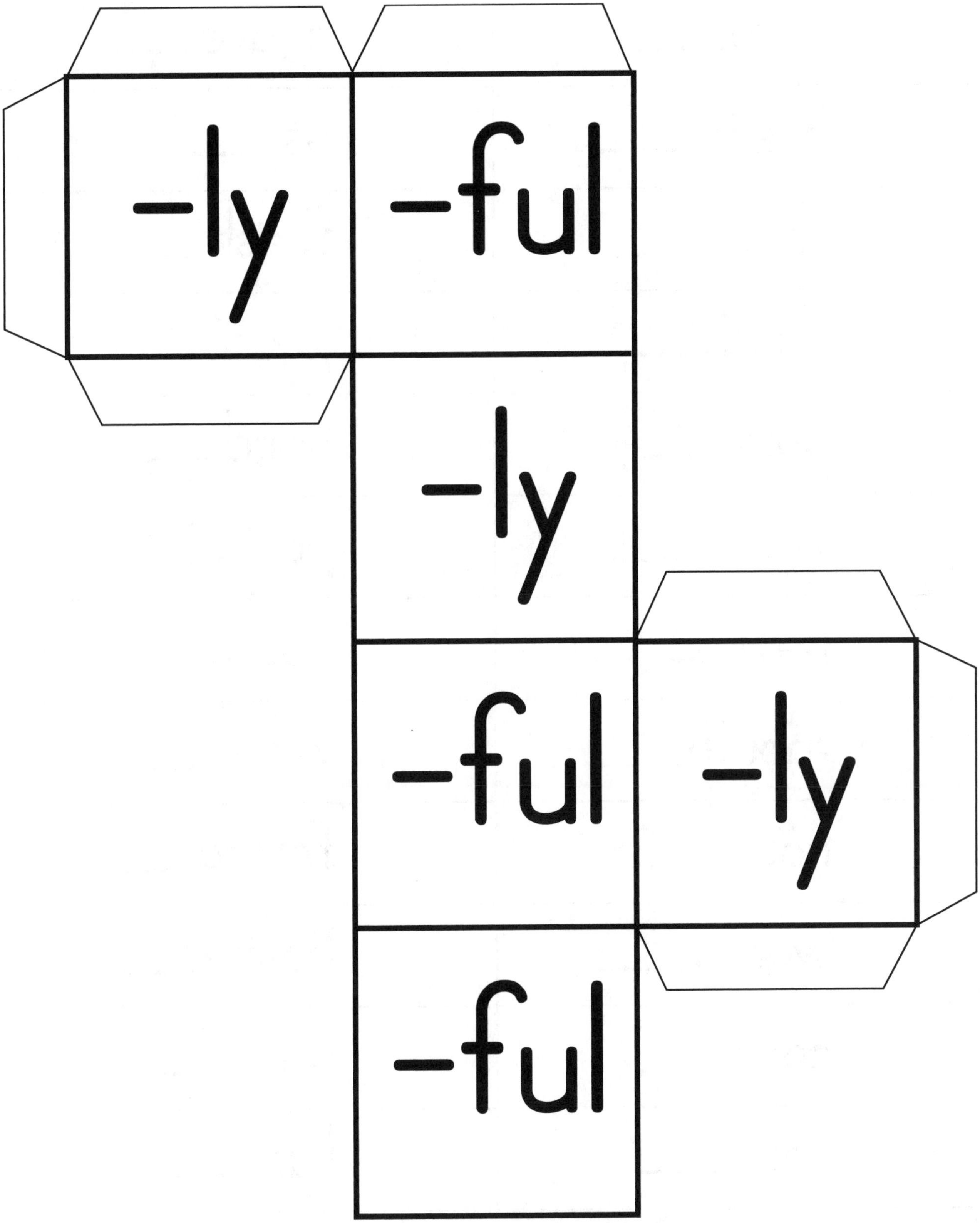

-ly

-ful

-ly

-ful

-ly

-ful

Suffix (-ful and -ly) Worksheet

RallyCoach

Instructions: Partners use worksheet with suffix cube.

arm___	brave___
bright___	use___
cheer___	fresh___
dead___	joy___
pain___	hard___
weak___	pocket___
new___	hope___
mouth___	wish___
hour___	friend___
warm___	basket___
color___	quick___
care___	light___

Doubling Final Consonants (-ed and -ing) Cube

RallyCoach

Instructions: Copy the cube pattern onto cardstock for each pair. Cut out, fold, and tape to form a cube. Partners take turns rolling the cube. The student rolling the cube chooses one incomplete word on the worksheet to make a word.

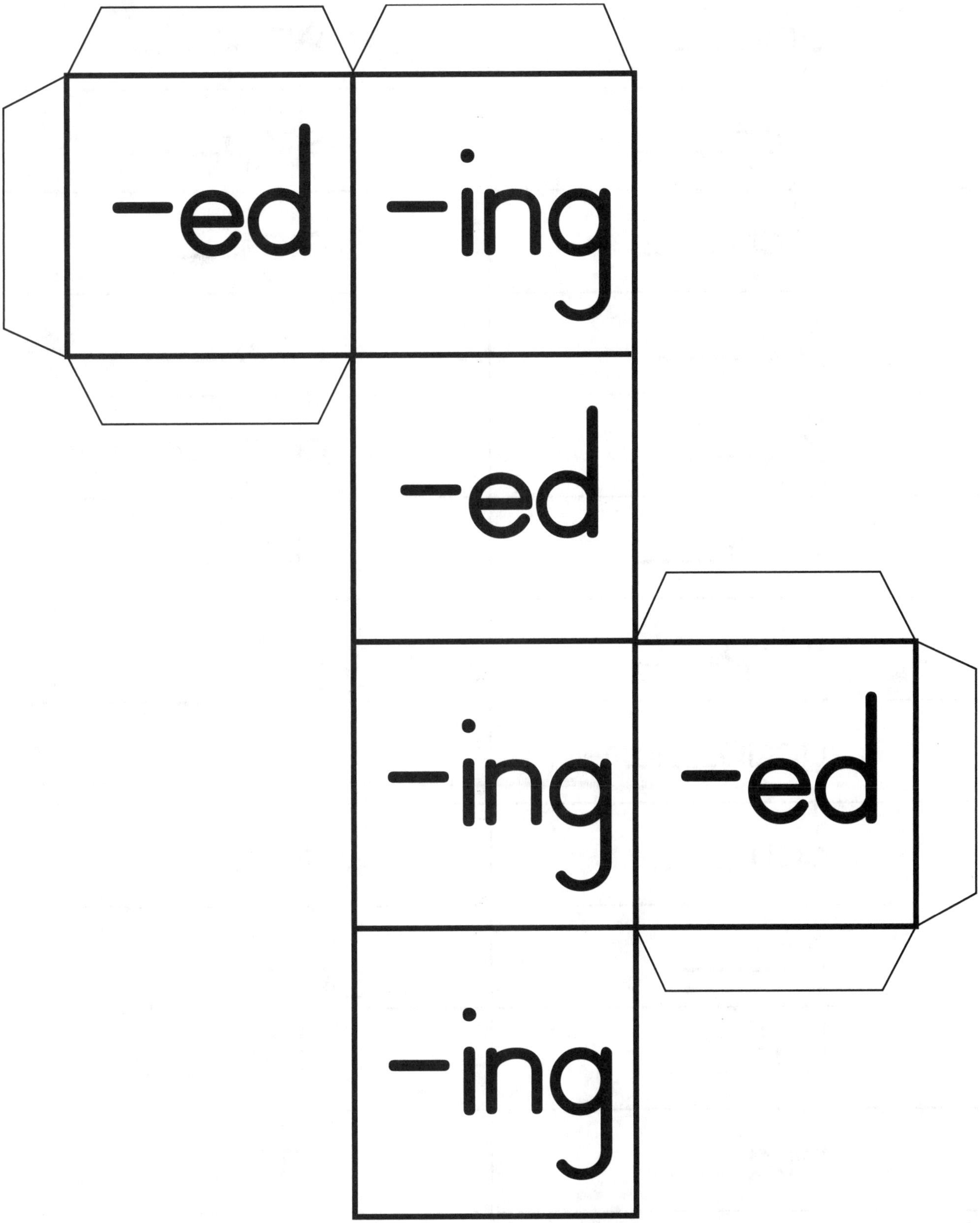

-ed

-ing

-ed

-ing

-ed

-ing

Doubling Final Consonants (-ed and -ing) Worksheet

RallyCoach

Instructions: Partners use worksheet with -ed/-ing cube.

grip___	wrap___
trap___	shop___
step___	dig___
trip___	rob___
jog___	chop___
trim___	run___
whip___	get___
grab___	fit___
can___	net___
sit___	plan___
bat___	ship___
beg___	hit___

Antonym/Synonym Cube

RallyCoach

Instructions: Copy the cube pattern onto cardstock for each pair. Cut out, fold, and tape to form a cube. Partners take turns rolling the cube. The student rolling the cube chooses a pair of words on the worksheet that fits the description "antonyms" or "synonyms."

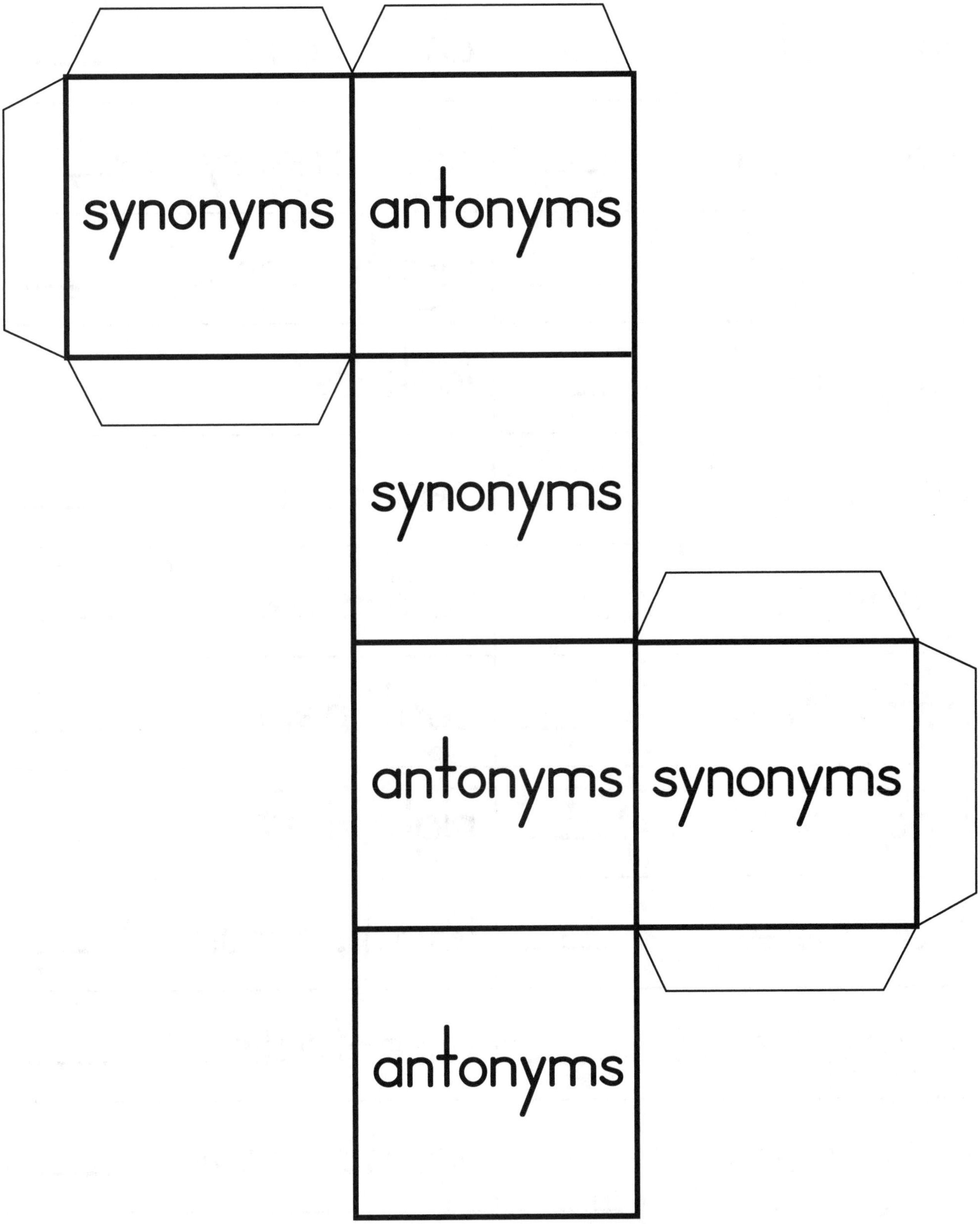

synonyms

antonyms

synonyms

antonyms

synonyms

antonyms

Antonym/Synonym Worksheet

RallyCoach

Instructions: Partners use worksheet with Antonym-Synonym Cube. Write *A* if the word pair are antonyms. Write *S* if the word pair are synonyms.

hot-cold ___	chef-cook ___
wet-moist ___	neat-messy ___
dark-light ___	right-correct ___
easy-hard ___	look-see ___
angry-mad ___	near-far ___
speak-talk ___	fast-slow ___
many-few ___	cent-penny ___
long-short ___	right-left ___
true-false ___	excellent-great___
strong-weak ___	wise-foolish ___
open-close ___	woman-lady ___

Spinner (er, ir, ur)

RallyCoach

Instructions: Copy the spinner onto cardstock for each pair. Add a plastic/metal spinner in the middle or use a spinner made from a paper clip and a pencil. (To make a paper clip spinner: Place a paper clip over the center of the spinner. Place the pencil point on the center point of the spinner, through the paper clip. Using the other hand, spin the paper clip around the pencil point.) Partners take turns spinning. The student spinning chooses an incomplete word on the worksheet to form a word.

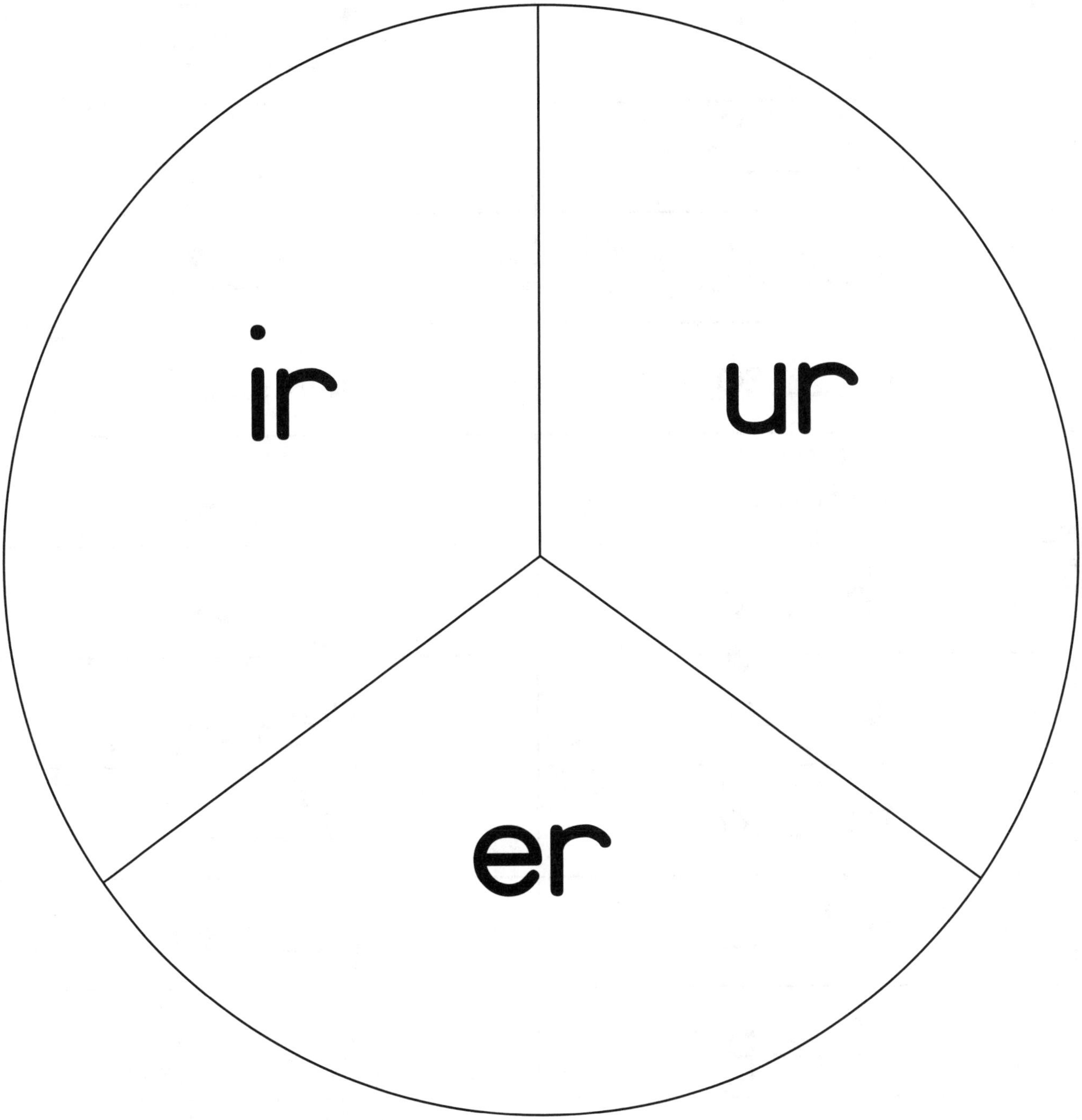

ir

ur

er

Worksheet (er, ir, ur)

RallyCoach

Instructions: Partners use worksheet with Spinner (er, ir, ur).

c___b	s___
d___t	t___tle
ret___n	f___
b___d	aft___
n___se	bik___
cold___	c___l
ch___p	g___l
b___n	cov___
th___d	st___
eat___	p___se
sl___p	g___m
t___n	sk___t

Spinner (aw, ew, ow)

RallyCoach

Instructions: Copy the spinner onto cardstock for each pair. Add a plastic/metal spinner in the middle or use a spinner made from a paper clip and a pencil. (To make a paper clip spinner: Place a paper clip over the center of the spinner. Place the pencil point on the center point of the spinner, through the paper clip. Using the other hand, spin the paper clip around the pencil point.) Partners take turns spinning. The student spinning chooses an incomplete word on the worksheet to form a word.

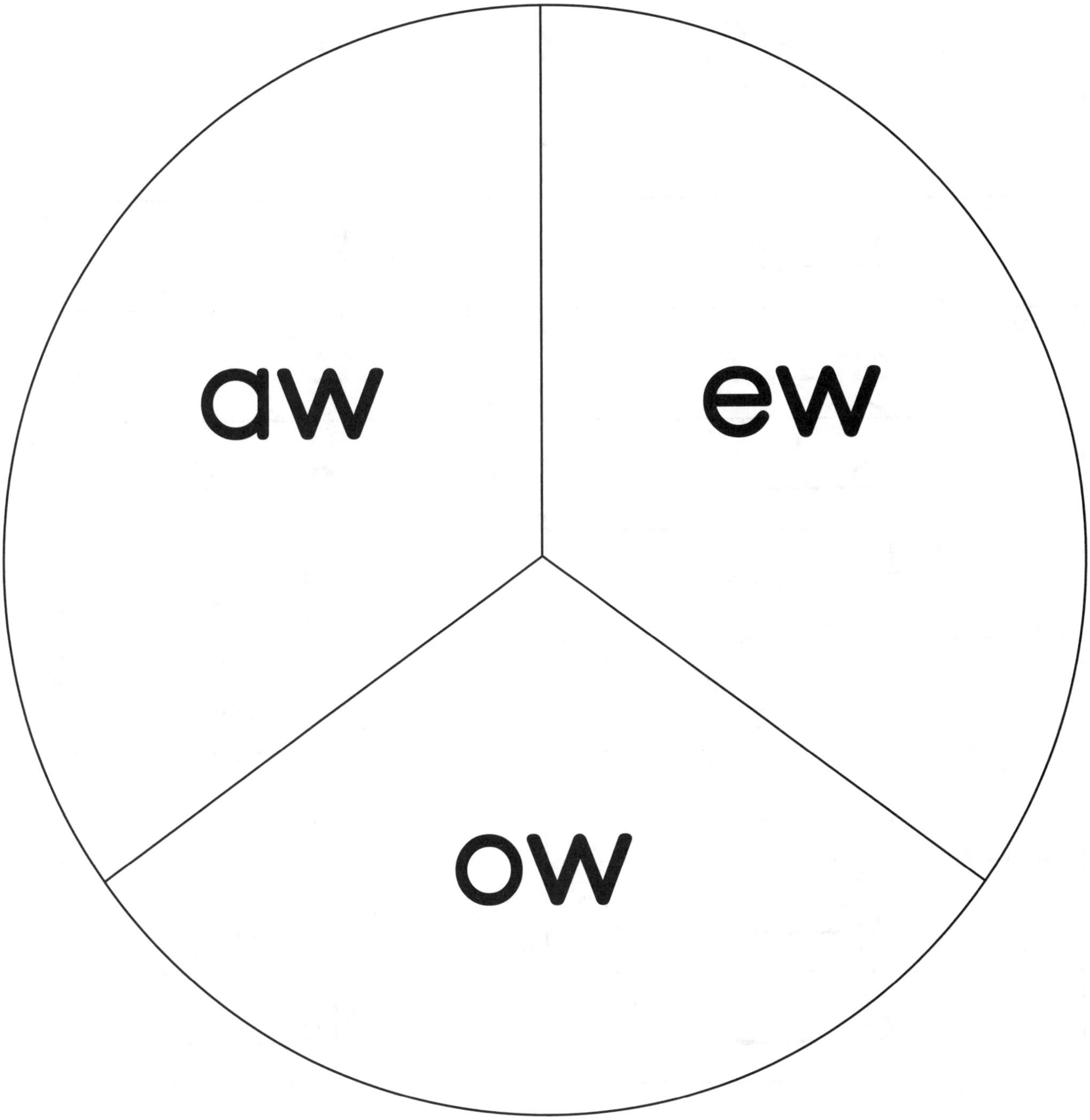

aw

ew

ow

Worksheet aw, ew, ow

RallyCoach

Instructions: Partners use worksheet with Spinner (aw, ew, ow).

ch___	c___
br___n	j___
f___	cr___
t___n	kn___
gr___	___ls
p___	d___
t___er	pl___
fl___	d___n
str___	n___
w___	s___
dr___	thr___
cr___	y___n

Contraction Spinner (not, is, will)

RallyCoach

Instructions: Copy the spinner onto cardstock for each pair. Add a plastic/metal spinner in the middle or use a spinner made from a paper clip and a pencil. (To make a paper clip spinner: Place a paper clip over the center of the spinner. Place the pencil point on the center point of the spinner, through the paper clip. Using the other hand, spin the paper clip around the pencil point.) Partners take turns spinning. The student spinning uses the word indicated by the spin and one word from the worksheet to make a contraction.

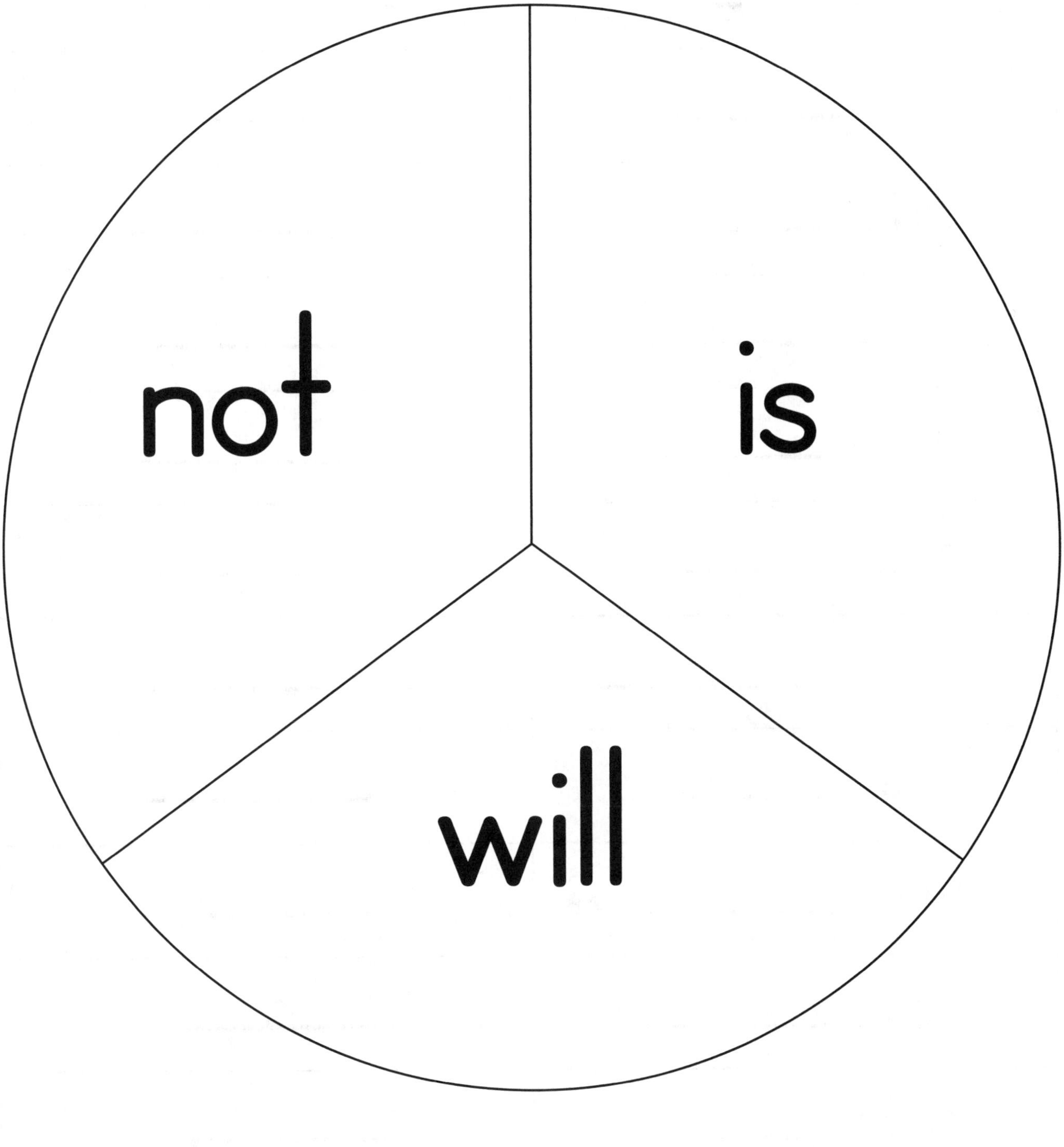

not

is

will

Contraction Worksheet (not, is, will)

RallyCoach

Instructions: Partners use worksheet with Contraction Spinner. Partners write word from Spinner in first column. The two words are written as a contraction in the second column.

Word from Spinner	Contraction
I________	________
she________	________
did________	________
do ________	________
is________	________
it________	________
here________	________
are________	________
we________	________
you________	________
have________	________

Contraction Worksheet (not, is, will)

RallyCoach

Instructions: Partners use worksheet with Contraction Spinner. Partners write word from Spinner in first column. The two words are written as a contraction in the second column.

Word from Spinner	Contraction
that__________	__________
can__________	__________
where__________	__________
could__________	__________
they__________	__________
should__________	__________
must__________	__________
there__________	__________
what__________	__________
does__________	__________
would__________	__________

Prefix (re-, un-) Sorting Mat

RallyCoach

Instructions: Copy one mat for each pair. Choose a word card. Add prefix (re- or un-) and write the word in the correct column.

Add re-	Add un-

Prefix (re-, un-) Word Cards

RallyCoach

Instructions: Copy one set of cards for each pair. Cut apart.

Word Cards ___turn	Word Cards ___plug
Word Cards ___port	Word Cards ___move
Word Cards ___roll	Word Cards ___word
Word Cards ___able	Word Cards ___lock
Word Cards ___heat	Word Cards ___cooked
Word Cards ___tidy	Word Cards ___set
Word Cards ___dress	Word Cards ___cycle
Word Cards ___act	Word Cards ___zip
Word Cards ___cover	Word Cards ___play
Word Cards ___wire	Word Cards ___do
Word Cards ___seen	Word Cards ___afraid
Word Cards ___kind	Word Cards ___run

Adding -s or -es Sorting Mat

RallyCoach

Instructions: Copy one mat for each pair. Choose a word card. Add *s* or *es* to the word and write it in the correct column.

Add -s	Add -es

Adding -s or -es Word Cards

RallyCoach

Instructions: Copy one set of cards for each pair. Cut apart.

Word Cards — ax__	Word Cards — boss__
Word Cards — cross__	Word Cards — dress__
Word Cards — rabbit__	Word Cards — hiss__
Word Cards — grass__	Word Cards — key__
Word Cards — door__	Word Cards — miss__
Word Cards — fox__	Word Cards — clock__
Word Cards — dish__	Word Cards — box__
Word Cards — bush__	Word Cards — lunch__
Word Cards — hand__	Word Cards — buzz__
Word Cards — tax__	Word Cards — crash__
Word Cards — can__	Word Cards — wish__
Word Cards — peach__	Word Cards — boy__

Plural Sorting Mat (f to v, y to i)

RallyCoach

Instructions: Choose a word from the word cards. Change f to v and add -es or change y to i and add -es to make a plural. Write the plural word in the correct column.

Change f to v and add -es	Change y to i and add -es

Plural Sorting Mat (f to v, y to i) Word Cards

RallyCoachRallyCoach

Instructions: Copy one set of cards for each pair. Cut apart.

Word Cards	Word Cards
half	berry
spy	poppy
self	loaf
buggy	penny
elf	fly
family	shelf
leaf	story
city	baby
thief	wolf

Compound Words

RallyCoach

Instructions: Copy one worksheet for each pair. Partners take turns choosing two words from the word cards to form a compound word. One word card is placed in each of the first two columns. The compound word they form is written in the last column.

Word 1	Word 2	Compound Word

Compound Word Cards

RallyCoach

Instructions: Copy one set of cards for each pair. Cut apart.

air	cut	finger	grand
fire	back	cracker	plane
suit	out	pa	hill
yard	motor	speed	hair
news	down	bed	case
nail	south	side	ear
cake	doors	cycle	paper
gate	room	video	pour
west	way	keeper	land
ache	shop	cup	sleep
stick	grass	walk	yard
bone	work	wish	tape

WORD STUDY **BlacKline**

Onset Blends and Rimes (Nonsense Words) Word Cards

RallyCoach

Instructions: Copy one set of cards for each pair. Cut apart. Partners take turns decoding nonsense words. A word card is chosen and a Wikki Stix® (formed in a circle) is placed around the onset blend or around the rime (depending on the instructional focus).

Word Cards	Word Cards
sket	brog
flim	blit
glem	fleg
glug	prag

Onset Blends and Rimes (Nonsense Words) Word Cards

RallyCoach

Instructions: Copy one set of cards for each pair. Cut apart. Partners take turns decoding nonsense words. A word card is chosen and a Wikki Stix® (formed in a circle) is placed around the onset blend or around the rime (depending on the instructional focus).

Word Cards	Word Cards
gran	grot
twet	drob
grag	glot
prem	sleg

WORD STUDY Blackline

Onset Blends and Rimes (Nonsense Words) Word Cards

Instructions: Copy one set of cards for each pair. Cut apart. Partners take turns decoding nonsense words. A word card is chosen and a Wikki Stix® (formed in a circle) is placed around the onset blend or around the rime (depending on the instructional focus).

Word Cards — twan	Word Cards — smig
Word Cards — crit	Word Cards — skub
Word Cards — plib	Word Cards — snab
Word Cards — smem	Word Cards — spog

Word Cards
(ir, er, ur)

RallyCoach

Instructions: Copy one set of cards for each pair. Cut apart. Partners take turns placing letter pattern cards in the word card blanks to make words.

Word Cards	Word Cards
b____d	h____l
f____	st____
wh____l	p____se
b____n	h____
eat____	s____

Word Cards
(ir, er, ur)

RallyCoach

Instructions: Copy one set of cards for each pair. Cut apart. Partners take turns placing letter pattern cards in the word card blanks to make words.

Word Cards	Word Cards
c___l	g___l
t___n	t___tle
c___b	cov___
g___m	d___t
aft___	sk___t

Letter Pattern Cards (ir, er, ur)

RallyCoach

Instructions: Copy one set of Letter Pattern cards for each pair on a different color of paper than the Word Cards. Partners take turns placing letter pattern cards in the word card blanks to make words.

Letter Pattern Cards ir	Letter Pattern Cards er	Letter Pattern Cards ur	Letter Pattern Cards ir	Letter Pattern Cards er	Letter Pattern Cards ur
Letter Pattern Cards ir	Letter Pattern Cards er	Letter Pattern Cards ur	Letter Pattern Cards ir	Letter Pattern Cards er	Letter Pattern Cards ur
Letter Pattern Cards ir	Letter Pattern Cards er	Letter Pattern Cards ur	Letter Pattern Cards ir	Letter Pattern Cards er	Letter Pattern Cards ur
Letter Pattern Cards ir	Letter Pattern Cards er	Letter Pattern Cards ur	Letter Pattern Cards ir	Letter Pattern Cards er	Letter Pattern Cards ur
Letter Pattern Cards ir	Letter Pattern Cards er	Letter Pattern Cards ur	Letter Pattern Cards ir	Letter Pattern Cards er	Letter Pattern Cards ur
Letter Pattern Cards ir	Letter Pattern Cards er	Letter Pattern Cards ur	Letter Pattern Cards ir	Letter Pattern Cards er	Letter Pattern Cards ur

Word Cards
(ai, aw)

RallyCoach

Instructions: Copy one set of cards for each pair. Cut apart. Partners take turns placing letter pattern cards in the word card blanks to make words.

Word Cards	Word Cards
r___n	fl___
cl___	gr___n
j___	dr___
str___	w___t
p___n	cr___l

Word Cards
(ai, aw)

RallyCoach

Instructions: Copy one set of cards for each pair. Cut apart. Partners take turns placing letter pattern cards in the word card blanks to make words.

Word Cards: y____n	Word Cards: tr____l
Word Cards: f____l	Word Cards: h____k
Word Cards: gn____	Word Cards: f____nt
Word Cards: f____n	Word Cards: sn____l
Word Cards: br____n	Word Cards: l____n

Letter Pattern Cards (ai, aw)

RallyCoach

Instructions: Copy one set of Letter Pattern cards for each pair on a different color of paper than the Word Cards. Partners take turns placing letter pattern cards in the word card blanks to make words.

Letter Pattern Cards	Letter Pattern Cards	Letter Pattern Cards	Letter Pattern Cards
ai	aw	ai	aw
Letter Pattern Cards	Letter Pattern Cards	Letter Pattern Cards	Letter Pattern Cards
ai	aw	ai	aw
Letter Pattern Cards	Letter Pattern Cards	Letter Pattern Cards	Letter Pattern Cards
ai	aw	ai	aw
Letter Pattern Cards	Letter Pattern Cards	Letter Pattern Cards	Letter Pattern Cards
ai	aw	ai	aw
Letter Pattern Cards	Letter Pattern Cards	Letter Pattern Cards	Letter Pattern Cards
ai	aw	ai	aw
Letter Pattern Cards	Letter Pattern Cards	Letter Pattern Cards	Letter Pattern Cards
ai	aw	ai	aw

SHOWDOWN
Activities

Word Study Showdown

Teams play Showdown to practice prefixes, suffixes, sounds of C, sounds of G, compound words, possessive words, and contractions.

STRUCTURE
Showdown

Activity Steps

1. Each team receives a Team Set of cards and every student receives a Student Set of cards.
2. The Team Set is placed facedown in the middle of the team. Students hold their Student Set in their hands.
3. The teacher selects one student to be the Showdown Captain for the first round.
4. The Showdown Captain selects the top card from the middle and reads it aloud.
5. Working alone, students individually identify an answer from their card set.
6. When finished, teammates signal they are ready.
7. The Showdown Captain calls, "Showdown!"
8. Teammates show their answers at the same time.
9. The Showdown Captain leads checking.
10. If correct, the team celebrates. If not, the teammates coach, then celebrate.
11. The person to the left of the Showdown Captain becomes the Showdown Captain for the next round.

Blacklines

Prefixes (re-, un-)

Showdown (Team Set)

Instructions: Copy one set of cards for each team. Cut apart.

Prefixes (re-, un-) ___equal	Prefixes (re-, un-) ___roll
Prefixes (re-, un-) ___able	Prefixes (re-, un-) ___do
Prefixes (re-, un-) ___happy	Prefixes (re-, un-) ___cycle
Prefixes (re-, un-) ___turn	Prefixes (re-, un-) ___true

Prefixes (re-, un-)

Showdown (Team Set)

Instructions: Copy one set of cards for each team. Cut apart.

Prefixes (re-, un-)	Prefixes (re-, un-)
___play	___move
___run	___lucky
___set	___plug
___count	___phrase

Prefixes (re-, un-)

Showdown (Team Set)

Instructions: Copy one set of cards for each team. Cut apart.

Prefixes (re-, un-)	___likely
Prefixes (re-, un-)	___seen
Prefixes (re-, un-)	___new
Prefixes (re-, un-)	___tidy
Prefixes (re-, un-)	___fair
Prefixes (re-, un-)	___said
Prefixes (re-, un-)	___build
Prefixes (re-, un-)	___heat

Prefixes (re-, un-)

Showdown (Student Set)

Note: This page has cards for four students (one team). Copy, cut apart, and give each student one "re-" and one "un-" card.

Prefixes (re-, un-)	Prefixes (re-, un-)	Prefixes (re-, un-)	Prefixes (re-, un-)
re-	un-	re-	un-
Prefixes (re-, un-)	Prefixes (re-, un-)	Prefixes (re-, un-)	Prefixes (re-, un-)
re-	un-	re-	un-

Suffixes (-ly, -ful)

Showdown (Team Set)

Instructions: Copy one set of cards for each team. Cut apart.

Suffixes (ly-, ful-) week___	Suffixes (ly-, ful-) friend___
Suffixes (ly-, ful-) pain___	Suffixes (ly-, ful-) night___
Suffixes (ly-, ful-) arm___	Suffixes (ly-, ful-) care___

Suffixes (-ly, -ful)

Showdown (Team Set)

Instructions: Copy one set of cards for each team. Cut apart.

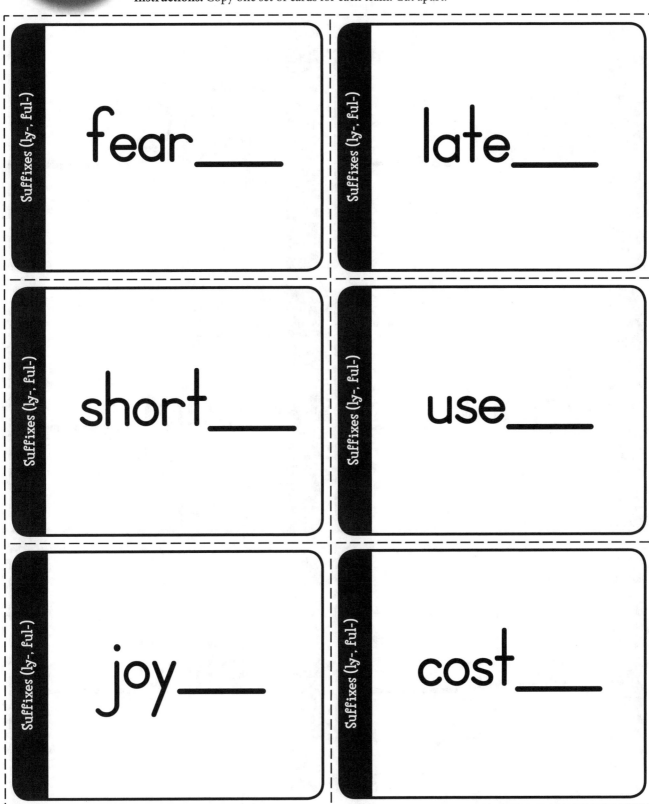

Suffixes (ly-, ful-) fear___	Suffixes (ly-, ful-) late___
Suffixes (ly-, ful-) short___	Suffixes (ly-, ful-) use___
Suffixes (ly-, ful-) joy___	Suffixes (ly-, ful-) cost___

Suffixes (-ly, -ful)

Showdown (Team Set)

Instructions: Copy one set of cards for each team. Cut apart.

Suffixes (ly-, ful-)	Suffixes (ly-, ful-)
elder___	plate___
thank___	part___
hour___	blind___

Suffixes (-ly, -ful)

Showdown (Team Set)

Instructions: Copy one set of cards for each team. Cut apart.

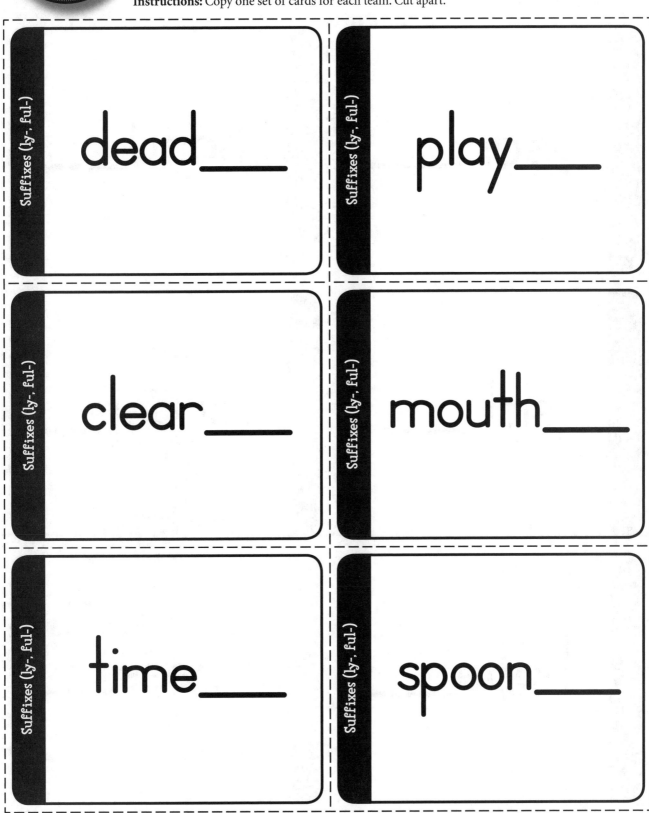

Suffixes (ly-, ful-) dead___	Suffixes (ly-, ful-) play___
Suffixes (ly-, ful-) clear___	Suffixes (ly-, ful-) mouth___
Suffixes (ly-, ful-) time___	Suffixes (ly-, ful-) spoon___

Suffixes (-ly, -ful)

Showdown (Team Set)

Instructions: Copy one set of cards for each team. Cut apart.

Suffixes (ly-, ful-) year___	Suffixes (ly-, ful-) hand___
Suffixes (ly-, ful-) sick___	Suffixes (ly-, ful-) wonder___
Suffixes (ly-, ful-) hope___	Suffixes (ly-, ful-) stress___

Suffixes (-ly, -ful)

Showdown (Student Set)

Note: This page has cards for four students (one team). Copy, cut apart, and give each student one "-ly" and one "-ful" card.

Suffixes (ly-, ful-)	Suffixes (ly-, ful-)	Suffixes (ly-, ful-)	Suffixes (ly-, ful-)
-ly	-ful	-ly	-ful
Suffixes (ly-, ful-)	Suffixes (ly-, ful-)	Suffixes (ly-, ful-)	Suffixes (ly-, ful-)
-ly	-ful	-ly	-ful

c as /s/ and /k/

Showdown (Team Set)

Instructions: Copy one set of cards for each team. Cut apart.

c as /s/ and /k/ — carpenter	c as /s/ and /k/ — castle	c as /s/ and /k/ — citizen	c as /s/ and /k/ — central
c as /s/ and /k/ — color	c as /s/ and /k/ — cents	c as /s/ and /k/ — cereal	c as /s/ and /k/ — cottage
c as /s/ and /k/ — circle	c as /s/ and /k/ — corner	c as /s/ and /k/ — cabin	c as /s/ and /k/ — center

c as /s/ and /k/

Showdown (Team Set)

Instructions: Copy one set of cards for each team. Cut apart.

c as /s/ and /k/ — celery	c as /s/ and /k/ — cider	c as /s/ and /k/ — cold	c as /s/ and /k/ — careful
c as /s/ and /k/ — cell	c as /s/ and /k/ — cool	c as /s/ and /k/ — city	c as /s/ and /k/ — collar
c as /s/ and /k/ — correct	c as /s/ and /k/ — curious	c as /s/ and /k/ — cycle	c as /s/ and /k/ — cage

c as /s/ and /k/

Showdown (Student Set)

Instructions: This page has cards for four students (one team). Copy, cut apart, and give each student one c as /s/ card and one c as /k/ card.

c as /s/ and /k/	c as /s/ and /k/	c as /s/ and /k/	c as /s/ and /k/
c =/s/	c =/k/	c =/s/	c =/k/
c as /s/ and /k/	c as /s/ and /k/	c as /s/ and /k/	c as /s/ and /k/
c =/s/	c =/k/	c =/s/	c =/k/

g as /j/ and /g/

Showdown (Team Set)

Instructions: Copy one set of cards for each team. Cut apart.

g as /j/ and /g/	g as /j/ and /g/
giant	girls
get	gum
gerbil	general
gel	gulp
garden	giraffe
gem	gift

g as /j/ and /g/

Showdown (Team Set)

Instructions: Copy one set of cards for each team. Cut apart.

g as /j/ and /g/ — guide	g as /j/ and /g/ — geese
g as /j/ and /g/ — gym	g as /j/ and /g/ — germs
g as /j/ and /g/ — goat	g as /j/ and /g/ — gallop
g as /j/ and /g/ — guess	g as /j/ and /g/ — ghost
g as /j/ and /g/ — gals	g as /j/ and /g/ — garlic
g as /j/ and /g/ — guitar	g as /j/ and /g/ — gentle

g as /j/ and /g/

Showdown (Student Set)

Note: This page has cards for four students (one team). Copy, cut apart, and give each student one g as /j/ card and one g as /g/ card.

g as /j/ and /g/)	g as /j/ and /g/)	g as /j/ and /g/)	g as /j/ and /g/)
g=/j/	g=/g/	g=/j/	g=/g/

g as /j/ and /g/)	g as /j/ and /g/)	g as /j/ and /g/)	g as /j/ and /g/)
g=/j/	g=/g/	g=/j/	g=/g/

Compounds, Possessives, Contractions

Showdown (Team Set)

Instructions: Copy one set of cards for each team. Cut apart. Showdown Captain reads the sentence. Students indicate which type of word is in the sentence using cards from Card Set 2. Students also use markerboards to write the identified word. Both the card and the markerboard are shown and the answers are stated at the same time.

Compounds, Possessives, Contractions

We were so excited to visit Ted's school on Monday.

Compounds, Possessives, Contractions

They were sure the idea wouldn't fit the plan.

Compounds, Possessives, Contractions

Kay and Sid visited the marketplace in the village.

Compounds, Possessives, Contractions

What happened to Carl's navy blue suit?

Compounds, Possessives, Contractions

It's going to be a warm and breezy day.

Compounds, Possessives, Contractions

We paid the taxes at the courthouse.

Compounds, Possessives, Contractions

Where did the dog bury its bone?

Compounds, Possessives, Contractions

You needn't read the entire book this evening.

Compounds, Possessives, Contractions

Fourteen monkeys swung from branches at the zoo.

Compounds, Possessives, Contractions

Showdown (Team Set)

Instructions: Copy one set of cards for each team. Cut apart. Showdown Captain reads the sentence. Students indicate which type of word is in the sentence using cards from Card Set 2. Students also use markerboards to write the identified word. Both the card and the markerboard are shown and the answers are stated at the same time.

Compounds, Possessives, Contractions	Mel's pet gerbil escaped from the cage last night.
Compounds, Possessives, Contractions	We can't seem to uncover the clues to the mystery.
Compounds, Possessives, Contractions	The new yardstick will help us measure the box.
Compounds, Possessives, Contractions	When the giant stomped his feet, the ground shook.
Compounds, Possessives, Contractions	Chad and Jade haven't discovered the surprise.
Compounds, Possessives, Contractions	It will be helpful to use the guidebook on the trip.
Compounds, Possessives, Contractions	Their new house is just about completed.
Compounds, Possessives, Contractions	We mustn't leave the door to the garage open.
Compounds, Possessives, Contractions	A tiny hummingbird hovered above the feeder.

Compounds, Possessives, Contractions

Showdown (Student Set)

Note: This page has cards for two students. Copy, cut apart, and give each student one set of cards.

Compounds, Possessives, Contractions	Compounds, Possessives, Contractions	Compounds, Possessives, Contractions
compound word	possessive word	contraction

Compounds, Possessives, Contractions	Compounds, Possessives, Contractions	Compounds, Possessives, Contractions
compound word	possessive word	contraction

NUMBERED HEADS TOGETHER

Activity

Word Wall Spelling

After spelling the word themselves, teammates put their "heads together" to ensure all members can correctly spell the word wall word. The teacher then calls a number and all students with that number share their team's spelling.

Numbered Heads Together

STRUCTURE

Note:
The Word Wall Cards on the following pages are not used for this activity. They are provided for your convenience to post on your word wall. However, before you begin this activity, make sure you take down word wall words students will spell.

Activity Steps

1. Students number off in small groups.
2. Teacher reads a selected word from the Word Wall List.
3. Students privately write the word on a markerboard or on a piece of paper.
4. Teacher says, "Heads Together!" and students lift up from their chairs to put their heads together, show their answers, and discuss until they reach consensus on the word spelling.
5. Everyone clears their boards and sits down when they agree.
6. The teacher calls out a number. All students with that number write the agreed-upon spelling of the word on their marker-boards.
7. All students with their number selected hold up their boards simultaneously. The teacher writes each group's spelling on the overhead.
8. The teacher leads the class in a discussion of each spelling by asking questions such as "Which way looks right?" "How do you know?" or "What was the tricky part or familiar part?"
9. Teammates celebrate or correct spelling on boards.
10. The process is repeated for each new word.

Note: "Additional Word Wall Words" provide extra word choices.

BlacKlines

Second Grade Word Wall List

Numbered Heads Together

Instructions: Words to be used with Word Wall Spelling.

a	go	or
all	had	see
am	have	so
an	he	they
and	his	this
are	in	to
as	is	up
at	it	was
be	like	we
but	me	were
by	my	what
can	not	with
do	of	you
for	on	your
from	one	

Second Grade Word Wall Cards

Instructions: Use the cards provided to create a Word Wall.

Second Grade Word Wall Cards and	Second Grade Word Wall Cards are	Second Grade Word Wall Cards as	Second Grade Word Wall Cards at
Second Grade Word Wall Cards a	Second Grade Word Wall Cards all	Second Grade Word Wall Cards am	Second Grade Word Wall Cards an

Second Grade Word Wall Cards

Instructions: Use the cards provided to create a Word Wall.

Second Grade Word Wall Cards do	Second Grade Word Wall Cards for	Second Grade Word Wall Cards from	Second Grade Word Wall Cards go
Second Grade Word Wall Cards be	Second Grade Word Wall Cards but	Second Grade Word Wall Cards by	Second Grade Word Wall Cards can

Second Grade Word Wall Cards

Instructions: Use the cards provided to create a Word Wall.

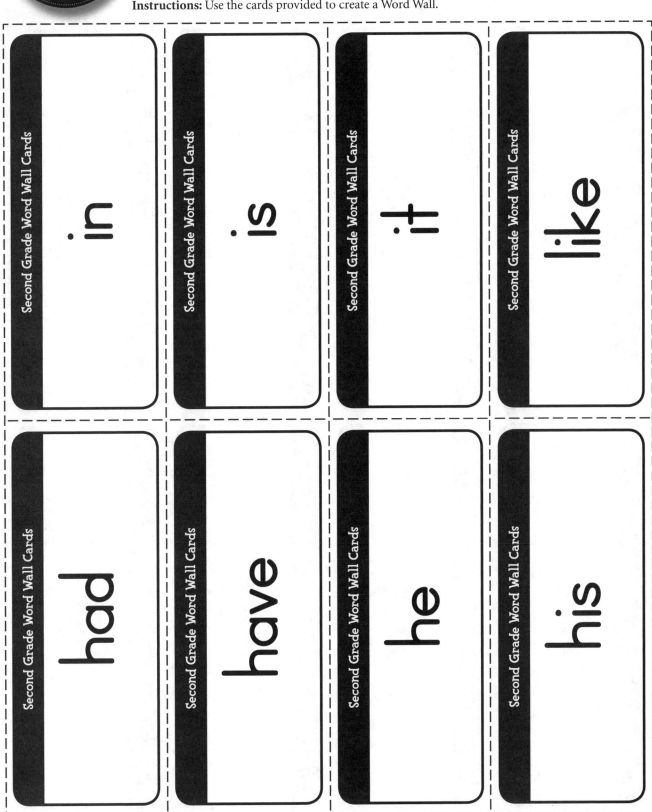

Second Grade Word Wall Cards in	Second Grade Word Wall Cards is	Second Grade Word Wall Cards it	Second Grade Word Wall Cards like
Second Grade Word Wall Cards had	Second Grade Word Wall Cards have	Second Grade Word Wall Cards he	Second Grade Word Wall Cards his

Second Grade Word Wall Cards

Instructions: Use the cards provided to create a Word Wall.

Second Grade Word Wall Cards on	Second Grade Word Wall Cards one	Second Grade Word Wall Cards or	Second Grade Word Wall Cards see
Second Grade Word Wall Cards me	Second Grade Word Wall Cards my	Second Grade Word Wall Cards not	Second Grade Word Wall Cards of

Second Grade Word Wall Cards

Instructions: Use the cards provided to create a Word Wall.

Second Grade Word Wall Cards

up

Second Grade Word Wall Cards

was

Second Grade Word Wall Cards

we

Second Grade Word Wall Cards

were

Second Grade Word Wall Cards

so

Second Grade Word Wall Cards

they

Second Grade Word Wall Cards

this

Second Grade Word Wall Cards

to

Second Grade Word Wall Cards

Instructions: Use the cards provided to create a Word Wall.

Second Grade Word Wall Cards with	Second Grade Word Wall Cards your	Second Grade Word Wall Cards	Second Grade Word Wall Cards
Second Grade Word Wall Cards what	Second Grade Word Wall Cards you	Second Grade Word Wall Cards	Second Grade Word Wall Cards

Second Grade
Additional Word Wall Cards

Instructions: Use the cards provided to create a Word Wall.

Second Grade Additional Word Wall Cards also	Second Grade Additional Word Wall Cards another	Second Grade Additional Word Wall Cards any	Second Grade Additional Word Wall Cards around
Second Grade Additional Word Wall Cards about	Second Grade Additional Word Wall Cards after	Second Grade Additional Word Wall Cards again	Second Grade Additional Word Wall Cards air

Second Grade Additional Word Wall Cards

Instructions: Use the cards provided to create a Word Wall.

Second Grade Additional Word Wall Cards

between

Second Grade Additional Word Wall Cards

big

Second Grade Additional Word Wall Cards

called

Second Grade Additional Word Wall Cards

came

Second Grade Additional Word Wall Cards

away

Second Grade Additional Word Wall Cards

back

Second Grade Additional Word Wall Cards

because

Second Grade Additional Word Wall Cards

been

Second Grade Additional Word Wall Cards

Instructions: Use the cards provided to create a Word Wall.

Second Grade Additional Word Wall Cards	Second Grade Additional Word Wall Cards	Second Grade Additional Word Wall Cards	Second Grade Additional Word Wall Cards
different	does	down	each
Second Grade Additional Word Wall Cards	**Second Grade Additional Word Wall Cards**	**Second Grade Additional Word Wall Cards**	**Second Grade Additional Word Wall Cards**
come	could	day	did

Second Grade Additional Word Wall Cards

Instructions: Use the cards provided to create a Word Wall.

Second Grade Additional Word Wall Cards first	Second Grade Additional Word Wall Cards found	Second Grade Additional Word Wall Cards get	Second Grade Additional Word Wall Cards give
Second Grade Additional Word Wall Cards end	Second Grade Additional Word Wall Cards even	Second Grade Additional Word Wall Cards every	Second Grade Additional Word Wall Cards find

Second Grade Additional Word Wall Cards

Instructions: Use the cards provided to create a Word Wall.

Second Grade Additional Word Wall Cards help	Second Grade Additional Word Wall Cards her	Second Grade Additional Word Wall Cards here	Second Grade Additional Word Wall Cards him
Second Grade Additional Word Wall Cards got	Second Grade Additional Word Wall Cards good	Second Grade Additional Word Wall Cards great	Second Grade Additional Word Wall Cards has

Second Grade Additional Word Wall Cards

Instructions: Use the cards provided to create a Word Wall.

Second Grade Additional Word Wall Cards	Second Grade Additional Word Wall Cards	Second Grade Additional Word Wall Cards	Second Grade Additional Word Wall Cards
its	just	know	last
home	how	if	into

Second Grade Additional Word Wall Cards

Instructions: Use the cards provided to create a Word Wall.

Second Grade Additional Word Wall Cards
look

Second Grade Additional Word Wall Cards
made

Second Grade Additional Word Wall Cards
make

Second Grade Additional Word Wall Cards
man

Second Grade Additional Word Wall Cards
left

Second Grade Additional Word Wall Cards
line

Second Grade Additional Word Wall Cards
little

Second Grade Additional Word Wall Cards
long

Second Grade Additional Word Wall Cards

Instructions: Use the cards provided to create a Word Wall.

Second Grade Additional Word Wall Cards much	Second Grade Additional Word Wall Cards must	Second Grade Additional Word Wall Cards name	Second Grade Additional Word Wall Cards never
Second Grade Additional Word Wall Cards may	Second Grade Additional Word Wall Cards men	Second Grade Additional Word Wall Cards more	Second Grade Additional Word Wall Cards most

Second Grade Additional Word Wall Cards

Instructions: Use the cards provided to create a Word Wall.

Second Grade Additional Word Wall Cards

off

Second Grade Additional Word Wall Cards

old

Second Grade Additional Word Wall Cards

only

Second Grade Additional Word Wall Cards

other

Second Grade Additional Word Wall Cards

new

Second Grade Additional Word Wall Cards

no

Second Grade Additional Word Wall Cards

now

Second Grade Additional Word Wall Cards

number

Second Grade Additional Word Wall Cards

Instructions: Use the cards provided to create a Word Wall.

Second Grade Additional Word Wall Cards part	Second Grade Additional Word Wall Cards people	Second Grade Additional Word Wall Cards place	Second Grade Additional Word Wall Cards put
Second Grade Additional Word Wall Cards our	Second Grade Additional Word Wall Cards out	Second Grade Additional Word Wall Cards over	Second Grade Additional Word Wall Cards own

Second Grade Additional Word Wall Cards

Instructions: Use the cards provided to create a Word Wall.

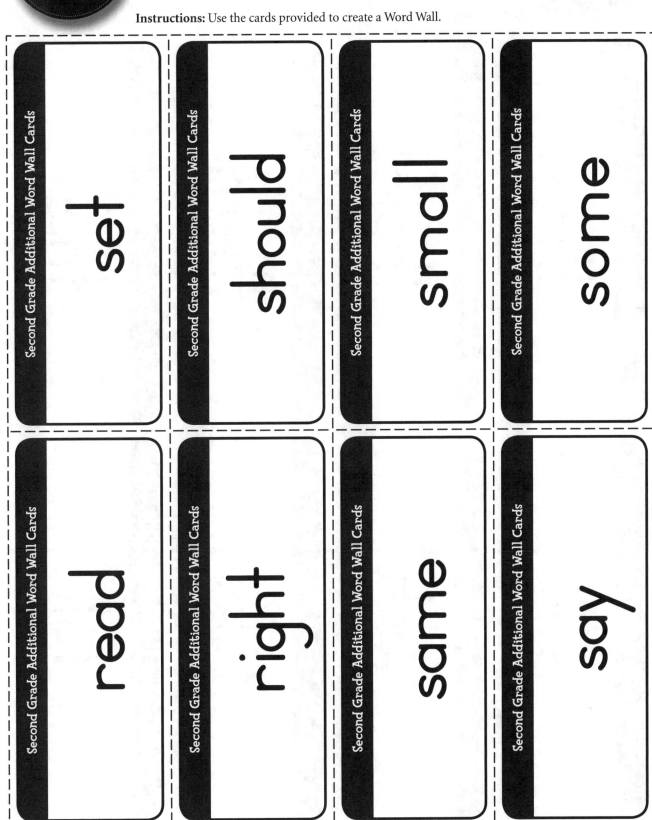

Second Grade Additional Word Wall Cards	Second Grade Additional Word Wall Cards	Second Grade Additional Word Wall Cards	Second Grade Additional Word Wall Cards
set	should	small	some
read	right	same	say

Second Grade Additional Word Wall Cards

Instructions: Use the cards provided to create a Word Wall.

Second Grade Additional Word Wall Cards than	Second Grade Additional Word Wall Cards their	Second Grade Additional Word Wall Cards them	Second Grade Additional Word Wall Cards then
Second Grade Additional Word Wall Cards still	Second Grade Additional Word Wall Cards such	Second Grade Additional Word Wall Cards take	Second Grade Additional Word Wall Cards tell

Second Grade Additional Word Wall Cards

Instructions: Use the cards provided to create a Word Wall.

Second Grade Additional Word Wall Cards
time

Second Grade Additional Word Wall Cards
too

Second Grade Additional Word Wall Cards
two

Second Grade Additional Word Wall Cards
under

Second Grade Additional Word Wall Cards
these

Second Grade Additional Word Wall Cards
think

Second Grade Additional Word Wall Cards
three

Second Grade Additional Word Wall Cards
through

Second Grade Additional Word Wall Cards

Instructions: Use the cards provided to create a Word Wall.

Second Grade Additional Word Wall Cards way	Second Grade Additional Word Wall Cards well	Second Grade Additional Word Wall Cards when	Second Grade Additional Word Wall Cards where
Second Grade Additional Word Wall Cards us	Second Grade Additional Word Wall Cards use	Second Grade Additional Word Wall Cards very	Second Grade Additional Word Wall Cards water

Second Grade Additional Word Wall Cards

Instructions: Use the cards provided to create a Word Wall.

Second Grade Additional Word Wall Cards words	Second Grade Additional Word Wall Cards work	Second Grade Additional Word Wall Cards would	Second Grade Additional Word Wall Cards write
Second Grade Additional Word Wall Cards which	Second Grade Additional Word Wall Cards who	Second Grade Additional Word Wall Cards why	Second Grade Additional Word Wall Cards will

Second Grade Blank Word Wall Cards

Instructions: Use the cards to add additional words.

Second Grade Word Wall Cards	Second Grade Word Wall Cards	Second Grade Word Wall Cards	Second Grade Word Wall Cards
Second Grade Word Wall Cards	Second Grade Word Wall Cards	Second Grade Word Wall Cards	Second Grade Word Wall Cards

Balanced Literacy

- Comprehension
- Word Study
- Fluency ✓
- Writing

Fluency

Fluency

Fluency is a part of an effective reading program. When a reader is fluent, energies are automatically channeled into comprehending the text instead of decoding words.

Reading fluency includes the following components:

- expression (stress, pitch, volume, clarity)
- phrasing (pauses, word groups)
- rate (just the right speed)
- accuracy (correct words and punctuation)

The fluency resources and materials at the beginning of this section are designed to be used in the suggested order to scaffold the learner and ensure understanding (*aloud* and *shared*). The remainder of the activities in this section are designed to provide fluency practice (*guided* and *independent*).

Table of Decoding Strategy Resources

		Balanced Literacy				
Page(s)	Resources	Aloud	Shared	Guided	Independent	Literature Circles
406	Decoding Strategy Resources/ Materials Description					
408	Decoding Strategy Bookmarks	●	●	●	●	●
409	Decoding Strategy Flashcards	●	●	●	●	●
411	Decoding Strategy Graph	●	●	●	●	●

Table of Fluency Resources

		Balanced Literacy				
Page(s)	Resources	Aloud	Shared	Guided	Independent	Literature Circles
	Fluency Descriptions and Lists					
414	Fluency Resources/Materials Descriptions					
415	Fluency Bookmarks	●	●	●	●	●
416	Fluency Graphics/Note Taking	●	●	●	●	●

Table of Fluency Activities

Page(s)	Activities	Blacklines	Aloud	Shared	Guided	Independent	Literature Circles
			Balanced Literacy				
418	**RallyCoach Activity**						
419	Expression	• Rubric and Graph	●	●	●	●	●
420	Phrasing	• Rubric and Graph	●	●	●	●	●
421	Accuracy	• Rubric and Graph	●	●	●	●	●
422	Rate	• Rubric and Graph	●	●	●	●	●
423	Fluency	• Continuum Worksheet	●	●	●	●	●
424	**Poems for Two Voices Activity**						
425	Mammals	• Copy of Poem	●	●			
426	Clouds	• Copy of Poem	●	●			
427	Blank Form	• Blank Worksheet	●	●			
428	**Quiz-Quiz-Trade Activity**						
429	Fluency Practice	• Sentence Cards	●	●	●		

Decoding Strategy Resources

Decoding Strategy Resources

Resources/Materials Descriptions

Decoding Strategy Bookmark (p. 408)

Learning to read requires that we guide each student in becoming an independent reader. Successful readers are able to pull appropriate strategies from a repertoire of choices when they come to a word they do not know. It is important to scaffold the instruction to help the students move from observation, to understanding, to practice, and finally, to independent implementation. As the teacher models decoding strategies during shared reading and interacts with students during guided reading, the Decoding Strategy Bookmark becomes a visual reference. The Decoding Strategy Bookmark will be a helpful tool for individual students during guided reading and independent reading.

The three questions listed at the top of the bookmark are to help students self-monitor their reading and to help them know when to apply a strategy(ies). Students should ask themselves the three questions. If they answer, "No," to one of the questions, they need to try various strategies until they can answer, "Yes" to all three questions. Eight decoding strategies are listed below the questions to serve as prompts.

Decoding Flashcards (pp. 409)

(Students will have all of the Decoding Flashcards available to them in an envelope or small plastic bag. The teacher may choose to focus on a few strategies at a time and have students work with only those particular cards until all the strategies have been introduced.)

The Decoding Flashcards can be used in various ways:

- **Shared Reading**
  As the teacher models a strategy(ies), the students can each identify the modeled strategy and hold up the appropriate flashcard(s). To help the students realize that good readers use multiple strategies, the teacher will model trying several different strategies until one works.

Resources/Materials Descriptions (continued)

- **Guided Reading**
  Periodically, the teacher may ask the students to locate a place in their text, where they needed to use a decoding strategy. Each student demonstrates and explains to the group the strategy(ies) attempted. The Decoding Flashcards are used to identify the strategy(ies) as the group listens and coaches.
- **Partner Reading**
  The above practice may also be used with partners using the **RallyCoach** structure.

Decoding Strategy Graph (p. 411)

The Decoding Strategy Graph provides an additional practice opportunity that allows students to compare strategies used frequently to those that might need strengthening. The graph can be used with the **RallyCoach** structure.

Decoding Strategy Bookmark

Does it make sense?

Does it sound right?

Does it look right?

Picture Clues

Mouth Ready

Patterns (Chunks)

Reread.
Fix.

Skip word.
Get clues.
Reread.

Think about what word makes sense.

Stretch through word.

Try vowel both ways. a e i o u

Decoding Strategy Bookmark

Does it make sense?

Does it sound right?

Does it look right?

Picture Clues

Mouth Ready

Patterns (Chunks)

Reread.
Fix.

Skip word.
Get clues.
Reread.

Think about what word makes sense.

Stretch through word.

Try vowel both ways. a e i o u

Picture Clues
Mouth Ready
Pattern (Chunk)
Reread. Fix.
Skip word.
Get clues.
Reread.
Think about
what word
makes sense.
a
e
i
o
u
Stretch through
the word.
Try vowel both
ways.

Does it make sense?	Does it sound right?	Does it look right?

Decoding Strategy Graph

	I use picture clues.	I get my mouth ready.	I know something about the word. (chunking/patterns)	I reread. I fix.	I skip the word, get clues, reread.	I think about what word makes sense.	I stretch through the word.	I try the vowel both ways. a e i o u	Does it make sense? Does it sound right? Does it look right?
12									
11									
10									
9									
8									
7									
6									
5									
4									
3									
2									
1									

Fluency Resources

Fluency Resources

Resources/Materials Descriptions

Fluency Bookmark (p. 415)
Fluency is automatic and accurate recognition of words in a text while using phrasing and expression in a way that makes reading sound like spoken language. The Fluency Bookmark is a visual prompting tool for students to use as they learn and practice the components of fluent reading.

Fluency Graphics/Note Taking (p. 416)
The fluency page provides flexible instructional uses. The teacher may have students attach their own labels, graphics, or notes to build mental connections as they become fluent readers.

Fluency Rubrics and Graphs (pp. 419-422)
The broad fluency components of expression, phrasing, rate, and accuracy have been defined through the rubric continuum to increase students' fluency knowledge, self-awareness, and monitoring of progress.

Students must be given opportunities to reread and practice if fluency is going to improve. The graph below each rubric provides students with a visual record for charting their own progress as they practice with a partner or individually.

Together, these two tools provide data for reflection and conversation between students and between student and teacher.

Fluency Continuum (p. 423)
After using the Rubrics and Graphs described above to create a solid understanding of fluency, the Fluency Continuum becomes another self-monitoring option for students.

Fluency
expression
· stress
· pitch
· volume
· clarity
phrasing
· pauses
· word groups
· punctuation
STOP
rate
· speed (just right)
accuracy
· right words
· correct pronunciation
Fluency
expression
· stress
· pitch
· volume
· clarity
phrasing
· pauses
· word groups
· punctuation
STOP
rate
· speed (just right)
accuracy
· right words
· correct pronunciation
Fluency
expression
· stress
· pitch
· volume
· clarity
phrasing
· pauses
· word groups
· punctuation
STOP
rate
· speed (just right)
accuracy
· right words
· correct pronunciation
Fluency
expression
· stress
· pitch
· volume
· clarity
phrasing
· pauses
· word groups
· punctuation
STOP
rate
· speed (just right)
accuracy
· right words
· correct pronunciation

Fluency Graphics/ Note Taking

Instructions: Copy for each student.

Fluency Graphics/Note Taking

expression

- stress
- pitch
- volume
- clarity

Fluency Graphics/Note Taking

Fluency Graphics/Note Taking

phrasing

- pauses
- word groups
- punctuation

Fluency Graphics/Note Taking

Fluency Graphics/Note Taking

rate

- speed (just right)

Fluency Graphics/Note Taking

Fluency Graphics/Note Taking

- right words
- correct pronunciation

Fluency Graphics/Note Taking

Fluency Activities

Fluency Scoring

Students read a text passage to a partner. The partner uses a rubric to score the reading on one dimension. Students practice rereading the same passage to improve their fluency and chart their progress.

Activity Steps

1. There are four rubrics provided to work on different dimensions of fluency. Each student receives a rubric sheet.
2. Partner A reads the text passage while Partner B listens carefully, paying special attention to the rubric scoring.
3. Partner B uses the rubric to score Partner A's reading. Partner B colors in the score in the "1st time" column of the graph. Then Partner B describes the score and how Partner A can improve.
4. Partner B then reads while Partner A listens.
5. Partner A scores the reading by filling in the graph and provides feedback to Partner B.
6. The process is repeated multiple times with the same text passage to improve fluency. There are 5 columns on the graph provided so students can graph their progress.

STRUCTURE
RallyCoach

Hint:
Tell students in advance that they will be scoring each other on their reading. The scores are used only as a way for students to provide each other constructive feedback and chart their progress.

BlacKlines

Expression Rubric

RallyCoach

Instructions: Copy for each student.

Score	1	2	3	4
Expression • Stress • Pitch • Volume • Clarity	No voice change	Voice changes sometimes	Voice changes most of the time when needed	Voice changes when needed

Expression Graph

RallyCoach

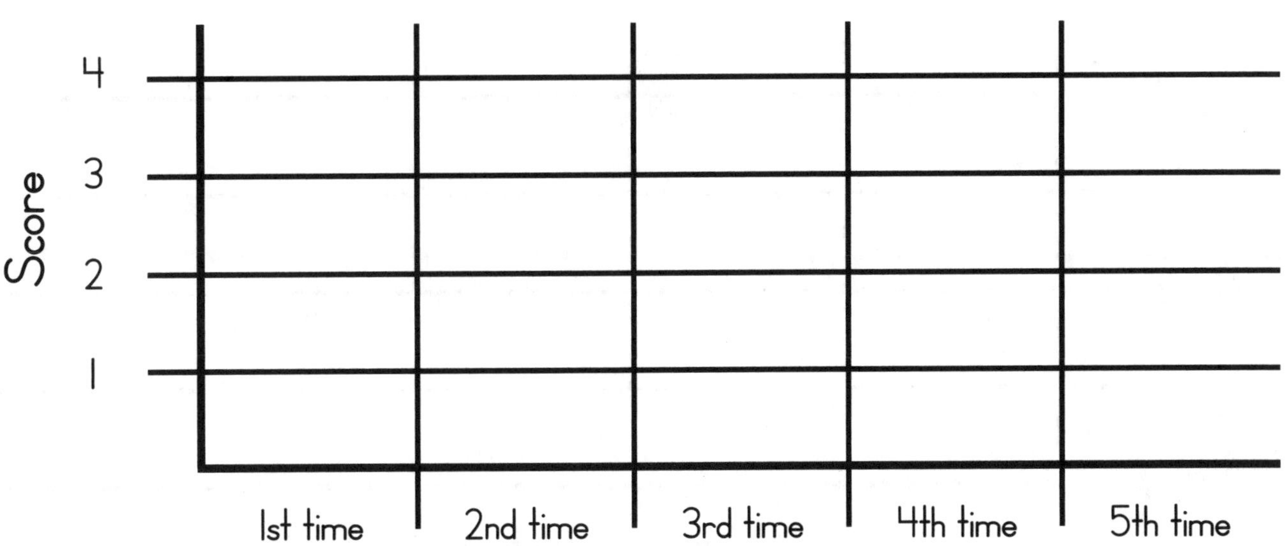

Name ____

Phrasing Rubric

RallyCoach

Instructions: Copy for each student.

Score	1	2	3	4
Phrasing • Pauses • Word Groups • Punctuation	Reads word by word and does not stop at punctuation	Reads in small chunks and sometimes stops at punctuation	Reads in larger chunks and usually stops at punctuation	Reads in long chunks and stops at punctuation

Phrasing Graph

RallyCoach

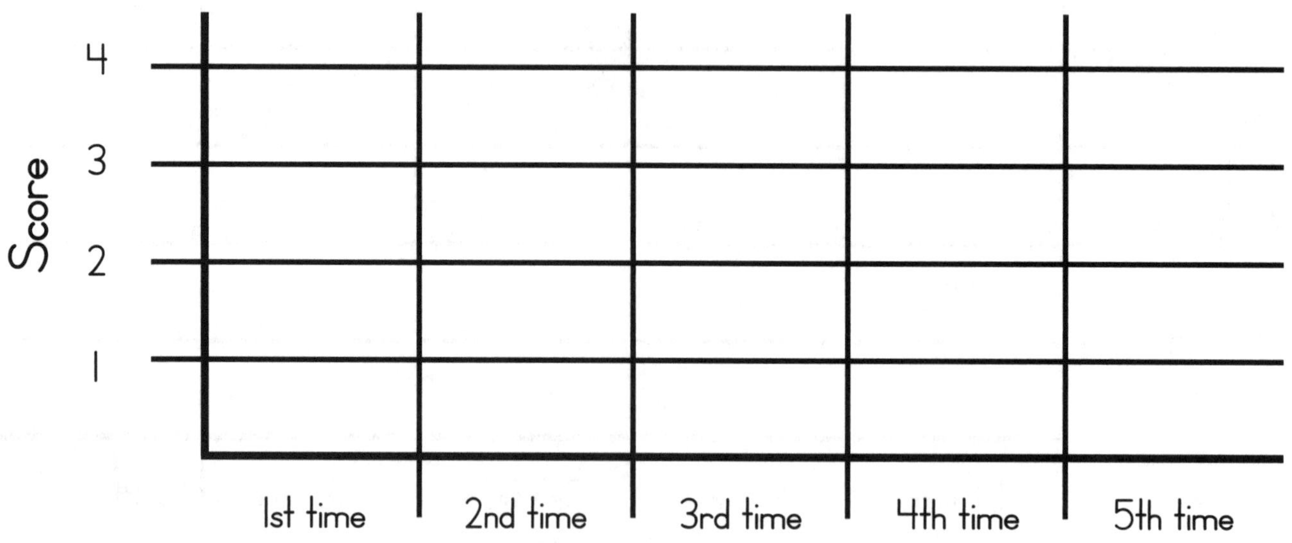

Name ____

Rate Rubric

RallyCoach

Instructions: Copy for each student.

Score	1	2	3	4
Rate • Speed (Just Right)	Reads too fast or too slow Hard to understand	Reads too fast or too slow sometimes	Reads "just right" most of the time	Keeps speed steady and "just right"

Rate Graph

RallyCoach

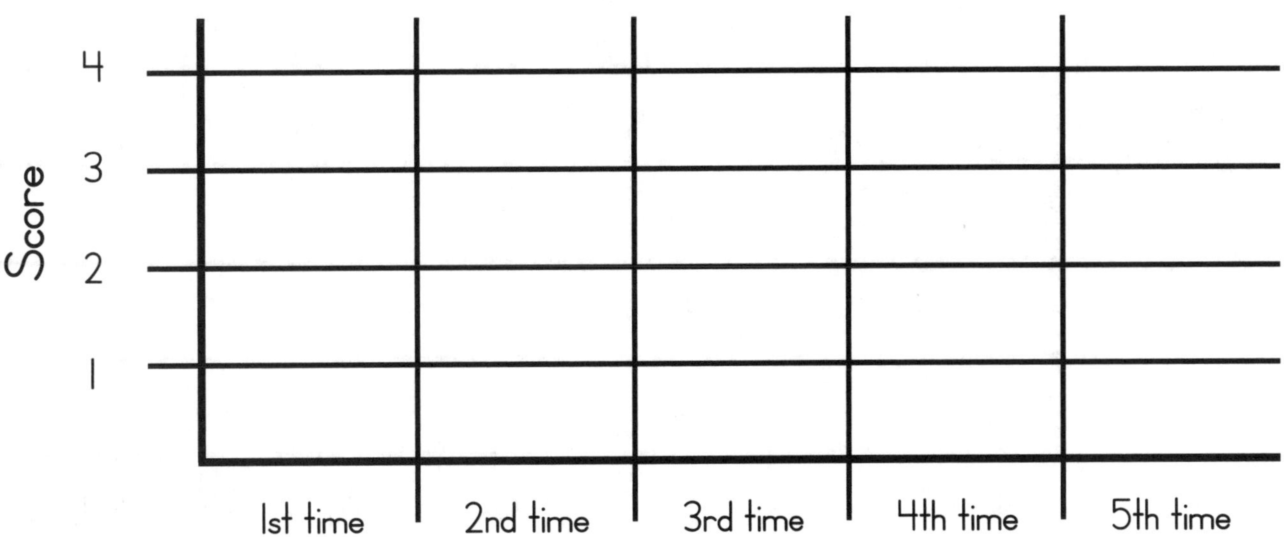

Name ____

Accuracy Rubric

RallyCoach

Instructions: Copy for each student.

Score	1	2	3	4
Accuracy • Right Words • Correct Pronunciation	Many errors	Errors, which sometimes change the meaning	Some errors, which do not change the meaning	Very few or no errors Words correctly pronounced

Accuracy Graph

RallyCoach

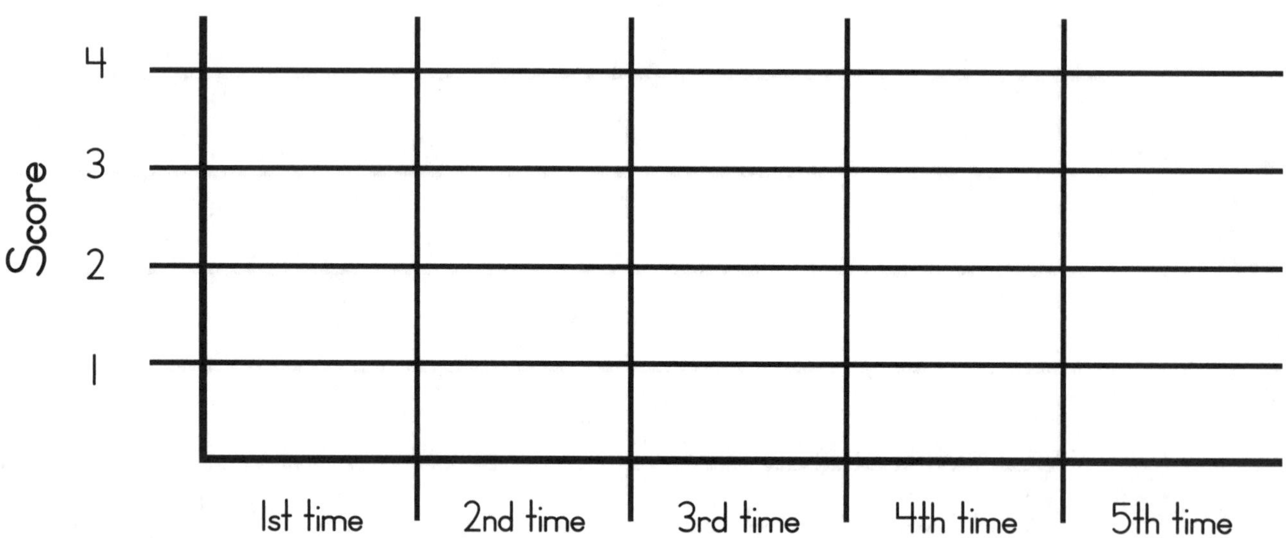

Name ______________________________

Fluency Continuum

RallyCoach

Instructions: Copy for each student.

Fluency Continuum

expression

- stress
- pitch
- volume
- clarity

Fluency Continuum

no | sometimes | most of the time | yes

Fluency Continuum

phrasing

- pauses
- word groups
- punctuation

Fluency Continuum

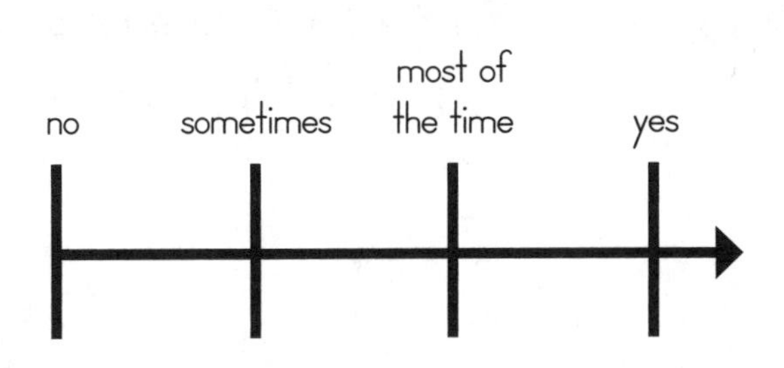

Fluency Continuum

rate

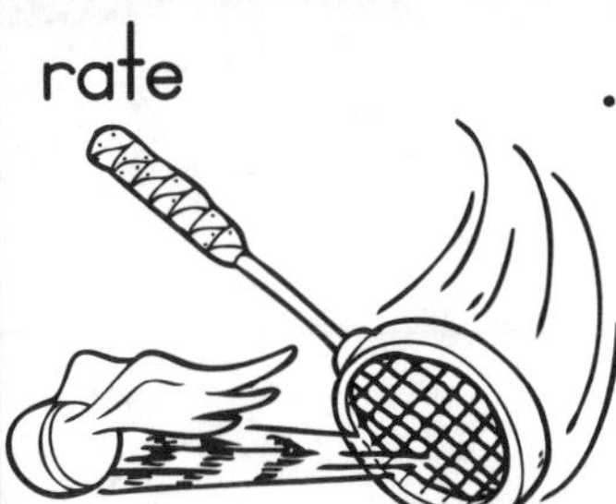

- speed (just right)

Fluency Continuum

no | sometimes | most of the time | yes

Fluency Continuum

accuracy

- right words
- correct pronunciation

Fluency Continuum

no | sometimes | most of the time | yes

POEMS FOR TWO VOICES

Activity

Fluency Poems

Partners present a poem—recited at times by one partner, the other partner, or both.

Activity Steps

1. The teacher provides students a poem. The poem has some lines labeled "A," some lines labeled "B," and some lines labeled, "AB." The teacher assigns pairs.
2. Pairs practice their poems. Partner A reads the A lines. Partner B reads the B lines. They read the AB lines in unison. Students listen carefully to their partners to keep the flow.
3. When ready, pairs read their poem to another pair.

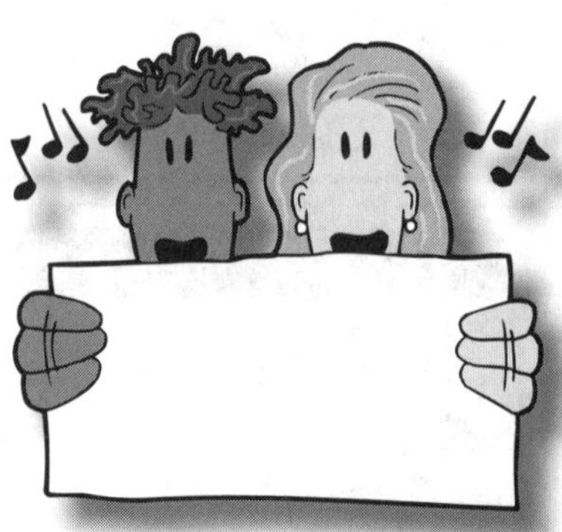

STRUCTURE

Poems for Two Voices

Blacklines

Mammals

Poems for Two Voices

Instructions: Copy for each student or pair.

A There are many kinds of mammals,
B Gigantic, big, medium, or small
A On land, in the air, and in the sea
B Some eat plants and some eat meat.
AB All have hair.
AB All breathe air.
A Their body temperature will stay the same,
B In sunshine, snow, ice, or rain.
A Most babies are born alive and well.
B They drink milk from their mothers for quite a long spell.
A A backbone in each one you will find,
B That's what makes them a group of the same kind.
A Aardvark . . .
B and anteater
A Hippopotamus . . .
B and horse
A Llama . . .
B and lion
A Dolphin . . .
B and dog
A Badger . . .
B and bat
A Whale . . .
B and walrus
A Cheetah . . .
B and chimpanzee . . .
AB and you and me!

Clouds

Poems for Two Voices

Instructions: Copy for each student or pair.

AB Clouds
A Very small drops of water
B Tiny pieces of ice
AB Held in the air
A Always moving
B Always changing shape.
AB Cirrus clouds
A High in the sky
B Thin and wispy
A Like delicate white feathers.
AB Cumulus clouds
B Fair weather clouds
A Puffy and lumpy
B Like cotton balls or popcorn.
AB Stratus clouds
A Gray sheets
B Covering most of the sky.
AB Clouds
A Important part of Earth's weather
B Carrying water
AB Falling to earth as rain or snow.

Blank Form

Poems for Two Voices

Names: ______________________________

____

Our Poem Is About: ______________________________

Instructions: Copy for each pair of students.

A ______________________________

B ______________________________

A ______________________________

B ______________________________

AB ______________________________

A ______________________________

B ______________________________

A ______________________________

B ______________________________

AB ______________________________

QUIZ-QUIZ-TRADE
Activity

Partner Fluency Practice

Students quiz a partner, get quizzed by a partner, and then trade cards to repeat the process with a new partner. Partners use cards to practice fluency using phrasing and expression.

Activity Steps

1. Each student receives a card with a sentence on the front and answer on the back.
2. All students stand up, put a hand up, and pair up.
3. Partner A asks Partner B to read the sentence.
4. Partner B reads the sentence with phrasing and expression.
5. Partner A follows on the back of the card as Partner B reads and praises or coaches.
6. Partners switch roles and read again.
7. After they have read both ways, partners trade cards, and raise their hands to find a new partner. The partner reading and trading proceeds for numerous pairings.

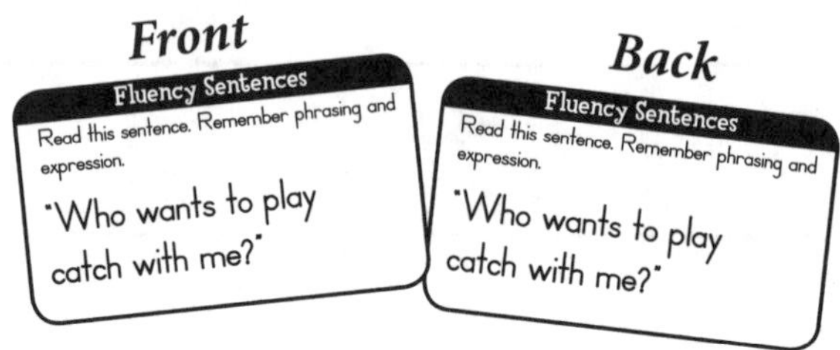
Front
Fluency Sentences
Read this sentence. Remember phrasing and expression.
"Who wants to play catch with me?"
Back
Fluency Sentences
Read this sentence. Remember phrasing and expression.
"Who wants to play catch with me?"

STRUCTURE

Quiz-Quiz-Trade

BlacKlines

Fluency Sentences

Quiz-Quiz-Trade

Instructions: Copy enough cards so each student has one card. Cut on dotted lines and fold in half.

Fluency Sentences

Read this sentence. Remember phrasing and expression.

If you want to go frog hunting, you will need to take a flashlight and go after dark.

Fluency Sentences

Read this sentence. Remember phrasing and expression.

If you want to go frog hunting, you will need to take a flashlight and go after dark.

Fluency Sentences

Read this sentence. Remember phrasing and expression.

Frogs never need to drink water because their skin takes in water instead.

Fluency Sentences

Read this sentence. Remember phrasing and expression.

Frogs never need to drink water because their skin takes in water instead.

Fluency Sentences

Read this sentence. Remember phrasing and expression.

"It's lunchtime!" yelled Mom.

Fluency Sentences

Read this sentence. Remember phrasing and expression.

"It's lunchtime!" yelled Mom.

Fluency Sentences

Read this sentence. Remember phrasing and expression.

"See you later," I exclaimed as I waved to my friend, Joe.

Fluency Sentences

Read this sentence. Remember phrasing and expression.

"See you later," I exclaimed as I waved to my friend, Joe.

Fluency Sentences

Quiz-Quiz-Trade

Instructions: Copy enough cards so each student has one card. Cut on dotted lines and fold in half.

Fluency Sentences

Read this sentence. Remember phrasing and expression.

"Who wants to play catch with me?"

Fluency Sentences

Read this sentence. Remember phrasing and expression.

"Who wants to play catch with me?"

Fluency Sentences

Read this sentence. Remember phrasing and expression.

"Go away!" I screamed to my brother.

Fluency Sentences

Read this sentence. Remember phrasing and expression.

"Go away!" I screamed to my brother.

Fluency Sentences

Read this sentence. Remember phrasing and expression.

I do NOT like snakes!

Fluency Sentences

Read this sentence. Remember phrasing and expression.

I do NOT like snakes!

Fluency Sentences

Read this sentence. Remember phrasing and expression.

Tigers, bears, zebras, camels, and gorillas are a few animals you will see at the zoo.

Fluency Sentences

Read this sentence. Remember phrasing and expression.

Tigers, bears, zebras, camels, and gorillas are a few animals you will see at the zoo.

Fluency Sentences

Quiz-Quiz-Trade

Instructions: Copy enough cards so each student has one card. Cut on dotted lines and fold in half.

Fluency Sentences

Read this sentence. Remember phrasing and expression.

"Hush!" whispered my mom.

Fluency Sentences

Read this sentence. Remember phrasing and expression.

"Hush!" whispered my mom.

Fluency Sentences

Read this sentence. Remember phrasing and expression.

Brrrr, it's cold outside!

Fluency Sentences

Read this sentence. Remember phrasing and expression.

Brrrr, it's cold outside!

Fluency Sentences

Read this sentence. Remember phrasing and expression.

"That clown is so funny!" laughed Molly.

Fluency Sentences

Read this sentence. Remember phrasing and expression.

"That clown is so funny!" laughed Molly.

Fluency Sentences

Read this sentence. Remember phrasing and expression.

Long, long ago, dinosaurs roamed the earth.

Fluency Sentences

Read this sentence. Remember phrasing and expression.

Long, long ago, dinosaurs roamed the earth.

Fluency Sentences

Quiz-Quiz-Trade

Instructions: Copy enough cards so each student has one card. Cut on dotted lines and fold in half.

Fluency Sentences	Fluency Sentences
Read this sentence. Remember phrasing and expression. Have you ever seen a rainbow?	Read this sentence. Remember phrasing and expression. Have you ever seen a rainbow?
Fluency Sentences Read this sentence. Remember phrasing and expression. What? You don't like to read!	**Fluency Sentences** Read this sentence. Remember phrasing and expression. What? You don't like to read!
Fluency Sentences Read this sentence. Remember phrasing and expression. "I'm late! I'm late!" shrieked Anna.	**Fluency Sentences** Read this sentence. Remember phrasing and expression. "I'm late! I'm late!" shrieked Anna.
Fluency Sentences Read this sentence. Remember phrasing and expression. Oh, no! It's raining!	**Fluency Sentences** Read this sentence. Remember phrasing and expression. Oh, no! It's raining!

Fluency Sentences

Quiz-Quiz-Trade

Instructions: Copy enough cards so each student has one card. Cut on dotted lines and fold in half.

Fluency Sentences

Read this sentence. Remember phrasing and expression.

Can you help me look for my book?

Fluency Sentences

Read this sentence. Remember phrasing and expression.

Can you help me look for my book?

Fluency Sentences

Read this sentence. Remember phrasing and expression.

I need eggs, milk, flour, cheese, and butter from the store.

Fluency Sentences

Read this sentence. Remember phrasing and expression.

I need eggs, milk, flour, cheese, and butter from the store.

Fluency Sentences

Read this sentence. Remember phrasing and expression.

"Watch out for that bee!" I screamed to my brother.

Fluency Sentences

Read this sentence. Remember phrasing and expression.

"Watch out for that bee!" I screamed to my brother.

Fluency Sentences

Read this sentence. Remember phrasing and expression.

Thank you for helping me.

Fluency Sentences

Read this sentence. Remember phrasing and expression.

Thank you for helping me.

Fluency Sentences

Quiz-Quiz-Trade

Instructions: Copy enough cards so each student has one card. Cut on dotted lines and fold in half.

Fluency Sentences

Read this sentence. Remember phrasing and expression.

Help! I need help!

Fluency Sentences

Read this sentence. Remember phrasing and expression.

Help! I need help!

Fluency Sentences

Read this sentence. Remember phrasing and expression.

"Where is my pencil?" I asked. "Has anyone seen it?"

Fluency Sentences

Read this sentence. Remember phrasing and expression.

"Where is my pencil?" I asked. "Has anyone seen it?"

Fluency Sentences

Read this sentence. Remember phrasing and expression.

Please bring me a drink of water.

Fluency Sentences

Read this sentence. Remember phrasing and expression.

Please bring me a drink of water.

Fluency Sentences

Read this sentence. Remember phrasing and expression.

"Let's jump rope," suggested Clare to Abby.

Fluency Sentences

Read this sentence. Remember phrasing and expression.

"Let's jump rope," suggested Clare to Abby.

Fluency Sentences

Quiz-Quiz-Trade

Instructions: Copy enough cards so each student has one card. Cut on dotted lines and fold in half.

Fluency Sentences

Read this sentence. Remember phrasing and expression.

Bob looked at Ben and asked, "Have you ever seen such a big dog?"

Fluency Sentences

Read this sentence. Remember phrasing and expression.

Bob looked at Ben and asked, "Have you ever seen such a big dog?"

Fluency Sentences

Read this sentence. Remember phrasing and expression.

My mom would NEVER let me wear that!

Fluency Sentences

Read this sentence. Remember phrasing and expression.

My mom would NEVER let me wear that!

Fluency Sentences

Read this sentence. Remember phrasing and expression.

I can't believe it!

Fluency Sentences

Read this sentence. Remember phrasing and expression.

I can't believe it!

Fluency Sentences

Read this sentence. Remember phrasing and expression.

"I'm so, so sorry!" I told Kate.

Fluency Sentences

Read this sentence. Remember phrasing and expression.

"I'm so, so sorry!" I told Kate.

Fluency Sentences

Quiz-Quiz-Trade

Instructions: Copy enough cards so each student has one card. Cut on dotted lines and fold in half.

Fluency Sentences

Read this sentence. Remember phrasing and expression.

"Mom! Let's go on the roller coaster," begged Hannah.

Fluency Sentences

Read this sentence. Remember phrasing and expression.

"Mom! Let's go on the roller coaster," begged Hannah.

Fluency Sentences

Read this sentence. Remember phrasing and expression.

"No, I don't like merry-go-rounds," stated David. "They make me dizzy."

Fluency Sentences

Read this sentence. Remember phrasing and expression.

"No, I don't like merry-go-rounds," stated David. "They make me dizzy."

Fluency Sentences

Read this sentence. Remember phrasing and expression.

Some spiders spin webs to catch their prey.

Fluency Sentences

Read this sentence. Remember phrasing and expression.

Some spiders spin webs to catch their prey.

Fluency Sentences

Read this sentence. Remember phrasing and expression.

Scott looked sick. "I want to go home," he groaned.

Fluency Sentences

Read this sentence. Remember phrasing and expression.

Scott looked sick. "I want to go home," he groaned.

Comprehension 

Word Study 

Fluency 

Writing 

Writing

Writing

Authors use four main text types to convey meaning in print:

- **Narrative**—to entertain
- **Expository**—to inform
- **Technical**—to tell how to...
- **Persuasive**—to convince

Expository writing is a great starting place for students. Children naturally write in expository form, informing us of what they know or are learning from their experiences. Many states are testing students' proficiency in comprehending expository text, which is often more challenging for students. Therefore, this section focuses on writing an expository piece with the goal of strengthening both expository reading and writing.

Writing and reading are reciprocal processes, each supporting the other. Understanding why and how authors use text features helps students apply these same organizational features in their own writing.

This writing section is organized in sequential lessons that will produce an expository piece of writing through a cooperative group learning process. The goal is for students to apply what they have learned through group work to their individual writing.

Note: The teacher should have his or her own ongoing piece of writing that is used for modeling in each lesson.

Table of Writing Resources

		Balanced Literacy				
Page(s)	Resources	Aloud	Shared	Guided	Independent	Literature Circles
444	Expository Writing Resource Descriptions					
446	Expository Writing Model	●	●	●	●	
447	Expository Writing Steps	●	●	●	●	
448	Six Trait Checklist for Expository Writing	●	●	●	●	
449	Six Trait Question Posters	●	●	●	●	

Table of Writing Activities

	Activities	Blacklines	Balanced Literacy: Aloud	Shared	Guided	Independent	Literature Circles
456	Expository Writing Stages	• Teacher Resource Lesson Guide					
457	**Inside-Outside Circle Activity**						
457	Prewriting Circles	• Prewriting Question Cards	●		●		
459	**Jot Thoughts Activity**						
459	Brainstorming Ideas	• Brainstorming Mat	●			●	
461	**RoundTable Consensus Activity**						
461	Sorting Ideas	• Sorting Mat	●	●	●		
463	**Solo Activity**						
463	Paragraph Writing	• SAMPLE Topic Sentence Form • SAMPLE Detail Sentences Form • Topic Sentence Form • Detail Sentences Form	●			●	
468	**RoundRobin Activities**						
468	Improving Details	• Six Ways to Improve Details • Detail Improvement Form	●	●	●	●	
471	**RallyCoach Activities**						
471	Word Choice Practice	• Word Choice—Powerful Verbs • Word Choice—Powerful Adjectives • Word Choice—Describing Words/Adjectives • Word Choice—Similes	●	●	●	●	

Table of Writing Activities (continued)

Page(s)	Activities	Blacklines	Balanced Literacy: Aloud	Shared	Guided	Independent	Literature Circles
480	**RallyCoach Activity**						
480	Sentence Writing Practice	• Sentence Mechanics • Sentence Mechanics Form	●	●	●	●	
484	**Team Stand-N-Share Activity**						
484	Hooks and Endings	• Hook Examples • Ending Examples • Hook and Ending Form—Sample • Hook and Ending Form	●	●	●	●	
489	**Two-Partner Edit Activity**						
448	Six Trait Feedback	• Six Trait Checklist for Expository Writing			●		
490	**Mix-Pair-Share Activity**						
490	Sharing Final Drafts				●		

Writing Resources

Expository Writing Resources

Writing Resources Descriptions

One key to scaffolding instruction is the inclusion of modeling. **The teacher should have his or her own ongoing piece of writing that is used for modeling in each lesson.** This permits the students to see the skill being used, creates a better understanding of what is expected, and allows for more effective application of the skill.

Expository Writing Model (p. 446)

The hook, fish, and tail graphics are visuals that can be used to increase the students' understanding of the parts of an expository writing piece.

- **Hook** = beginning sentence(s) that engages the reader and makes him or her want to continue reading
- **Fish (Mighty Middle)** = the topic sentences and supporting details that provide the information and facts relating to the topic
- **Tail End** = the ending gives the writing natural closure

Expository Writing Steps (p. 447)

The organization of expository writing is necessary to move the reader through the text: hook, mighty middle, and ending. As you notice, the writer will start with the informational part of the piece first (mighty middle). Once the writer has organized his or her information, the teacher will use focus lessons to help students revise to produce a quality writing piece. The beginning hook comes next. The writer will create a hook that will draw the reader in and make him or her want to continue reading. Because the writer has already written the mighty middle and knows the information he or she is presenting to the reader, it will be easier for him or her to write an appropriate hook. The tail end comes last. The purpose of the ending is to bring the writing to a satisfying closure, tying up loose ends for the reader.

Writing Resources Descriptions (continued)

Six Trait Checklist for Expository Writing (p. 448)

Ideas, organization, voice, word choice, sentence fluency, and conventions are six trait writing components used to evaluate the student's writing performance. In this section, a six trait checklist is provided to increase student awareness of qualities that make up each component. After students complete their writing, the students can evaluate their writing by placing an "X" on the line indicating the qualities used in their writing. This visual will help students realize which areas they need to work on for improvement. Once the students have experience self-evaluating and have a clear understanding of the characteristics that make up each trait, the teacher can move students from a checklist to a rubric.

Six Trait Question Posters (p. 449)

The six traits, and easy-to-understand questions that reinforce each trait, have been made into posters that can be used for classroom wall displays, overhead transparencies, and/or individually held up next to the teacher's enlarged writing text. During this shared writing time, the students can focus their attention on the teacher as she or he answers the questions, revises, and evaluates the writing piece. The individual posters allow the teacher to scaffold the instruction by concentrating on one or two traits at a time. Students will soon understand that answering "yes" to the questions given for each trait will not only strengthen the writer's skill, but will also increase the reader's engagement as he or she reads the piece.

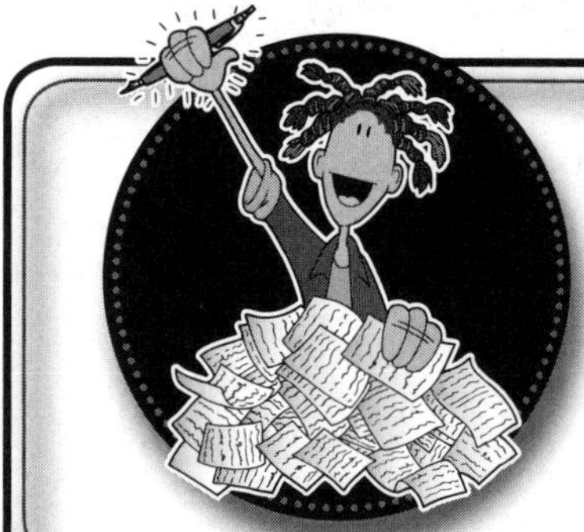

Expository Writing Model

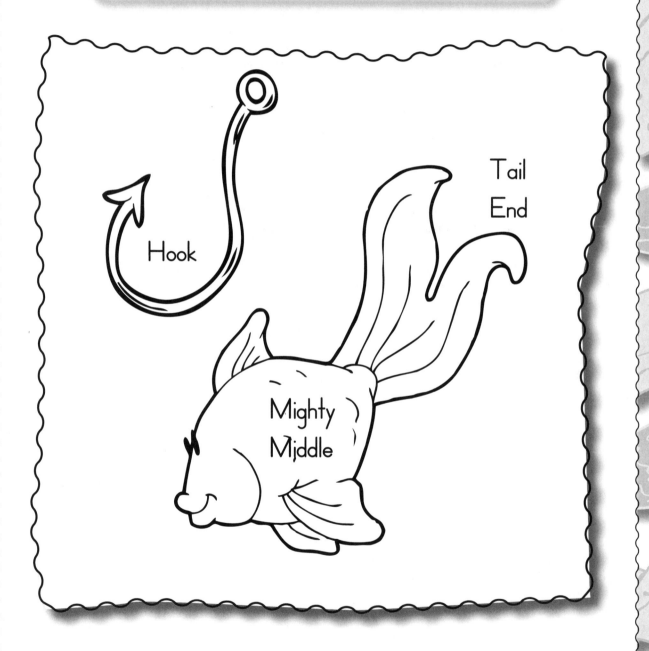

Hook

Tail
End

Mighty
Middle

Expository Writing Steps

Hook

Mighty Middle

Ending

Finished Writing Piece

1. Mighty Middle

- The "Mighty Middle" is the action of the writing.
- Students should begin their writing piece at the action. This will help keep their topic narrowed.
- Focus lessons will be added after the students have their "Mighty Middle" draft completed.

2. Hook

- Hook the readers with a statement or two that will make them want to continue reading: use a question, bold words, quotation, expression, riddle, etc.

3. Ending (Tail)

- The ending will restate, answer, or relate to the beginning hook, giving natural closure to the writing piece.

Six Trait CheckList for Expository Writing

Name______________________________ **Date**____________________

Instructions: The teacher determines how many of the six traits to evaluate. The student and/or teacher can evaluate a piece of writing by placing an '*X*' on each line, indicating the skill(s) being used to strengthen each trait. Copy for each student.

Ideas

Will the reader learn something new?
☐ YES ☐ NO

Do I have enough information?
☐ YES ☐ NO

Does it all make sense?
☐ YES ☐ NO

Organization

Does my beginning 'hook' the reader?
☐ YES ☐ NO

Is my paper easy to follow?
☐ YES ☐ NO

Does the ending wrap up the paper?
☐ YES ☐ NO

Voice

Does the writing sound like me?
☐ YES ☐ NO

Can the reader tell that I care about the topic?
☐ YES ☐ NO

Will the reader want to read more?
☐ YES ☐ NO

Word Choice

Do my words help the reader visualize?
☐ YES ☐ NO

Did I use interesting/powerful words?
☐ YES ☐ NO

Did I use NEW words?
☐ YES ☐ NO

Sentence Fluency

Is my writing easy to read?
☐ YES ☐ NO

Do my sentences begin in different ways?
☐ YES ☐ NO

Did I use some long and some short sentences?
☐ YES ☐ NO

Conventions

Did I leave spaces between words?
☐ YES ☐ NO

Did I use periods and question marks in the right places?
☐ YES ☐ NO

Did I use capital letters correctly?
☐ YES ☐ NO

Did I spell word wall words correctly?
☐ YES ☐ NO

Six Trait Question Posters

Ideas

Adapted from Six Trait Writing Model: NWREL (Northwest Regional Educational Lab)

Ideas

Will the reader learn something new?

☐ YES ☐ NO

Do I have enough information?

☐ YES ☐ NO

Does it all make sense?

☐ YES ☐ NO

Six Trait Question Posters

Organization

Adapted from Six Trait Writing Model: NWREL (Northwest Regional Educational Lab)

Organization

Does my beginning "hook" the reader?

☐ YES ☐ NO

Is my paper easy to follow?

☐ YES ☐ NO

Does the ending wrap up the paper?

☐ YES ☐ NO

Six Trait Question Posters

Voice

Adapted from Six Trait Writing Model: NWREL (Northwest Regional Educational Lab)

Voice

Does the writing sound like me?

☐ YES ☐ NO

Can the reader tell that I care about the topic?

☐ YES ☐ NO

Will the reader want to read more?

☐ YES ☐ NO

Six Trait Question Posters

Word Choice

Adapted from Six Trait Writing Model: NWREL (Northwest Regional Educational Lab)

Word Choice

Do my words help the reader visualize?

☐ YES ☐ NO

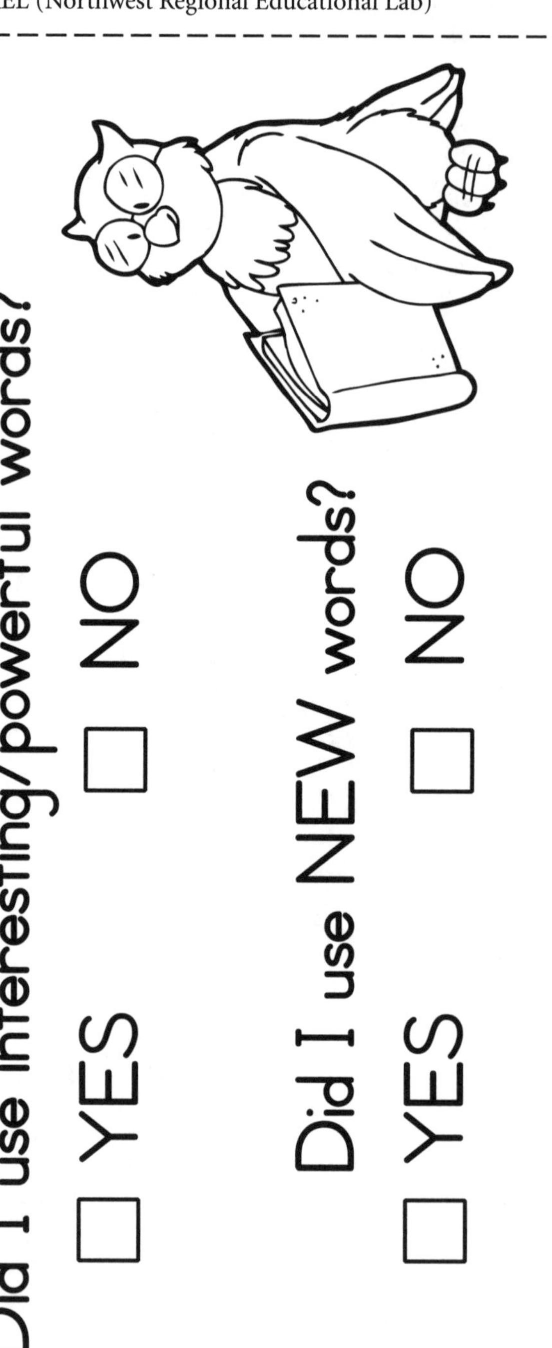

Did I use interesting/powerful words?

☐ YES ☐ NO

Did I use NEW words?

☐ YES ☐ NO

Six Trait Question Posters

Sentence Fluency

Adapted from Six Trait Writing Model: NWREL (Northwest Regional Educational Lab)

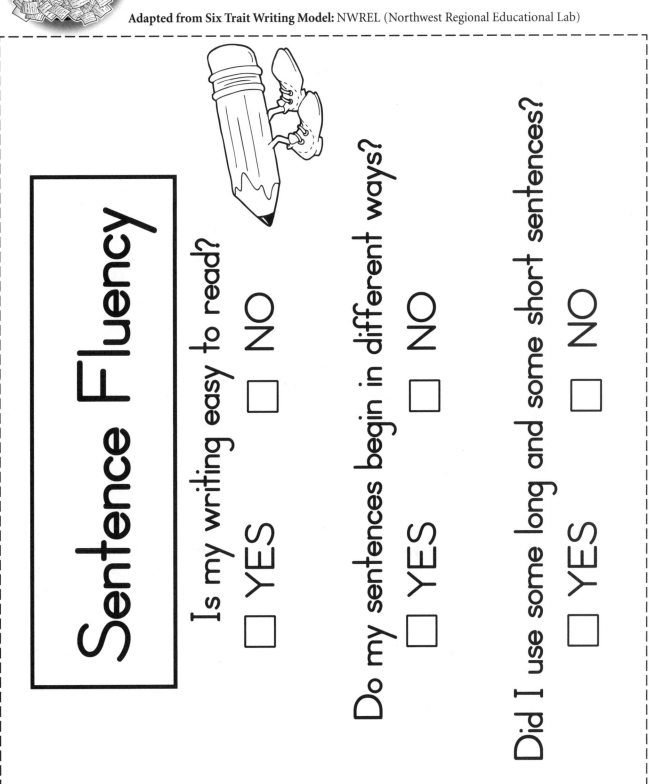

Sentence Fluency

Is my writing easy to read?

☐ YES ☐ NO

Do my sentences begin in different ways?

☐ YES ☐ NO

Did I use some long and some short sentences?

☐ YES ☐ NO

Six Trait Question Posters

Conventions

Adapted from Six Trait Writing Model: NWREL (Northwest Regional Educational Lab)

Conventions

Did I leave spaces between words?

☐ YES ☐ NO

Did I use periods and question marks in the right places?

☐ YES ☐ NO

Did I use capital letters correctly?

☐ YES ☐ NO

Did I spell word wall words correctly?

☐ YES ☐ NO

Writing Activities

Resource Lesson Guide

The following writing activities are sequenced to take students through the stages of writing an expository piece. The first time through this process, each team will be researching, brainstorming, and sorting information on the same topic. Individually, they will be writing sentences and paragraphs for their own writing piece. After students are familiar with the structures, they will be prepared to follow the same guided format with individual topics.

Prewriting (pp. 457–462)

- **Prewriting Circles**—Students ask partners prewriting questions to focus them on their writing topic.
- **Brainstorming Ideas**—Students brainstorm ideas related to their writing topic.
- **Sorting Ideas**—Students sort ideas into categories that will be developed into complete sentences.

Writing (p. 463–467)

- **Paragraph Writing**—Students develop their ideas into a topic sentence and supporting detail sentences.

Editing & Rewriting (pp. 468–488)

- **Improving Details**—Students learn six ways to improve their detail sentences and then work to improve their own detail sentences.
- **Word Choice Practice**—Students practice word choice and then work to improve the word choice in their expository writing.
- **Sentence Writing Practice**—Students practice rewriting sentences for mechanics and fluency.
- **Hooks and Endings**—Students write beginning hooks and endings to their expository writing pieces.

Peer Feedback (p. 489)

- **Six Trait Feedback**—Students get feedback from peers, focusing on the six traits.

Sharing (p. 490)

- **Sharing Final Drafts**—Students share their final drafts with peers as an audience.

PREWRITING

Activity

Prewriting Circles

The amount of writing that students produce is in proportion to the amount of talking and processing that they get to do before they write. In this activity, students form two concentric circles so that pairs face each other. Using the questions provided, students ask their partner a question. The circles rotate multiple times so students share with multiple partners. This activity helps students focus on their topic, expand their writing ideas, and write in complete sentences. Prior to this activity the teacher decides if the whole class will have the same topic or if each team will have a different topic.

STRUCTURE

Inside-Outside Circle

Activity Steps

1. Time is given to choose a topic and read about the topic.
2. Students form pairs and each student is given one Prewriting Question Card.
3. One student from each pair moves to form one large circle.
4. Remaining students find and face their partners. (The class now stands in two concentric circles.)
5. The Inside Circle students ask the Outside Circle students the question on their question card. The Outside Circle students respond.
6. Partners switch roles: Outside Circle students ask the questions and Inside Circle students respond.
7. Students trade cards, then the Inside Circle students rotate clockwise to face a new partner to ask and answer a new prewriting question.

Blackline

Prewriting Question Cards

Inside-Outside Circle

Instructions: Make enough copies of this blackline so that each student has one card. Cut out the question cards and give each student one card. Students use cards to ask partners prewriting questions during Inside-Outside Circle.

Prewriting Questions	Prewriting Questions	Prewriting Questions
What topic are you planning to write about?	What do you already know about this topic?	What questions do you still have about this topic?

Prewriting Questions	Prewriting Questions	Prewriting Questions
What is the most important idea to get across to your readers?	Where could you find more information about this topic?	What will readers find interesting about this topic?

Prewriting Questions	Prewriting Questions	Prewriting Questions
What does this topic remind you of?	If you could add a photograph to your writing about this topic, what would it be?	What information about this topic will you not include in your writing?

Prewriting Questions	Prewriting Questions	Prewriting Questions
How can you present the topic so that it is not boring to read?	What words do you want to include in your writing about this topic?	What would be a good title for your writing? Why?

Brainstorming Ideas

Students brainstorm in teams using Jot Thoughts. They write one word, phrase, or sentence about their topic, read it aloud to the team, then place the idea on a mat with the topic in the center of the table. This process frees students' minds to generate information without worrying about organization. Creative and varied responses are encouraged as students read their ideas aloud to spark additional ideas.

STRUCTURE

Jot Thoughts

Activity Steps

1. Each team gets a Brainstorming Mat. They write the writing topic in the center of the mat. Students each have sticky notes and a pen.
2. Students write the ideas that come to mind on the sticky note, and place it on the mat. They announce their idea to the team.
3. The team tries to completely cover the mat with ideas about the topic.

Sample Brainstorming Mat

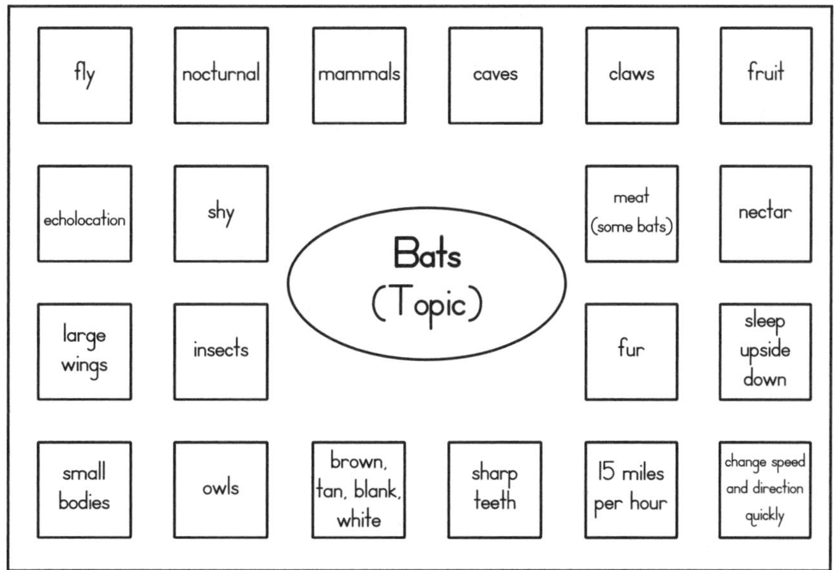

BlacKline

Brainstorming Mat

Jot Thoughts

Instructions: Write your writing topic in the center of this mat. As a team, brainstorm ideas relating to the topic on sticky notes and place them on the mat. Announce your idea to teammates as you place it on the mat. (Make one copy per team.)

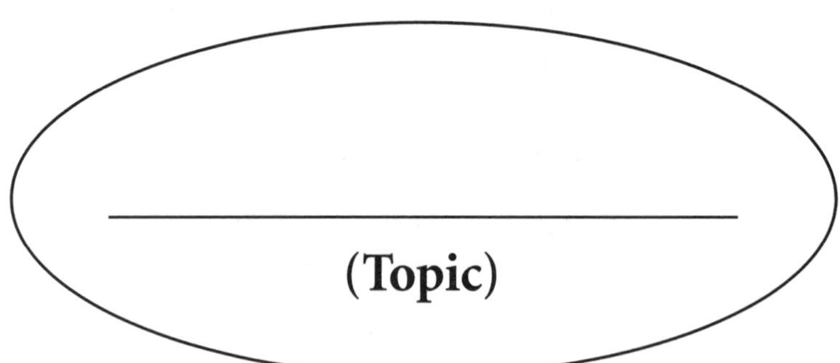

Sorting Ideas

After students have generated numerous ideas relating to the topic, they use RoundTable Consensus to physically sort the ideas into categories on a sorting mat. The concrete aids help students organize expository information into groups that are later developed into paragraphs.

STRUCTURE

RoundTable Consensus

Activity Steps

1. Each team gets a Sorting Mat and their ideas generated from the previous activity.
2. The first student selects a sticky note, places the note on the Sorting Mat, and announces the possible category or reason for sorting.
3. Teammates show agreement or lack of agreement with thumbs up or thumbs down.
4. If there is agreement, the team celebrates and the next student places the next idea on the sorting mat. If there is not consensus, students discuss the idea until they reach agreement.
5. When all items are sorted, students take turns labeling each category, checking for consensus before writing.

Appearance	Locomotion
large wings; fur; sharp teeth; small bodies; brown, tan, blank, white	fly; echolocation; 15 miles per hour; change speed and direction quickly
Diet	________
insects; fruit; nectar; meat (some bats)	

Sample Sorting Mat

BlacKline

Sorting Mat

RoundTable Consensus

Instructions: Students take turns sorting ideas into like categories. Once all ideas are sorted, students label categories. Make one copy per team.

WRITING

Activity

Paragraph Writing

Now that students have their ideas sorted into categories, they are ready to develop each category into a paragraph. To do this, they independently write the topic sentence of a paragraph, followed by supporting detail sentences.

STRUCTURE

Solo

Activity Steps

1. Copy the Topic Sentence Form on light-colored paper and the Detail Sentences Form on a different light-colored paper. Give both sheets to each student.
2. Using the Sample Topic Sentence Form, model for students how to fill out their Topic Sentence Form.
3. Students complete their Topic Sentence Form by writing the 1) Topic, 2) Question, and 3) Topic Sentence. Then, they cut out the topic sentence for later use.
4. Next, model for students how to turn an idea into a complete written sentence using the Sample Detail Sentences Form.
5. Students select three individual sticky notes and write them as three complete detail sentences on the form.
6. Students cut the three detail sentences apart and select their favorite sequence. Then, they tape the sentences together in the preferred sequence, and tape the topic sentence on top.

BlacKlines

SAMPLE
Topic Sentence Form

Instructions: Use this form to model how to develop a topic sentence.

Topic

Appearance

Question

What does a bat look like?

Topic Sentence

Bats are mammals with brown, black, tan or white furry bodies.

SAMPLE
Detail Sentences Form

Instructions: Use this form to model how to develop detail sentences.

#1 The body of the largest bat is half the size of a cat. The body of the smallest bat is the size of a jelly bean.

(Example of Comparison)

#2 Bats have two large wings. They are made of long arm bones and five finger bones with skin stretched between.

2nd finger
thumb (1st finger)
3rd finger
4th finger
5th finger
wing

(Example of Text Feature Diagram)

#3 Bats have sharp teeth. Their teeth can crunch the bones of fish, frogs, and mice.

Topic Sentence Form

Instructions: Write your paragraph topic in the box below. Then write the topic as a question. Then write the question as a topic sentence. Cut out your topic sentence. (Make one copy per student.)

Topic

____

Question

____

____

____

Topic Sentence

____

____

____

____

Detail Sentences Form

Instructions: Write a detail sentence in each box below. Cut them out, then sequence them in the best order. Number the sentences in order from 1–3. Tape them together in the sequence you like. Then, tape your Topic Sentence (page 466) on top. (Make one copy per student.)

#______

#______

#______

Improving Details

Students have each written a paragraph about the topic. Now, their task is to improve their paragraphs by adding details to text. The teacher models how to improve details. Students work independently to add details and share their improvements with teammates.

Activity Steps

1. Using the Six Ways to Improve Details form, share with students the various ways they can improve their writing.
2. Students select one detail sentence they have written. They select which of the six methods they plan to use to improve the information. The Detail Improvement Form on page 470 is used to record the improvements.
3. Students then share the new and improved sentence with teammates.
4. Teammates hold up 1–6 fingers to guess which idea for improvement their teammate used. The student informs the team which method he or she used and congratulates students who guessed correctly.
5. They repeat the process for the other two sentences, choosing different ways to improve their other sentences.
6. If improvements were made, revise the writing on the original detail sentence form or cut and tape the detail improvement form sentences on top of the originals.

STRUCTURE

RoundRobin

Blacklines

Six Ways to Improve Details

Instructions: Use this form to share with students six ways to write and improve detail sentences.

Comparison

A bat's wings are very different from a bird's wings.

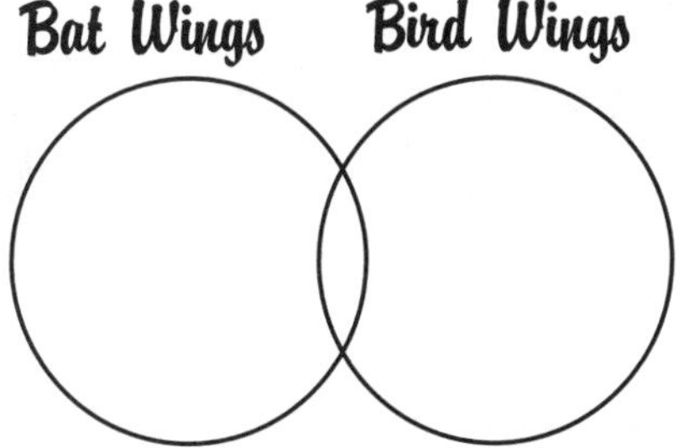

Personal Experience

Once we had bats in our attic. They got in through a broken window. I saw them hanging upside down when they were sleeping.

Number Word

Some bats can fly **15** miles per hour. They can also fly as high as **10,000** feet.

Description

When a mother bat gives birth, she has her head up and hangs by her thumb claws. She makes a basket with her tail, and the new-born bat pup slides from her body into the basket. Then the mother bat hangs her head down again.

Text Feature

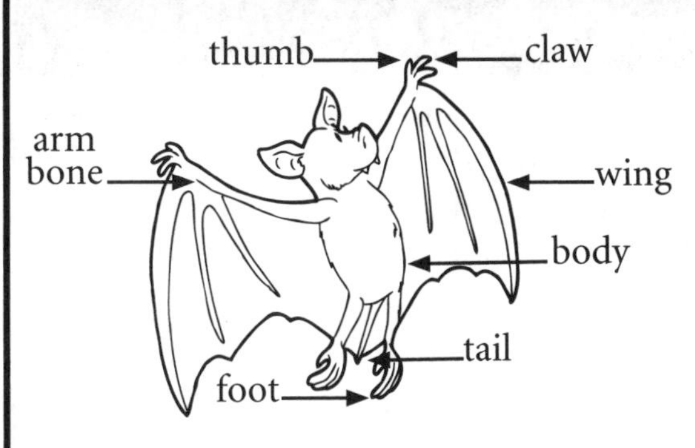

Specific Name or Example

There are many different kinds of bats. Kitti's Hog-Nosed Bat is the smallest bat. The Giant Flying Fox Bat is the largest bat.

Detail Improvement Form

Instructions: Rewrite your three detail sentences below. For each sentence, pick one of the 6 ideas for improvement. Write the idea for improvement number in the circle. If needed, use the box to add text features. Share one sentence at a time with teammates and see if they can pick which idea for improvement you used.

6 Ways to Improve My Sentences

1. **Comparison**
2. **Personal Experience**
3. **Number Word**
4. **Description**
5. **Text Feature** (graph, diagram, chart, definition, picture)
6. **Specific Name or Example**

Detail Sentence #1

Detail Sentence #2

Detail Sentence #3

Word Choice Practice

Partners continue to improve their writing by adding descriptive language to engage the reader. Students brainstorm and share word choice ideas. Blacklines are included to practice verb choice, adjective choice, description, and similes. Students return to their writing to revise after each word choice activity.

STRUCTURE
RallyCoach

Activity Steps

1. Each pair receives a mat and a set of word cards. They place the word cards facedown between them.
2. Partner A turns over the first card and reads it aloud. He or she then places the card on the correct heading on the sorting mat.
3. Partner B is the coach. The coach makes suggestions.
4. Partners switch roles.

Blacklines

Word Choice Powerful Verbs

RallyCoach

Instructions: Sort the powerful verbs into the correct columns according to their meanings.

walk	talk	look

Word Choice
Powerful Verbs

Instructions: Give each team one copy of this Blackline. Students cut out the word cards and sort them in columns according to their meanings.

stroll	march	roam
glare	hike	view
remark	watch	parade
skip	reply	report
exclaim	jabber	ask
shuffle	gaze	march
strut	state	examine
stare	explain	mutter
admire	demand	travel
hop	observe	spy
sight	whisper	spot
call	search	pace

Word Choice
Powerful Adjectives

RallyCoach

Instructions: Sort the powerful adjectives (describing words) into the correct columns according to their meanings.

little	happy	big

Word Choice
Powerful Adjectives

Instructions: Give each team one copy of this Blackline. Students cut out the word cards and sort them in columns according to their meanings.

teeny	huge	massive
glad	content	petite
lively	small	thrilled
microscopic	merry	towering
minute	narrow	miniature
enormous	cheery	mammoth
immense	grand	pleased
joyful	wee	lofty
cheerful	soaring	jolly
tiny	compact	high

Word Choice
Describing Words/Adjectives

RallyCoach

Instructions: Sort the describing words/adjectives into the correct columns.

_____cat	_____butterfly	_____rain

Word Choice
Describing Words/Adjectives

RallyCoach

Instructions: Give each team one copy of this Blackline. Students cut out the word cards and sort them in columns according to the nouns they might describe.

flashy	hovering	hungry
fluttering	clawing	glittering
calico	pelting	meowing
darting	symmetrical	light
drizzling	shimmering	graceful
gliding	pouring	licking
striped	sprinkling	colorful
cold	purring	delicate
pouncing	changing	floating
napping	stormy	hissing
freezing	winged	gushing
flying	curious	gentle
heavy	glistening	sudden
multicolored	cuddly	lazy
sleepy	sparkling	falling

Word Choice Similes

RallyCoach

Instructions: Sort the word cards into columns to make appropriate similes.

slow as______	hot as______	soft as______

Word Choice Similes

RallyCoach

Instructions: Give each team one copy of this Blackline. Students cut out the word cards and sort them in columns to make appropriate similes.

a turtle	a baby chick	a burning fire
a puffy cloud	a sidewalk in summer	a teddy bear
an oven	a cup of coffee	a dripping faucet
syrup	a red hot stove	a fuzzy blanket
a freshly baked cookie	a cotton ball	a bowl of soup
a sizzling skillet	a melting ice cube	a line in a store
a kitten	a rabbit's fur	a buggy
molasses	a snail	the sun
baby's skin	a campfire	a sweater
a pillow	a traffic light	a boring day

EDITING & REWRITING

Activity

Sentence Writing Practice

Partners practice correcting sentences in pairs. Blacklines are provided to practice sentence mechanics. A form is provided for the teacher to create additional practice sentences. Students return to their writing to revise as needed.

Activity Steps

STRUCTURE

RallyCoach

1. Each pair receives a set of sentence strips. They place the sentence strips facedown between them.
2. Partner A turns over the first sentence strip and reads it aloud. He or she then makes one correction and explains why the correction was made.
3. Partner B is the coach. The coach makes a suggestion or agrees.
4. Using the same sentence strip, Partner B makes another correction and explains why the correction was made while Partner A coaches.
5. Partners continue passing the sentence strip back and forth until all corrections are made.
6. Repeat process with new sentence strip.

BlacKlines

Sentence Mechanics

RallyCoach

Instructions: Cut out sentence strips. Partner A reads one sentence strip and makes one correction and explains why. Partner B offers suggestions or agrees. Using the same sentence strip, Partner B makes another correction and explains why. Partners continue passing the sentence strip back and forth until all corrections are made. Repeat process with new sentence strip.

Sentence Mechanics

1. have you ever been to africa

Sentence Mechanics

2. it often rains in april

Sentence Mechanics

3. zoey is going swimming on friday

Sentence Mechanics

4. mr field is a new teacher at south creek elementary school

Sentence Mechanics

5. on Thursday sam bought shoes socks pants and a shirt at the midtown mall

Sentence Mechanics

6. debs birthday is october 3

Sentence Mechanics

7. mrs fish went to the beach to study seashells crabs and seaweed

Sentence Mechanics

RallyCoach

Instructions: Cut out sentence strips. Place them facedown between you and your partner. Partner A turns over the first one, reads it, and describes how to rewrite the sentence. Partner B offers suggestions or agrees. Partner A then rewrites the sentence. Switch roles for each sentence strip.

Sentence Mechanics

8. my address is 987 cole street in topeka kansas

Sentence Mechanics

9. on thanksgiving day connie baked a huge turkey to share with her family from hill city

Sentence Mechanics

10. jed steve kevin and mike watched the football game at the mountain stadium

Sentence Mechanics

11. we will look for a recipe book mystery book and informational book at bobs book store

Sentence Mechanics

12. miss ann t gregg and mrs pam s stevens will sing a duet at memorial concert hall

Sentence Mechanics

13. mike's dog buddy practiced catching a ball

Sentence Mechanics

14. where did you put the craft materials alex bought on tuesday

Sentence Mechanics Form

Instructions: Use this Blackline to create your own sentence strips for partners to practice correcting.

Sentence Mechanics

Sentence Mechanics

Sentence Mechanics

Sentence Mechanics

Sentence Mechanics

Sentence Mechanics

Sentence Mechanics

EDITING & REWRITING

Activity

Hooks and Endings

Students learn to write paragraph openers to "hook" the reader and endings to give the writing a natural closure. Teams investigate other writing samples and share what hooks and endings writers use.

Activity Steps

1. Students look through expository magazines, such as *National Geographic Kids* and *Ranger Rick*, noticing different ways authors begin articles.
2. Using RoundTable, the team generates a list of hooks.
3. After teams have enough time to collect multiple ideas, the teacher asks the class to stand.
4. The teacher calls on a standing student.
5. The selected student states one idea from the team list.
6. The student in each team who is holding the team list either adds the item to the list, or if it is already listed, checks it off. The teacher also makes a master list of student ideas.
7. Teammates pass their team list one teammate clockwise.
8. Teams sit when all their items are shared. While seated they add each new item as it is stated using RoundTable. When all teams are seated, Team Stand-N-Share is complete.
9. The teacher may use the Hook Examples blackline to share additional hook ideas.
10. Students repeat the process examining and sharing ending ideas.
11. Finally, students use the Hook & Ending Form to write a new hook and ending for their paper.
12. Students cut apart and tape their hook and ending to the beginning and end of their writing.

STRUCTURE

Team Stand-N-Share

Blacklines

Hook Examples

Instructions: Use this form to share effective writing hooks with students.

- **Question**
  Have you ever walked into a cave or barn and had a bat fly at you?
- **Riddle**
  I am furry, small, warm-blooded, and can fly. What am I?
- **Exclamation**
  It's a bird. It's a plane. It's Superman . . . NO, it's a B-A-T!
- **Onomatopoeia**
  E-e-e-e! The squeaking of a bat bounces off the cave wall.
- **Alliteration**
  Swooping . . . Swishing . . . Swerving . . . Bats fly . . . .
- **Exaggeration**
  I stepped into the dark, abandoned barn when a million flapping wings came toward my head.
- **Description**
  I thought I was alone. I was exploring a damp, dark cave, when the beam of my flashlight shone on hundreds of tiny, furry bodies hanging upside down from the cave ceiling.

Ending Examples

Instructions: Use this form to share effective writing endings with students.

- **Answer to Beginning Question**
  So the next time you walk into a cave or old barn, you may see a real, live bat.

- **Reference Back to Riddle**
  So now you know the answer to my riddle. A BAT is a furry, small, warm-blooded mammal that can fly.

- **Generalization**
  Bats are unusual and interesting mammals.

- **Personal Comment**
  I find bats scary, but fascinating.

- **Restatement of Main Idea**
  So after reading, "All About Bats," it's easy to tell why they are mammals.

- **Challenge to the Reader**
  Be sure to check out the library for more information on this extremely interesting animal.

Hook & Ending Form Sample

Instructions: Use this form to write a new hook and ending.

Type of Hook Onomatopoeia

Hook

Bats dive, swoop, and swerve through the dark night sky.

(Example of Onomatopoeia)

Middle

Type of Ending Challenge to the reader

Ending

Be on the lookout! You may actually be lucky enough to see a small flying mammal swishing through the sky the next time you are out at night.

(Example of a Challenge)

Hook & Ending Form

Instructions: Use this form to write a new hook and ending.

Type of Hook ______________________________

Hook

____

____

____

____

____

Middle

Type of Ending ______________________________

Ending

____

____

____

____

____

PEER FEEDBACK
Activity

Six Trait Feedback

Students share their writing with peers and receive feedback on six specific traits of their writing.

STRUCTURE
Two-Partner Edit

Activity Steps

1. Using their taped drafts, students stand up, put a hand up, and pair up with a classmate.
2. The pair sits down at a table, each with their Six Trait Checklist (page 448).
3. Partner A reads his or her writing.
4. Partner B provides feedback on one of the six traits by reading each statement under the trait, discussing it, and marking "Yes" or "No" by the statement.
5. Students switch roles and Partner A provides feedback to partner B.
6. Students thank each other and then pair up with another partner to examine the next trait. The process continues for six pairings, each focusing on a different trait.
7. After receiving feedback, students revise and write a final draft.

Blacklines

SHARING
Activity

Sharing Final Drafts

Students pair with classmates to share their writing and receive feedback.

Activity Steps

1. Each student takes his or her final draft, stands up, puts a hand up, and mixes in the classroom.
2. The teacher calls, "Pair."
3. Students pair up with the person closest to them, who is not from their team, and give a high five.
4. Students take turns sharing their expository writing pieces by reading them to their partners using RallyRobin. Students provide feedback to their partners. The feedback can be:
    - Open-ended reactions
    - Praise
    - Response to a provided gambit: "From your writing, I learned…"
    - Copycat gambit: Students repeat after the teacher a flattering phrase such as "Your expository writing was well written and tremendously informative!"
5. Students can do multiple rounds of peer sharing.

STRUCTURE
Mix-Pair-Share

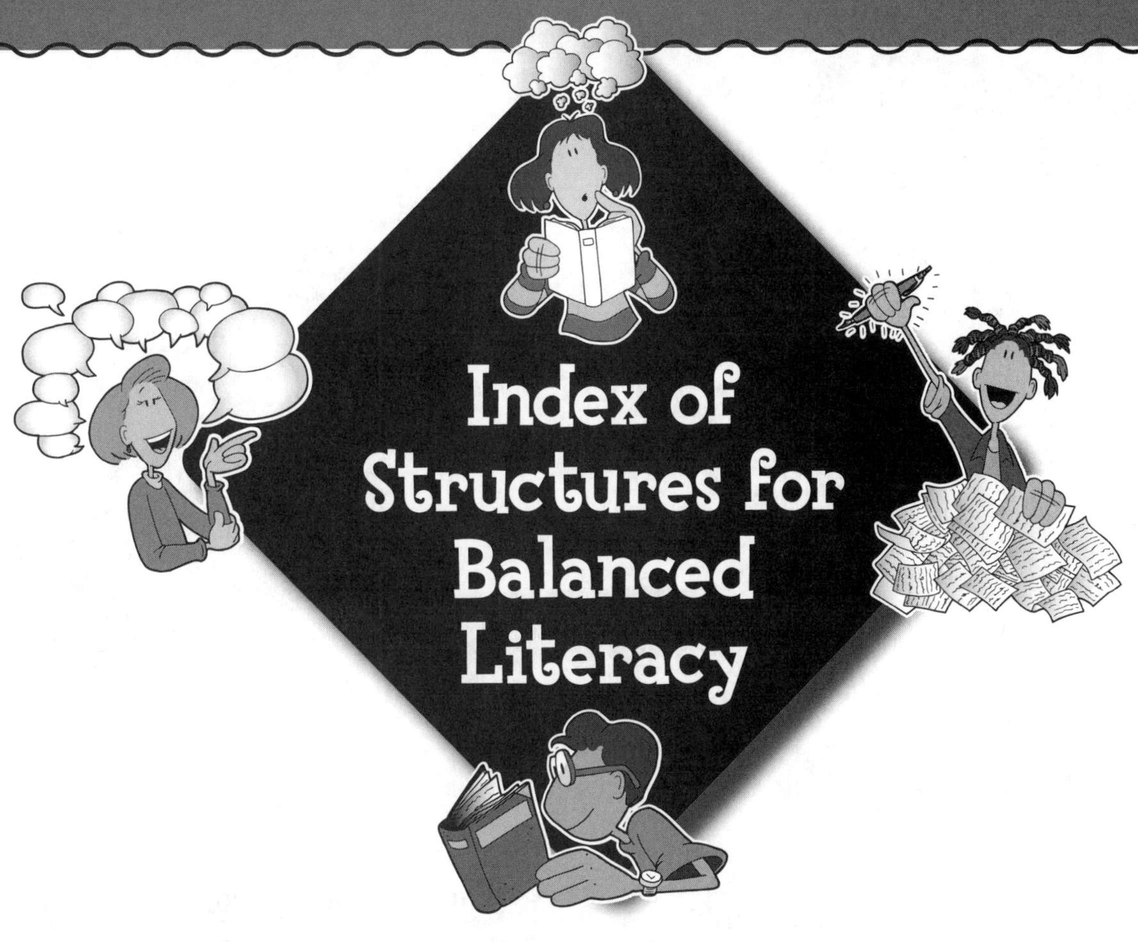

Structure — **Page(s)**

Structure

Fan-N-Pick

Teammates play a card game to respond to questions. Roles rotate with each new question.

Setup

- *Each team receives a set of question cards.*

Steps

1. Student #1 holds question cards in a fan and says, "Pick a card, any card!"
2. Student #2 picks a card, reads the question aloud, and allows five seconds of think time.
3. Student #3 answers the question.
4. Student #4 responds to the answer:
   - For right or wrong answers, Student #4 checks and then either praises or tutors.
   - For questions that have no right or wrong answer, Student #4 does not check for correctness, but praises and paraphrases the thinking that went into the answer.
5. Students rotate roles, one person clockwise for each new round.

Fan-N-Pick Activities and Blacklines

Structure

Find My Rule

Students induce a rule from examples provided by the teacher.

Steps

1. Teacher places one item in each area of the category frame.
2. Teacher asks, "What is my rule for placing items?" and provides think time.
3. Students RallyRobin with their shoulder partners to generate possible rules the teacher is using.
4. Teacher places two more objects in the category frame.
5. Teacher again says, "What is my rule?" and provides think time.
6. Students RallyRobin with their face partners to generate possible rules.
7. Teacher places more objects in the category frame, each time having teams discuss possible rules.
8. Teacher says, "Don't tell me your rule, instead name an item that fits in each category," and calls a number. Students with that number stand to share their items. The teacher confirms correct answers.
9. When most students seem to know the rule, the teacher calls on one student to verbalize the rule for the class.
10. Teacher confirms the rule.
11. Teacher presents new items one at a time, each time calling for students to hold up fingers indicating the category for the item.
12. Teacher congratulates the class.

Find My Rule Activities and Blacklines

Structure

Find Someone Who

Students circulate through the classroom, forming and reforming pairs, trying to "find someone who" knows an answer, then they become "someone who knows."

Setup

- *The teacher prepares a worksheet or questions for students.*

Steps

1. Students mix in the class, keeping a hand raised until they find a new partner that is not a teammate.
2. In pairs, Partner A asks a question from the worksheet; Partner B responds. Partner A records the answer on his or her own worksheet and expresses appreciation.
3. Partner B checks and initials the answer.
4. Partner B asks a question. Partner A responds. Partner B records the answer on his or her own worksheet and expresses appreciation.
5. Partner A checks and initials the answer.
6. Partners shake hands, part, and raise a hand again as they search for a new partner.
7. Students repeat Steps 1–6 until their worksheets are complete.
8. When their worksheets are complete, students sit down. Seated students may be approached by others as a resource.
9. In teams, students compare answers. If there is disagreement or uncertainty, they raise four hands to ask a team question.

Find Someone Who Activities and BlacKlines

Structure

Inside-Outside Circle

Students rotate in concentric circles to face new partners for sharing, quizzing, or problem solving.

Setup

- *The teacher prepares questions or provides a question card for each student.*

Steps

Note: When played with cards, Steps 3–6 are Quiz-Quiz-Trade.

1. Students form pairs. One student from each pair moves to form one large circle in the class facing outward.
2. Remaining students find and face their partners (class now stands in two concentric circles).
3. Inside circle students ask a question from their question card; outside circle students answer. Inside circle students praise or coach. (Alternative: The teacher asks a question and indicates inside or outside student to answer to their partner).
4. Partners switch roles: Outside circle students ask, listen, then praise or coach.
5. Partners trade question cards.
6. Inside circle students rotate clockwise to a new partner. (The teacher may call rotation numbers: "Rotate Three Ahead." The class may do a "choral count" as they rotate).

Variation: Inside-Outside Line. Students stand in two straight lines facing each other. One line rotates, and the other remains in place. Rotating students rotate to a new partner and rotate to the back of their line when they pass the last student in the fixed line.

Inside-Outside Circle Activity and Blacklines

Structure

Jot Thoughts

Teammates "cover the table," writing ideas on slips of paper.

Setup

- *Students each have multiple slips of paper (e.g., pre-cut sticky notes, cut-up bond paper).*

Steps

1. Teacher names a topic, sets a time limit, and provides think time (e.g., In three minutes, how many questions can you write that have the answer 17? What are ways we could reduce poverty?).
2. Students write and announce as many ideas as they can in the allotted time, one idea per slip of paper.
3. Each slip of paper is placed in the center of the table; students attempt to "cover the table" (no slips are to overlap).

Jot Thoughts Activities and Blacklines

Structure

Listen-Sketch-Draft

Students sketch content chunk by chunk, create and compare summaries, and finally draft a statement of the main idea.

Steps

1. Students listen while teacher presents the first chunk of information.
2. Teacher stops presenting and calls for each student to sketch the most important details.
3. Students share sketches using:
   - RoundRobin
   - Timed Pair Share
4. Students draft a main idea statement, based on the information shared in Step 1. While students draft their main idea, teacher circulates and monitors.
5. The process is repeated for the next chunk.
6. When all chunks have been presented, students draft a summary statement.
7. Students compare their summaries with a partner or teammates praising ideas.

Listen-Sketch-Draft Activity and BlackLines

Structure

Mix-Pair-Share

The class "mixes" until teacher calls, "pair." Students find a new partner to discuss or answer the teacher's questions.

Setup

- *Teacher prepares questions to ask students.*

Steps

Hint: For oral lists (Name animals that live in the rain forest.), use RallyRobin. For longer in-depth responses (How do you think we can save the rain forest?), use Timed Pair Share.

1. Students mix around the room.
2. Teacher calls, "Pair."
3. Students pair up with the person closest them and give a high five. Students who haven't found a partner raise their hands to find each other.
4. Teacher asks a question and gives think time.
5. Students share with their partners using:
    - Timed Pair Share
    - RallyRobin

Optional: Students may practice greetings or affirmations during Step 1.

Mix-Pair-Share Activity

Structure

Numbered Heads Together

Teammates put their "heads together" to reach consensus on the team's answer. Everyone keeps on their toes because their number may be called to share the team's answer.

Setup

- *Teacher prepares questions or problems to ask teams.*

Steps

1. Students number off.
2. Teacher poses a problem and gives think time. (Example: How are rainbows formed? Think about your best answer.")
3. Students privately write their answers.
4. Students stand up and "put their heads together," showing answers, discussing, and teaching each other.
5. Students sit down when everyone knows the answer or has something to share.
6. Teacher calls a number. Students with that number answer simultaneously using:
   - AnswerBoard Share
   - Chalkboard Responses
   - Choral Practice
   - Response Cards
   - Finger Responses
   - Manipulatives
7. Classmates applaud students who responded.

Variations:

Paired Heads Together. Students are in shoulder partner pairs. After teacher asks a question, pairs huddle to improve the answers they have each written. Teacher then calls for either A or B to share their best answer with their face partner.

Traveling Heads Together. Traveling Heads starts the same as Numbered Heads, but when the teacher calls a number, the students with that number on each team stand, then "travel" to a new team to share their answers. For fun, seated students beckon for a standing student to join their team.

Stir-the-Class. Teams stand around the outside of the class with spaces between teams. Teammates stand shoulder-to-shoulder. The teacher poses a question, then students write their own answers on an AnswerBoard or slip of paper. Teammates huddle to reach consensus, then unhuddle when done. The teacher selects a number and tells students with that number how many teams to rotate forward to share their answer.

Structure

Numbered Heads Together (continued)

Teammates put their "heads together" to reach consensus on the team's answer. Everyone keeps on their toes because their number may be called to share the team's answer.

Numbered Heads Together Activities and BlacKlines

Structure

Poems for Two Voices

Partners create and present a poem they recite using one voice, the other voice, or both.

Steps

1. The teacher assigns each pair a poem topic.
2. Partners work together to write their poem.
3. Partners label each line of their poem, A, B, or AB, representing who will read each line.
4. Pairs rehearse their poems.
5. Pairs recite their poems to another pair or to the class.

Note: Students may progress through three stages:
1. Teacher provides poem and AB scripting.
2. Teacher provides poem, and students provide AB scripting.
3. Students create or select poem and script it.

Poems for Two Voices Activities and BlackLines

Structure

Quiz-Quiz-Trade

Students quiz a partner, get quizzed by a partner, and then trade cards to repeat the process with a new partner.

Setup

- *The teacher prepares a set of question cards for the class, or each student creates a question card.*

Steps

1. The teacher tells students to "Stand up, put a hand up, and pair up."
2. Partner A quizzes B.
3. Partner B answers.
4. Partner A praises or coaches.
5. Partners switch roles.
6. Partners trade cards and thank each other.
7. Repeat steps 1–6 a number of times.

Text structure **resources are included in the Comprehension Resource Section on pages 29 and 32. Prefix/ Suffix and homophone resources are included in the Word Study Resource section on pages 176–177; 179–181.*

Quiz-Quiz-Trade Activities and Blacklines

(*continued on next page*)

Structure

Quiz-Quiz-Trade (continued)

Students quiz a partner, get quizzed by a partner, and then trade cards to repeat the process with a new partner.

Quiz-Quiz-Trade Activities and BlacKlines

Structure

RallyCoach

Partners take turns, one solving a problem while the other coaches.

Setup

- *Each pair needs one set of high-consensus problems and one pencil.*

Note: RallyCoach may be used with worksheet problems, oral problems provided by the teacher, or manipulatives.

Steps

1. Partner A solves the first problem.
2. Partner B watches and listens, checks, coaches if necessary, and praises.
3. Partner B solves the next problem.
4. Partner A watches and listens, checks, coaches if necessary, and praises.
5. Partners repeat taking turns solving successive problems.

Variation
Pairs Check. After solving two problems, pairs check their answers with the other pair in their team.

RallyCoach Activities and BlacKlines

(continued on next page)

Structure

RallyCoach (continued)

Partners take turns, one solving a problem while the other coaches.

RallyCoach Activities and BlacKlines

(*continued on next page*)

Structure

RallyCoach (continued)

Partners take turns, one solving a problem while the other coaches.

RallyCoach Activities and BlacKlines

Structure

RoundRobin

In teams, students take turns responding orally.

Steps

1. Teacher poses a problem to which there are multiple possible responses or solutions, and provides think time.
2. Students take turns stating responses or solutions.

RoundRobin Activities and Blacklines

Structure

RoundTable Consensus

In teams, students take turns answering questions or placing cards, checking for consensus each time.

Steps

1. Teacher provides or students generate question cards or manipulatives.
2. One student answers using manipulatives, if necessary.
3. The student checks for consensus.
4. The teammates show agreement or lack of agreement with thumbs up or down.
5. If there is agreement, the students celebrate and the next student responds. If not, teammates discuss the response until there is agreement and then they celebrate. If no agreement is reached, the card is set aside to be discussed later.
6. Play continues with the next student answering.

RoundTable Consensus Activities and BlacKlines

Structure

RoundTable Consensus (continued)

In teams, students take turns answering questions or placing cards, checking for consensus each time.

RoundTable Consensus Activities and Blacklines

Structure

Showdown

When the Showdown Captain calls, "Showdown!" teammates all display their own answers. Teammates either celebrate or tutor, and then celebrate.

Setup

- *Teams each have a set of question cards stacked facedown in the center of the table.*

Steps

1. The teacher selects one student on each team to be the Showdown Captain for the first round.
2. The Showdown Captain draws the top card, reads the question, and provides think time.
3. Working alone, all students, including the Showdown Captain, write their answers.
4. When finished, teammates signal they're ready.
5. The Showdown Captain calls, "Showdown."
6. Teammates show and discuss their answers.
7. The Showdown Captain leads the checking.
8. If correct, the team celebrates; if not, teammates tutor, then celebrate.
9. The person on the left of the Showdown Captain becomes the Showdown Captain for the next round.

Modifications: Rather than cards, students can play Showdown with oral questions from the teacher, or from questions on a handout or questions displayed by a projector. Students display their responses on a dry-erase board.

**Text Type, Text Structure, and Fact/Opinion resources are included in the Comprehension Resource Section on pages 27–29, 31–33. Prefix, Suffix, Compound Word, and Contraction resources are included in the Word Study Resource section on pages 176–178, 182–191.*

Structure

Showdown (continued)

When the Showdown Captain calls, "Showdown!" teammates all display their own answers. Teammates either celebrate or tutor, and then celebrate.

Showdown Activities and BlacKlines

Structure

Solo

Students write, read, draw, solve problems, or practice something on their own.

Steps

1. Teacher provides problem or activity for students.
2. Students engage in activity alone.

Solo Activities and BlacKlines

Structure

Talking Chips

Teammates place Talking Chips in the center of the table to make sure everyone contributes to the team discussion.

Setup

- *Teams have talking chips (maximum: two chips each).*

Steps

1. The teacher provides a discussion topic and provides think time.
2. Any student begins the discussion, placing one of his/her chips in the center of the table.
3. Any student with a chip continues discussing, using his/her chip.
4. When all chips are used, teammates each collect their chips and continue the discussion using their talking chips.

Modifications: Students may be given just one chip each, or two chips. Students with no chips left must wait until teammates have used all their chips before they all collect their chip(s) and continue the discussion.

Talking Chips Activity and Blacklines

Structure

Team Line-Ups

Students line up within their teams.

Setup

- *Teacher may prepare Line-Up cards or manipulatives for each team.*

Steps

1. Teacher gives teammates a problem.
2. Within their teams, teammates line up in order of their answers.

Team Line-Ups Activity and BlacKlines

Structure

Team Stand-N-Share

Teams check off or add each idea as it is shared by other teams, sitting down to show every teams' ideas have been shared.

Setup

- *Teams generate a list of items to share.*

Steps

1. All students stand near their teammates.
2. The teacher calls on a standing student holding the team list.
3. Selected student states one idea from the team list.
4. The student in each team, who is holding the team list, either adds the item to the list, or if it is already listed, checks it off.
5. Students pass their team lists one teammate clockwise.
6. Steps 2–5 are repeated.
7. Teams sit when all their items are shared. While seated, they add each new item using RoundTable. When all teams are seated, all items have been shared and Team Stand-N-Share is complete.

Variations

Pair Stand-N-Share. Pairs generate ideas, and then play as a pair.

Individual Stand-N-Share. Each student plays with her/his own list of ideas.

Team Stand-N-Share Activity and BlackLines

Structure

Timed Pair Share

In pairs, students share with a partner for a predetermined time while the partner listens. Then partners switch roles.

Steps

1. The teacher announces a topic, states how long each student will share, and provides think time.
2. In pairs, Partner A shares; Partner B listens.
3. Partner B responds with a positive gambit.
4. Partners switch roles.

Hint: The teacher provides positive response gambits to use in Step 3:

Copycat response gambits
- "Thanks for sharing!"
- "You are interesting to listen to!"

Complete the sentence gambits
- "One thing I learned listening to you was…."
- "I enjoyed listening to you because…."
- "Your most interesting idea was…."

Timed Pair Share Activity and BlacKlines

Structure

Two-Partner Edit

After writing, students discuss and edit their work with a partner, then again with a second partner.

Steps

1. Students write alone on a topic.
2. When complete, students go to a predetermined area of the room to find another student who has finished writing.
3. Students pair up and find a place to sit, shoulder to shoulder.
4. In each pair, Student A reads his or her writing.
5. Students discuss the writing while Student A makes edits.
6. Students switch roles: Student B reads and makes edits.
7. Students thank their shoulder partner.
8. Students stand up, hand up, pair up.
9. With their new partner, students each read, discuss, and re-edit their papers.

Two-Partner Edit Activity and Blacklines

Notes

Notes

Notes